THE HISTORY OF CRIME AND CRIMINAL JUSTICE

MEN AND VIOLENCE

GENDER,

HONOR,

AND RITUALS

IN MODERN EUROPE AND

AMERICA

Edited by

PIETER SPIERENBURG

OHIO STATE UNIVERSITY PRESS

Library of Congress Cataloging-in-Publication Data

Men and violence : gender, honor, and rituals in modern Europe and
America / edited by Pieter Spierenburg.
p.   cm. — (The history of crime and criminal justice)
Includes bibliographic references and index.
ISBN 0-8142-0752-9 (cl : alk. paper). — ISBN 0-8142-0753-7 (pa : alk. paper)
1. Masculinity — Case studies.   2. Violence — Case studies.
3. Honor.   4. Social classes.   5. Dueling — Case studies.
6. Lynching — Case studies.   I. Spierenburg, Petrus Cornelis.
II. Series: History of crime and criminal justice series.
HQ1090.M4285   1998
303.6'081 — dc21   97-34278
                                                       CIP

Text and jacket design by Gary Gore.
Type set in Cochin by G & S Typesetters, Inc.
Printed by Braun-Brumfield, Inc.

The paper in this publication
meets the minimum requirements of
American National Standard for Information Sciences —
Permanence of Paper for Printed Library Materials.
ANSI Z39.48–1992.

9   8   7   6   5   4   3   2   1

CONTENTS

Acknowledgments   vii

Masculinity, Violence, and Honor: An Introduction   1
PIETER SPIERENBURG

Part One: Elite Dueling

1   The Taming of the Noble Ruffian: Male Violence
    and Dueling in Early Modern and Modern Germany   37
    UTE FREVERT

2   Men of Steel: Dueling, Honor, and Politics in Liberal Italy   64
    STEVEN HUGHES

3   The End of the Modern French Duel   82
    ROBERT NYE

Part Two: Popular Duels

4   Knife Fighting and Popular Codes of Honor
    in Early Modern Amsterdam   103
    PIETER SPIERENBURG

5   Homicide and Knife Fighting in Rome, 1845–1914   128
    DANIELE BOSCHI

6   Fights/Fires: Violent Firemen in the Nineteenth-Century
     American City   159
     AMY SOPHIA GREENBERG

     Part Three: Violence and the State

7   The Victorian Criminalization of Men   197
     MARTIN J. WIENER

8   White Supremacist Justice and the Rule of Law: Lynching,
     Honor, and the State in Ben Tillman's South Carolina   213
     STEPHEN KANTROWITZ

9   "The Equal of Some White Men and the Superior of Others":
     Masculinity and the 1916 Lynching of Anthony Crawford in
     Abbeville County, South Carolina   240
     TERENCE FINNEGAN

     References   255
     Contributors   275
     Index   277

ACKNOWLEDGMENTS

The editor expresses his thanks to Steve Hughes for improving the English of two chapters written by nonnative speakers.

Helpful comments on an earlier version of the introduction were given by David Johnson and Jeff Adler (the series editors), by Florike Egmond, and by Randolph Roth (who reviewed the manuscript).

Masculinity, Violence, and Honor: An Introduction

PIETER SPIERENBURG

Few would deny that men and violence are closely related. In practically every historical setting, violent crime has been overwhelmingly a male enterprise, and today this is no different. Criminal violence, however, is only part of the story; not every act of aggression or bloodshed is always condemned. It is commonly known that, in various situations, violence may be honorable. Less clear, however, is the way in which aggressive behavior, or the abstention from aggressive behavior, can contribute to the construction of masculinity and male honor.

Our ignorance on such issues can be attributed in part to the evolution of gender studies, which have tended in the past to relegate men to the margins. When gender arose as an issue in the humanities and social sciences, women were the focus of attention, and practitioners of women's history tended to write individual or collective biographies of women. This descriptive orientation was an understandable reaction to a traditional historiography that implicitly was always about men. During the last ten years, however, the focus shifted: the production of narratives about women gave way to a more theoretical approach, problematizing relations between women and men and their representation. In this new approach, gender is analyzed as a crucial factor in the historical process, next to such factors as social stratification or ethnic affiliation.[1] Even more recently, it is acknowledged that studying gender also means posing the problem of male culture and masculinity.[2] Men can be studied explicitly as men, the male gender, rather than implicitly as the merchants or politicians with whom historians happen to have dealt for so long.[3] Presently, there is a growing international interest in the history of masculinity, to which this volume wants to contribute.

Masculinity is a very broad subject. This volume looks at it from one crucial angle: violence and honor, which have played a prominent role in male cultures. For one thing, in societies with pronounced notions of honor and shame, a person's reputation often depends on physical bravery and a forceful response to insults. Second, notions of honor and shame are characteristically gendered. In almost every society, male honor is considered to be quite different from female honor. Men may take pride in attacking fellow men, whether they use this force to protect women or for other reasons. Passivity, in violent and peaceful situations, is a cardinal feminine virtue. Anthropologists as well as historians have studied concepts of honor, including the changing interrelationships of male honor and violence.[4] Of course, masculinity is not necessarily bound up with physical bravado in all societies at all times. An important research question precisely concerns the conditions under which male cultures may become less prone to violence.

To pose that question is to acknowledge that human behavior takes shape in social and cultural interaction and that it is not programmed by biological factors.[5] The contributors to this volume all agree that the level of aggression and its changing nature have to be explained primarily with reference to the society in which they manifest themselves. This equally applies to conceptions of honor. Honor has at least three layers: a person's own feeling of self-worth, this person's assessment of his or her worth in the eyes of others, and the actual opinion of others about her or him.[6] The criteria of judgment depend on the sociocultural context. The search for different standards of honor and masculinity, then, is a cross-cultural as well as a diachronic enterprise. This book makes a modest beginning with it. As it focuses on change over time, a few words about geographic scope are in order here.

The observation of a relationship between physical force and male honor primarily derives from the western experience. In some nonwestern cultures this link appears to be much weaker: honorable men do not react to insults with an aggressive response, and when they do, it is often viewed negatively. According to anthropologist Frank Henderson Stewart, the concepts of honor prevalent among the Bedouins, and possibly in the Arab world as a whole, are fundamentally different from the European model. In contemporary Bedouin societies no particular connection between male honor and violence exists.[7] Among the Djuka from the Surinam rain forest it counts as a stain upon a man's honor if he fights out a conflict or reacts to an insult with violence. Only in the case of adultery is the aggrieved husband accorded a limited right to beat up his rival. All other conflicts have to be solved through the institution of the palaver. This attitude has characterized the Djuka for at least two hundred and fifty years, Thoden van Velzen argues, and it is connected to the uxorilocal organization of their society.[8] Conversely, in Japan the samurai have cherished a warrior ethos for centuries. A samurai's honor depended on his reputation for bloodshed and his aggressive lifestyle. Although this elite group was gradually pacified, as was the European aristocracy, in Japan the process of pacification took a longer time and it was half-hearted.[9] To a much greater extent than among the early modern European aristocracy, the social identity of the Tokugawa samurai depended on their origins as a warrior caste. Thus, considerable differences exist between cultures. The contributions to this volume, however, deal exclusively with western Europe and the United States since the early modern era.

Even then, the range of questions is sufficiently broad, and no satisfactory answers can be given to all of them. What follows is a tentative review of the historical evidence on violence, notions of honor, the body, and gender in the western world since the late Middle Ages. To present this within the confines of an introductory chapter requires a solid framework. The review will be guided by a theoretical approach that proceeds from a long-term perspective. Its principal aim is to indicate the extent to which the individual essays of this volume inform us about elements or episodes of major historical developments. The basic framework of these developments is set out first; then the focus is on the volume's respective parts.

Gender, Honor, and the Body

Violence does not stand by itself. Because of its physicality it belongs to the wider field of the history of the body and its symbolic representation. Insofar as honor relates to violence, it equally relates to this wider field. Honor originally depended on the body or, in Blok's words, the physical person.[10] Appearance was crucial for one's reputation. Honorable men were symbolically associated with strong, awe-inspiring animals. So we have the body, honor, and gender, and they are all related. Bodies, being male or female with few exceptions, form the basis of gender; gender gives rise to a dual concept of honor; honor shapes the experience of the body. The inherent circularity ensures that no element of this triangle is the principal determinant. The relationship is one of interdependence: if there is a change in one element, the others are likely to change, too. Nevertheless, in order to come to grips with these complex interdependencies, we may break them down into developments in three areas: the body and gender, gender and honor, and honor and the body.

For the body and gender the crucial periods seem to have been the Middle Ages and the late eighteenth century. Important work has been done on the first period.[11] Although the authors concerned criticize one another on points of detail, they agree that the medieval concept of sexual differences left room for much ambiguity.[12] In the view of contemporaries, to be male or female largely depended on character and habits. In accordance with this, the process of generation did not just offer two possibilities. Human specimens such as a virago, an effeminate man, or a hermaphrodite could be born just as easily.[13] The body's sexual identity had fluid boundaries. Christ's body in particular was often pictured as half female. His side wounds, a source of food, were likened to Mary's breasts.[14] Thomas Laqueur offers a model to account for these observations: in this period, gender came first. In medieval people's minds, the sociocultural experience of being male or female, or anything in between, had primacy, and biological sex was made to fit it. Essentially, this concept of sexual differences persisted during the early modern period. From the middle of the eighteenth century onward, however, the relationship was reversed. Sex came first now. Biology was seen as the basis of character, and biology left room for just two sexes. Sexual identity and, as a consequence, gender identity became much more strictly demarcated.[15] This new view was especially pronounced toward the end of the nineteenth century. As Robert Nye writes in this volume, doctors and biologists elaborated a standard anatomical and physiological model of masculinity, defining its features as hygienic norms to which all men should comply. Masculinity and femininity became binary opposites.

When this stricter demarcation of the sexes and gender roles was elaborated, the contrast between male and female honor weakened. Since the early modern period, notions of female and male honor gradually converged. Of course, they remained distinct to some extent. The process of convergence had two main aspects: the active-passive contrast in gender roles became less pronounced and men, like women before them, had to take moral standards into account. Women's honor had always been based primarily on issues of morality. Foremost, it depended on a reputation of chastity, but in the sixteenth and seventeenth centuries a clean slate with respect to sorcery was important, too. A chaste woman was a modest woman, true to the demand of passivity.[16] For men, on the other hand, the domain of sex originally meant activity: the protection of one's own womenfolk from predators and trying to seduce others' womenfolk. This attitude not only prevailed among elite men but also among men of lower social status. Popular customs testify to this at least until the sixteenth century. When a cuckolded husband was subjected to the ritual of charivari, for example, he was mocked as a loser by his fellow men rather than burdened with moral outrage.[17] Attitudes slowly changed during the early modern period. Restrictive demands on men, especially from religious moralists, became stronger.[18] Obviously, the male gender role continued to take a more active stance than the female, but the quest for sexual adventure was increasingly proscribed from it. By the nineteenth century, male honor, too, had become associated with sexual self-restraint, at least among the middle classes.[19]

Thus, a shift in the way the body and gender were perceived was accompanied by a transformation in concepts of gender and honor. That transformation, however, seems to have come about more gradually, extending over a period roughly from the sixteenth century to the nineteenth. The two changes were loosely related rather than connected in a cause-and-effect relationship. In this complex web of interdependent developments, the third area to be reviewed, that of honor and the body, was involved, too. In that case, we are talking primarily, but not exclusively, of male culture.

Honor can be oriented inward or outward. Association with the body means being linked to the body's outer appearance in particular. The outside is considered to reflect inner qualities, so appearance takes primacy. Conversely, in its spiritualized form, honor is linked primarily to inner virtues. It depends on an evaluation of a person's moral stature or psychological condition, in which outer appearance plays a much less significant part. Inward and outward are two end-poles of a continuum. The conceptions of honor prevailing in a particular society are never located completely at one end or the other, but always somewhere between these extremes. In western Europe over the last three hundred years or so, concepts of honor appear to have moved in the direction of spiritualization. By implication, their association with the body was strongest before this process of change set in. During most of the preindustrial period, male honor depended on a reputation for violence and bravery. An honorable man commanded respect; as a patron, he protected his clients and he dealt roughly with an enemy who dared to encroach upon his property.[20] In the streets he kept rivals at a distance, at arm's length at least.[21] When insulted, he was prepared to fight.[22] Well into the seventeenth century, these attitudes were manifest in almost every European country where the subject has been investigated.

The gradual change in the direction of spiritualization did not just mean the reduction or removal of the element of force from the prevalent concept of honor. The change also had a positive side, in the sense that something else took the place of force. Thus, by the seventeenth century, economic solidity was a major supplementary source of honor for men.[23] A reputation for engaging in sloppy affairs would greatly diminish a man's honor; *thief* was a common word of insult. Clearly, this implies the rise of a new ideal of masculine behavior. As Martin J. Wiener notes in this volume, the earliest attacks on "traditional manhood" can be traced back to the sixteenth century. For other historians, the decisive moment was at the end of the nineteenth century and the beginning of the twentieth, when a gentler and more domesticated type of man emerged; they speak of the breakthrough of a "new masculinity."[24] It can be argued, however, that taking pride in not being considered a thief was the earliest manifestation of a "new masculinity." It preceded its later counterpart by some three centuries.

The concept of "new masculinity" helps us to avoid equating the spiritualization of honor with its feminization. That would be an unwarranted simplification. For one thing, female honor, too, once seems to have carried more explicitly physical connotations. Views of chastity and unchasteness were suffused with bodily imagery. In sixteenth-century Italy, for example, a close analogy existed between the female body and the house. Forcing a stranger's door was the same, symbolically, as piercing a hymen.[25] Women and men shared such images. An explicitly physical act of defamation was performed a couple of times in Nuremberg around 1500, when an unchaste woman stood the risk of having her nose injured or even cut off. In most cases, this was done by one woman to another woman who had had an affair with her husband.[26] This custom was echoed in early seventeenth-century London: a few women threatened to slit the nose of their husbands' mistresses, but actual violence only amounted to a scratch on the face, called the whore's mark.[27] In seventeenth-century Burgundy, a woman considered dishonorable might be robbed of her headdress by another woman: a symbolic act whose physical connotations are somewhat less explicit.[28] A similar custom, knocking off an unchaste woman's cap, was practiced by women and men in the small coastal town of Wilster in Holstein in the early seventeenth century.[29] So it is likely that, over time, notions of female chastity became more interiorized and less linked to the body. If that was the case, women were also involved, though to a lesser extent than men, in the process of spiritualization of honor.

This process was reinforced by the efforts of religious moralists, in Spain, Britain, and the Netherlands among other countries.[30] As honor was gradually spiritualized, it came to be associated more firmly with what many people conceived to be the body politic.[31] Next to the inward-outward dimension, long-term change involves the social hierarchy. A person's status usually matters for the type of honor he is able to acquire. To protect "his people" is a more obvious duty for a rural patron than for an urban artisan, who has no clients to protect in the first place. For this artisan, it is important to prevent any rumor of being a thief. On the other hand, economic solidity may be a less crucial value for men who occupy a still lower position in the social hierarchy, such as the journeymen of early modern Germany. Their honor primarily lay in generosity, bravery, and comradliness.[32]

Social Stratification and the Duel

Social stratification, then, is a crucial factor influencing concepts of honor as well as definitions of masculinity. Consequently, social stratification is a major theme in most of the essays that follow. The contributions to this volume document the last few centuries of the very long term just sketched, with Ute Frevert's article and mine going back furthest in time. Frevert, especially, is concerned with the issue of stratification. It is her principal argument that, whereas the duel's association with masculine values is a historical constant, the social composition of the groups most apt to duel changed over time. In the early modern period, dueling flourished exclusively among the nobility, whether army officers or not. In the course of the nineteenth century, however, bourgeois men increasingly adopted this custom as a means of solving conflicts. Consequently, the bourgeoisie rejected its civilian origins to some extent. Frevert shows that academia played the role of intermediary. During the seventeenth century the universities were increasingly exposed to aristocratic influences. Students became eager duelists, hoping to challenge an army officer. The persistence of this student tradition and, later, the militarization of German culture go a long way to explain how it was possible that the bourgeoisie adopted the duel so easily as a habit of their own.

For Germany, Frevert describes this changing social recruitment of duelists as a more or less continuous process. Earlier historians spoke of the emergence of the bourgeois duel in terms of revival. Notably, this seems to be true for France. The duel became fashionable again among the country's elites by the mid-nineteenth century, following upon a phase of relative marginalization, marked by its retreat to the world of the military, at the end of the ancien régime.[33] As Robert Nye points out, dueling was taken up by the Republican opposition in the Second Empire. In Italy, unification seems to have provided the custom with a new impulse, although we cannot underpin this with hard figures. Before 1870 there is nothing approaching the meticulous collection of statistics by Iacopo Gelli, which Steven Hughes uses as his main source. Whatever the frequency of dueling, however, there can be no doubt about the prominent participation of bourgeois men. In Italy journalists were eager participants, next to military men who were often of middle-class origin. In France, the military was much less involved. The officer corps, Robert Nye argues, hardly indulged in dueling; instead, the custom was favored among civilians, who preferred the sword as a weapon. They cherished a national myth according to which France was the home country of the duel and the épée was its weapon par excellence.

Whether or not the term *revival* is appropriate, the bourgeoisie embraced dueling throughout nineteenth-century Europe. Their acceptance may have been facilitated by a new legitimating argument. Against the duel's critics, who found it a brutalizing ritual, the custom's defenders argued that, quite to the contrary, it was a civilizing force. Such arguments were elaborated notably in France, and Nye renders them thus: the modern duel civilizes its participants in two ways. First, it promotes mutual regard between men and pacifies interpersonal relations, by giving men confidence in their personal force. Second, the duel encourages self-mastery, teaching a man the forms to observe in his interactions with others. The men endowed with the greatest courage were regarded as the least likely to issue or provoke dueling challenges. This situation, still according to the French apologists, would lead to fewer rather than to more duels. Comparable arguments were heard in Italy. German protagonists added another nuance to this view. The duel, they argued, establishes a "fraternal bond" between its participants. Having experienced and survived it, former enemies are like brothers. Indeed, Frevert has found real-life examples of this sense of bonding. Especially in the nineteenth century, fighting out a conflict in a benign manner was supposed to bring people together. In this view, the civilizing element does not lie in any curbing of violence per se but in a decrease in the intensity of personal conflict.

Several qualifications can be made to the idea that the duel promoted civilized behavior. If we take it at face value, we must assume that the prospect of having to face an opponent in arms restrained men in social intercourse; they thought twice before they said a wrong word. With the advantage of historical hindsight, we can say that the idea takes for granted a measure of sensitization to violence. The implicit assumption is that honorable men actually do not want to fight at all and do everything they can to avoid it. In this way, the duel's defenders acknowledged that, deep in their hearts, they found the habit distasteful. In reality, therefore, the measure of civilization already reached affected contemporary views of dueling. A parallel situation prevailed some hundred years previously with attitudes toward judicial torture: even the conservatives, torture's defenders, took for granted that most people disliked the practice. They wanted to direct the public's compassion to the respectable citizenry who, in their view, would greatly suffer from crime if penal procedure were reformed.[34] In both instances, in the late eighteenth century and the late nineteenth, people who tolerated a violent custom nevertheless recognized that this violence was intrinsically distasteful and should therefore be kept to a minimum.

A second qualification is that contemporary views about civilizing

forces are not necessarily in line with the technical sense in which Norbert
Elias uses the term *process of civilization.* Yet, the development of dueling
can be related to this process. Ute Frevert argues this explicitly, speaking of an increasing regulation and disciplining of the duel. Between the
sixteenth and nineteenth centuries the duel changed from a relatively an-
archic fight into a completely stylized ritual of violence, bound to exact
rules and practiced with the consent of both parties. Although the contributions on Italy and France do not cover this very long term, they contain
another important observation: dueling codes in the late nineteenth and
early twentieth centuries were more genteel than their predecessors. The
combatants usually were not expected to go on until the inevitable end.
Frenchmen mostly fought "at first blood," and in Italy duelists incurred
relatively light wounds. This had been different still in England during the
first half of the nineteenth century: Englishmen then fought with accurate
pistols at short distance from each other, which resulted in a death rate
of about 15 percent.[35] Hence, the middle of the nineteenth century appears as the crucial moment of change. This also applies to the German-
speaking countries. Although German dueling codes continued to stress
that death must be an inherent risk, they no longer obliged the combatants passively to wait for each other's shots.[36] Willingness to risk one's life
was a more important element than a possible victory. In all three countries it mattered less who won than that honor was saved by shedding
(some) blood. While Hughes and Nye are not dealing with the origins of
this attitude, Frevert's data suggest that it was new in the bourgeois period, having emerged in the middle of the eighteenth century. No doubt,
the lesser violence of late nineteenth- and early twentieth-century duels
was a precondition for viewing them as promoters of civilization.

The conclusions about dueling and the bourgeoisie are relevant to a
more general argument about honor and the social hierarchy. In a highly
stratified society, the elite only acknowledges a claim to honor from its
own (male) members. For a long time historians took this to imply that
common people had no concept of honor, but this is questionable even for
the feudal period. In preindustrial Europe, common people reflected
about their reputations constantly, but higher groups had no interest in
them. Conversely, lower groups usually recognized middle- and upper-
class persons as honorable, but this had little relevance for their own
honor games: a lower person could never hope to diminish (to "steal") a
higher person's honor. The definition of who was honorable and how
much so largely took place within one's peer group.

This situation had partly changed in the second half of the nineteenth century. By that time, middle and upper classes shared a common honor code. Even in Germany, with its strong barriers between social groups, middle-class academics and army officers together belonged to the *Satis-faktionsfähige Gesellschaft*. Integration of bourgeoisie and aristocracy went farthest in France, as Robert Nye makes clear. Members of the upper middle classes intermarried with old nobles and laid claim to equal political and social status. The honor attached to membership of this new alliance of notables was shared by all. Gelli, the Italian journalist, did not even identify nobles as a separate group in his statistics. In his view, a loosely defined class of "gentlemen" could lay claim to honor. At the same time, gentlemen were not prepared to grant "true honor" to mere shopkeepers or workers. Steven Hughes points out that the leniency of the courts toward duelists had an obvious class bias. When a peasant or an urban worker had killed an opponent in a fair fight, he was punished as severely as any killer. Recognition that such a conflict could be an affair of honor—which, according to Daniele Boschi's data, it could very well be— would be scandalizing to elite values. Despite this, the merger of noble and bourgeois honor in the nineteenth century was a step in a gradual process of greater intergroup recognition of honor. Internationally, the exact trajectory of this process is little understood yet. It may have gone farthest in France, as exemplified by Georges Breittmayer's new dueling code with which Nye's essay concludes. Writing in the winter of 1917–18, Breittmayer decreed that anyone of draft age could duel and hence belonged to the same honor group. He only excluded men who had avoided military service or engaged in disreputable activities during the war. This was a more democratic code than ever adhered to in Italy, let alone Germany, but it came too late. It was overdue not only because the duel was about to die but also because society was changing. Ultimately, honor is exclusive by nature; it presupposes infamy or, at least, lesser honor. If all were honorable, no one would be really honorable. Democratization, then, may explain the lesser importance of honor codes in the twentieth century.

To conclude, over the long term, the social hierarchy affects the degree of exclusiveness of the claim to possess honor. In addition, the social hierarchy affects honor in another fundamental way: the extent to which it is a personal or a collective attribute. In that case, the question is whether the actions of individual persons contribute to the honor of the group to which they belong. In a conflict between students and artisans in Göttingen in

1790, for example, the collective honor of both groups was at stake.[37] The
volunteer firemen whom Amy Greenberg depicts so vividly, whether
fighting or not fighting, were upholding their company's honor. Nations
are particularly large groups. A final observation from the contributions
on dueling concerns the intimate association of honor codes with nationalism in the late nineteenth century. More than previously, honor was tied
to the nation. The French fought duels to take revenge on the Germans
who had defeated them in 1870–71, the Germans to assert their newly
won national self-consciousness, and the unified Italians to show that the
Ethiopians had better watch out next time. Conversely, nationalism could
allow the Italians just as well to refrain from dueling: from 1914 to 1918
they postponed their personal grievances to concentrate on the war effort.
It was not until the rise of the fascist regime that dueling was suppressed.
Mussolini's men also struck against the Mafia, which cherished its own
peculiar blend of honor and ritual violence. For the fascists, honor was
tied solely to the nation.

Throughout Europe, honor had become less of a personal attribute by
1900. In earlier days, one person's actions had repercussions for the honor
of his family at the most; now they had repercussions for a much larger
group, the nation in particular. The duel's opponents, finally, saw honor as
completely depersonalized: it was a kind of alien monster, preferably ex-
acting the lives of both duelists.[38] The nationalist concept of honor was
echoed in America at the level of individual states. Stephen Kantrowitz
points this out for South Carolina: in the 1890s, Governor Tillman wavered between condoning mob violence and insisting that the law should
be in control. He and other whites realized that South Carolina's collective honor depended on a reputation for proper legal procedure, hoping to
reassure either northern businessmen or possible political allies in the national arena. The theme of nationalism anticipates that of the state, discussed below. First, however, we have to take a closer look at the subject
of ritual, which not only characterized the elite duel but also played a crucial role in popular practices.

Ritual Violence: Popular and Elite Forms

In recent historiography, ritual has been analyzed primarily with reference to the social world of villages and urban neighborhoods. It is an om-
nipresent theme in the literature on preindustrial local communities. As an

element of human behavior, ritual may be connected with all three areas discussed earlier: the body, honor and gender. Here we must concentrate on ritual's relation to violence. In earlier publications I have proposed a model that included the hypothesis that long-term trends moved in the direction of a marginalization of ritual aspects of violence and a growing prominence of instrumental aspects. Instrumental violence means violence used as a means to an end, as in robbery or rape.[39] This is not the place to develop my model further; what ought to be discussed is the extent to which the contributions to the present volume shed light on the rituals of violence. An activity can be labeled as ritual according to various criteria. The ritual character may lie in a specific sequence of events while the activity is carried out; it may also lie, simultaneously or alternatively, in the particular time of the year when the activity takes place. Both criteria apply to violent activities just as much. A combat of one man against another, for example, may proceed according to a prearranged sequence of steps. Mock battles between the youths of neighboring villages, on the other hand, were usually connected to the seasonal calendar. The fighting of American volunteer firemen, too, was linked to specific events, notably fires. Ritual violence may even become a form of theater, as did the festive battles on the bridges of Venice in the seventeenth century.[40]

Thus, the repertoire of ritual violence comprised different forms, not only over time but also synchronically. Even women partook of that repertoire. In male popular culture, two types of ritual violence were notorious: collective unarmed fights, settled by boxing and/or wrestling, and the armed "fair" combat. Both types are dealt with in this volume; the second, the popular duel, is a recent historical discovery.

In my essay I have identified a substantial number of the homicide cases tried by the Amsterdam court in the seventeenth and eighteenth centuries as popular duels. These cases involved an "honorable" combat of one knife fighter against another. Such a combat was a ritual event, started off by a challenge from the insulted party and fought according to a code of fairness. The fighters tested each other's strength and thus their manhood. Although not as stylized as the elite sword or pistol duel, the knife duel was its lower-class counterpart. The participants occupied a social position along the border of the "respectable" and the nonrespectable segment of the urban lower classes. People who considered themselves respectable did not use a knife as a weapon; they would ward off an attacker with a stick. After 1720 the popular duel with knives disappeared from the Amsterdam court records, indicating its decline. In some rural areas of the Netherlands, on the other hand, knife fighting continued to be customary until the beginning of the nineteenth century.

No surprise for the Romans. As Daniele Boschi shows, a knife culture was alive and flourishing in Rome even around 1900. He observes that homicidal incidents frequently began for trivial reasons that often touched on matters of honor. Next to "classic" tavern conflicts and street brawls, Boschi's cases include homicidal incidents arising from tensions in the neighborhood, at the workplace, and within the family. Whatever the incident's origin, many offenders had either a previous criminal record or a reputation for easily losing self-control when drunk. The first characteristic also applied to a sizable minority of offenders in my file. The second, however, was a rare occurrence there: no particular character traits of Amsterdam killers around 1700 were recorded. Thus, whereas Amsterdam's popular duelists were a distinct group primarily in terms of their marginal social status, Rome's knife fighters were defined as a group partly in psychological terms. This suggests that, despite the similarity in knife cultures, the standards of acceptance of violence were different. In Rome around 1900, some measure of inner restraint on serious aggression must have been common among even the lowest social groups, so that individuals lacking these psychological restraints were branded as deviants. Indeed, Boschi observes that such violent men were ostracized within the working class: to associate with them was often a stain on the honor of more self-controlled working people. This implies a greater isolation than that experienced by Amsterdam knife fighters two centuries earlier.

Whereas Rome's rowdies were condemned as individuals, the riotous firemen of antebellum America, engaging in collective violence, received bad press as a group. Of course, knife fighters also constituted a group, but they were not organized as such. The knife culture's opponents had no other option than to suppress it; it would have been impossible to transform the concepts of honor of the bearers of that culture in the direction of greater peacefulness. Precisely that possibility was open in the case of the fire companies. At first, companies who considered themselves honorable freely attacked companies branded as dishonorable. But not everyone shared this attitude. Leading members as well as contemporary observers argued that a company's honor should be maintained by keeping up a reputation of orderliness, not violence. In St. Louis, for example, an entire company counted as dishonored if it accepted as a member a fireman expelled from another company for misconduct. Because of the firemen's obvious public task, demands to reform their manners from the middle classes may have had a stronger impact than similar appeals to knife fighters would have had. Indeed, Greenberg remarks that aspiring citizens of St. Louis wished their city to emulate the sphere of "gentility" which they felt characterized Boston and New York at the time. Despite such pressures, in the end the fire companies themselves, or their leaders, did not succeed in establishing a reputation for orderliness. So they were disbanded. Fire fighting without fighting was accomplished by replacing the volunteer companies with professional ones (where, presumably, the threat of dismissal was used to enforce peaceable behavior). It should be added that the establishment of professional companies cannot be explained solely as a reaction to the disorderliness of the volunteer firemen. This becomes clear from Amy Greenberg's account of the situation in San Francisco, whose volunteer company was quickly disbanded after just one riot. This was an obvious pretext, and more structural factors must have been involved in the shift to professional fire fighting throughout America.

In dealing with collective violence, Greenberg's contribution raises the question of numbers. How many people may legitimately participate in a violent encounter? With fistfights, which are relatively harmless, the number of participants does not matter too much. Even then, however, an affray between two parties of very unequal size would usually damage the honor of the larger group. So, what about more serious clashes? Ritual sequences and concepts of honor are often connected to a code of fairness. And again, exactly what we consider fair has changed over time. Throughout Europe, the codes of fairness underwent a diachronic development involving the lower classes as well as the elites. To illustrate this development, we must return to the duel.

In the duel, the number of participants is two by definition. This would be self-evident to a nineteenth-century bourgeois or his aristocratic predecessor a century earlier. Likewise, a one-on-one combat was required from honorable knife fighters in Amsterdam around 1700. However, as Frevert points out, in the early seventeenth century the seconds sometimes joined in the duel, despite its name. They were considered auxiliaries to the principals. Earlier still, some really unequal struggles had been within the domain of honor. The scene was that of the vendetta. The ritual revenge of one clan upon another precluded a concern for an equal contest. The Dutch province of Zeeland in the fifteenth century is a good example. In one incident, in 1498, two brothers and two of their cousins pursued just one man, named Hallinck Cornelis. Because Hallinck was armed with a pike, he managed to kill one of his assailants. Thereupon the other three went to the home of Hallinck's aged father, broke down the door, dragged the old man from his bed, stabbed him seventeen times, and finished him off by smashing his head with a club.[41] The same attitude prevailed among the regional elite of Friuli until the middle of the sixteenth century. Enemies from rival clans were butchered, as if they were prey in a hunting party. Ambushes were quite common. When the expelled leader of a once powerful faction was killed in Villach in 1512, ten men jumped on him from their hiding place, drove him to a corner, and offered his archenemy the opportunity to deal the final blow. From the 1560s onward the Friulian nobles preferred the duel when they were in conflict.[42]

Ostensibly, notions of what is fair and honorable and what is not were changing. Possibly, the change can be explained by bringing in the family. In ancient Dutch and North Italian vendetta ritual, treacherous murders were considered excusable by the community as long as they served to vindicate the collective honor of the clan. When the motive was revenge, almost anything was allowed. Amsterdam knife fighters around 1700 usually had personal grudges only. They upheld their individual honor. This may be taken as running counter to the conclusion, reached above, that honor became less of a personal attribute over time. In the Middle Ages personal honor and family honor were one and the same. Perhaps the Amsterdam knife fights represented an intermediate phase in which the sense of honor was personal at its most extreme. On the other hand, the knife fighters may have been an exceptional group. They were lone rangers to some extent, who fought primarily for a reputation in their peer group. To their aristocratic contemporaries, on the other hand, personal honor was equally linked to family honor. This link is relatively constant over time.[43] The longer process consisted of honor's increasing association with larger social groups. So, if the code of fairness became stricter over time, the explanation must lie elsewhere. We must rather think of a "civilizing process" in Elias's sense: the emergence of the aristocratic and the popular duel meant that fighting rituals became less "wild" and driven by emotional impulses.[44]

We know that the aristocratic duel originated in Italy in the early sixteenth century. For the popular duel, the Amsterdam evidence, from 1650 onward, is the oldest. Examples of peasants calling upon an enemy to leave his house and follow the challenger to the fields probably refer to less stylized fights.[45] Although it is possible that knife fights bound to ritual codes were an independent tradition among the lower classes, they might actually have originated in imitation of the elite duel. Ute Frevert suggests the latter possibility, discussing a few cases of ordinary people challenging each other to a rapier combat in seventeenth-century Germany and a case of a guild member engaged in a duel with a Danish officer. While the popular duel's origins may not be that remote, the timing of its demise, on a European scale, varied from one place to another; indeed, it varied according to town, region, or country. Within the Netherlands, the custom of knife fighting had a longer life in rural Groningen and Brabant than in Amsterdam (and possibly in other towns in the western part of the country). In Rome and in most of Italy to the south of Lombardy, knife fights were still endemic by the late nineteenth century. It would be too simple, however, to say that the knife culture disappeared earlier in northern than in southern Europe. Some provinces of Finland in the nineteenth century were notorious for knife fighting.[46] Finnish society remained relatively violent well into the twentieth century, even though we do not hear of an honor code.[47]

Conversely, a traditional code of honor may be in operation without frequent recourse to violence. An early example is the verbal dueling practiced in Italy in the second half of the sixteenth century.[48] A situation in which honor was combined with a low frequency of violence also has been observed in a study of loan-sharking in Philadelphia from the 1920s to the 1970s. Sharks and their clients inhabited a masculine world; they shared an honor code, in which trustfulness and keeping a man's word were central values. Appeals to that code were more frequent than violent coercion as means to get payment and for obvious reasons. In this business, too many broken limbs would serve as a counter-advertisement.[49] It may be assumed, however, that clients under pressure of payment often sensed the threat of physical coercion. The potential for violence was greater than the actual recourse to it. This probably also applies to earlier historical situations that are less well documented. Among the dueling-prone groups of fin de siècle Europe as well as the people with knives in Amsterdam around 1700, a certain potential for violence and demanding satisfaction existed, but a greater or smaller part of this potential remained submerged. Actual violence need not always ensue. When it did not, the available sources usually remain silent. Disagreements during drinking bouts that were laughed away did not make it to the courtroom. Newspapers seldom reported when a gentleman had decided that a particular insult was too minor to be taken as an encroachment upon his honor.

Violent Men and the State

So far, the role of the state has been underplayed. Political processes are a possible explanatory factor in any account of long-term cultural change. In most of the discussion up to now, the state was present already. Its leaders felt ambivalent toward the elite duel. At the same time, various courts were unequivocally bent on the suppression of knife fighting. Around 1860, American cities substituted professional for amateur fire brigades. The courts' concern extended to still other forms of "traditional" violence. In England, and probably in other European countries as well, these forms of violence were criminalized more intensely during the nineteenth century.

That is the subject of Martin Wiener's essay. The creation of a new standard of masculinity is his central problem, more so than that of honor codes. Taking a close look at the institutions of social control in nineteenth-century Britain, he finds that the end result of their activities was an increasing criminalization of men: "The early Victorian reconstruction of womanhood was paralleled and complemented by a much less well known reconstruction of manhood." Wiener emphasizes that his account of this process is not intended as a balanced one; rather, it functions as a complement to existing accounts focused on the treatment of women. He argues that the disappearance of female criminals in the nineteenth century, which other historians have noted as well, was largely an artefact of the increasing visibility of male criminals. Typically male forms of behavior, in particular those involving violence, were increasingly proscribed by law. Consequently, a growing proportion of serious criminal prosecutions and punishments were aimed at men.

Consequently, Wiener rejects what he calls a "power essentialism": the assumption that gender relations are always and everywhere structured in such a way that men collectively exercise power and benefit from it, while women are its collective objects and victims. This is well taken: although the objects of discipline were men, most of the agents of discipline were also men. Judges, journalists, members of Parliament, and doctors, though not all moral entrepreneurs, were male. The rejection of essentialism does not mean that power was absent in the process that Wiener describes. As a rule, the agents of discipline occupied a higher position in the social hierarchy than the objects of discipline. In the process that the former set in motion, they reconstructed their own and others' manhood. Social class, then, was another crucial factor. Wiener acknowledges this in his choice of words. Speaking of "the domestication of men into gentility and a culture of sensibility," he is referring implicitly to middle-class men, while elsewhere he speaks of "the civilization of the crowd." The criminalization of dueling is an example of discipline aimed at men from the upper echelons of society, and indeed the duel disappeared in England around the middle of the nineteenth century. Violence directed at women was increasingly criminalized as well. The member of Parliament who, in 1856, spoke of "unmanly assaults" in this connection and who wanted to reform "the character of our own sex" could hardly have said it more clearly: the issue was the creation of a new masculinity. It was created, Wiener concludes, at the expense of a masculinization of crime.

While the leaders of the British state, from a position of strength, self-consciously strove to curb male violence, a quite different situation prevailed around the turn of the century in South Carolina. The chapters written by Stephen Kantrowitz and Terence Finnegan both deal with this state, but the issues they raise are characteristic of the postbellum South as a whole. Foremost among these issues, evidently, is that of race. Reflections about masculinity were a key feature of race relations in the New South, although they were complicated by conflicts — couched in terms of honor — between state power and local justice.

Kantrowitz focuses on the period 1890–94 when Ben Tillman, a wealthy planter and dissident Democrat, served as governor. He was from Edgefield County, called "bloody Edgefield" by one historian because of its tradition of excessive violence.[50] Indeed, before his election, Tillman and his ardent supporters had tried to accomplish their aim, the establishment of a white supremacist order, using intimidation and force. As governor, Tillman was torn between two loyalties: he remained committed to white supremacy, which might include condoning mob violence against black people, but at the same time he was obliged to show that South Carolinians respected the rule of law. That obligation made him condemn lynching explicitly in his inaugural address. His subsequent confrontation with lynch-happy communities can be interpreted partly as a conflict between state power and local autonomy. Tillman's statist stance was far from principled. During his administration he took a step back, declaring that he approved of lynching, and was even prepared to take a leading role in it, when a man of any color had assaulted a virtuous woman of any color (and he and his supporters agreed that no black woman could ever be virtuous). On balance, then, Tillman steered a course between fighting the mob and leading the mob. He insisted that the state's power be respected, but he also made it clear to white men that the preservation of their honor had primacy over the formalities of the law.

Terence Finnegan's essay takes the story up to the 1910s. He offers a thick description of a notorious lynching incident, in which political antagonisms as well as racial psychology figured prominently. The racial hatred that Abbeville whites felt toward Anthony Crawford was due in large part to his remarkable material success. Crawford was a literate, fifty-six-year-old former slave, who owned over four hundred acres of cotton land west of the town of Abbeville. His prosperity was well known in the white community. On at least two occasions one of the local papers ran a story about the success of his farming operations. The immediate reason for his lynching was relatively trivial: a disagreement over the price of cottonseed. Ultimately, however, the white men who murdered Crawford felt that this black man had challenged their manhood by his economic success. On a Saturday in October 1916 a mob heavily beat Crawford, ritually maltreated his body while he was lying on the ground, and finally hanged him after he was dead. If nothing else, the mob showed that those southerners, mentioned in Kantrowitz's essay, who advocated a "civilizing" of the lynching ritual, had not had much success yet. Crawford's lynching had far-reaching consequences for Abbeville County: whites were unable to stem the migratory flow of black labor out of the county, which increased greatly after the event.

Thus, the last two contributions do more than just discuss the role of the state. They raise crucial questions about the state, honor, and gender within the context of the history of the American South. It is worth looking at these three themes in greater detail, starting with gender.

A central argument in Stephen Kantrowitz's essay refers to what he calls the rape-lynch complex. The historical literature on the South has paid ample attention to white men's anxieties about black men ravishing white women. The rape of a white woman, more often alleged than real, was an offense to her honor as well as to her husband's, and it challenged the honor and masculinity of all white men. The importance of this anxiety was greater than a mere statistical computation of reported motives for lynching would show. Kantrowitz argues that sexual fears were embedded in a more encompassing concern for white men's patriarchal authority. The rape-lynch complex certainly held sway over the minds of white southerners around 1900. It can hardly be a coincidence that Tillman considered the defense of a white woman's honor to be the only motive justifying an infringement upon the state's monopoly on punishment. And, as Finnegan mentions, critics of lynching feared that black men would take revenge for the violence done to them by raping white women. Yet, Finnegan is skeptical about a "psychosexual explanation" for lynching, as he calls it. In an earlier article, he argues that lynching functioned to deny political rights to blacks.[51] Nevertheless, it is clear that feelings of injured manhood played a part in the murder of Anthony Crawford, who was considered "uppity" by white residents of Abbeville. Throughout the South, Terence Finnegan says, white men viewed "uppity" black men as contesting their own manhood; such blacks were successful, not servile.

Hence, even in cases in which female honor was not explicitly referred to, standards of masculinity were involved nonetheless. It may be questioned whether the frequency with which lynched black males were accused of having raped a white woman should be the decisive factor in assessing the value of a psychosexual explanation for the *entire episode* of lynching. To understand why it occurred at all, we probably have to take into account marital and male/female relations among southern whites. Did the marital life of the white middle classes change in the nineteenth century in a way parallel to marital changes among the European middle classes?[52] If so, this may have caused unconscious tensions in southern white men, which they projected onto black men. This hypothesis requires further research on the family and marriage in the South.[53]

Honor is an obvious theme in relation to southern culture. The South was a classical honor-and-shame society, particularly in the antebellum period.[54] Of all such societies, the American South perhaps is the best documented. Moreover, the South's white elites were relatively violence-prone in a manner reminiscent of the medieval European aristocracy. Clearly, the process of spiritualization of honor had not taken root there. In the 1980s, two eminent historians, Bertram Wyatt-Brown and Edward

Ayers, have published about violence and honor in the antebellum South.[55] Wyatt-Brown explains that a strong association with the body underlay the prevailing concept of honor. The imperative of its violent defense pervaded southern life. Contemporaries were said to subscribe to the classical statement that it is better to die than to lose one's honor. It could be lost, for instance, by not reacting to a physical insult such as having one's nose pulled.[56] White men of all social classes shared the honor-and-shame culture (and their women shared it by association, unless they were evangelicals).[57] Whereas lower-class men might challenge each other to fistfights, ritual or not, elite men settled matters by way of a pistol duel. The planters were at least as violent as their social inferiors.

Having returned to the subject of dueling, we must take another look at Europe, where the history of the state's response to dueling was far from linear. France's rulers were bent on suppressing the custom from the beginning of the seventeenth century. Later, Louis XIV was the first monarch who consciously attempted to transform the nobility's conceptions of honor, maintaining that service to the king was the source of supreme honor. In several other countries of early modern Europe, ruling groups similarly attempted to get rid of the duel. They considered it a public infringement on the state's internal monopoly on violence. On the other hand, the authorities in the German lands, notably Prussia, were rather ambivalent. This emerges clearly from many of Frevert's quotations. Well into the nineteenth century, princely advisers wavered between condoning the duel as a necessary instrument to uphold a person's honor and condemning it as a form of private justice. They were conscious of belonging themselves to the elite "entitled to satisfaction." However, it will not do simply to consider the Prussian response to dueling as lagging behind that in western European states. The liberal elites of France and Italy in the second half of the nineteenth century again were in a position similar to that of the Prussian nobility. They were the ruling class, and yet they were positively inclined to this ritual of private settlement. They even saw it as a form of national duty. This poses a problem for any analysis of state formation processes.

As a way to circumvent the problem, it may be supposed that, say, in late nineteenth-century France the state's monopoly on violence was so firmly established that a duel a year or so could not jeopardize it. After all, "common" murders and assaults were more frequent: the monopoly is never absolute. Another route toward explanation is to amend the theory of state formation processes, in order to make room for episodes of increased tolerance of violence. This is the solution adopted by Elias in his discussion of Germany's *Satisfaktionsfähige Gesellschaft*.[58] A third possibility is to follow Hughes's argument that the revival of dueling in liberal Italy can be explained as a "normal" process, intimately related to the early stages of parliamentarism. The new, liberal elite used dueling as a means of setting limits on behavior and legitimizing their own status. He points out that in France, England, and the southern United States, too, the heyday of the modern duel coincided with nascent parliamentarism.[59] As attractive as this argument sounds, the American South may have to be excluded from it.

Dueling in the southern United States formed part of an unbroken tradition of violence. This tradition persisted after 1865 in changed form. Some disagreement exists about whether the Civil War ended dueling. According to Dickson Bruce, the "hierarchical and carefully ordered world" from the antebellum period "had lost its strength." Therefore, sporadic attempts failed to revive the duel after the war.[60] Ayers, on the other hand, says that the custom was still alive in the 1870s; only from the 1880s onward was dueling considered no longer honorable.[61] In any case, intensified racial violence, notably lynching, took the duel's place after the Civil War. There is an intriguing similarity in the state of South Carolina's attitude toward lynching at the end of the nineteenth century and the state of Prussia's attitude toward dueling at the beginning. In both cases, the administration cherished a general principle (racial hegemony, an elitist honor code), which led it to favor a practice (lynching, dueling) which it had to condemn at the same time. In South Carolina, an obvious way to proceed was to promote the state's honor over the citizens' individual honor. As Stephen Kantrowitz shows, Tillman condemned local vigilante justice because it suggested that the state's protection was inadequate, which, by implication, meant a stain upon the state's honor.

The southern culture of violence and honor, then, must be related to the pace of state formation on the American continent. State formation processes in America were quite different from European developments. In America the process of monopolization of violence lagged behind, compared with Europe, and in its turn the South lagged behind the North. I made this point earlier with respect to punishment, but it is equally relevant for attitudes toward violence.[62] The crucial factor, as noted above, is the lack of pacification among the elites in the South, certainly in the antebellum period.

The pacification of the elites formed a major cornerstone of European state formation processes during the early modern period. Europe's aristocracies turned, in Elias's words, from a class of warriors into a class of courtiers.[63] As just suggested, the later revival of dueling formed only a partial countertendency to these early modern developments. In most of Europe, the elites were gradually pacified after the era of the vendetta. Although slower in areas such as Scotland, this process increasingly affected the upper and middle classes.[64] The top groups usually led the way. Thus, Louis XIV had "tamed" the court nobility, but at the same time the older attitudes still prevailed in two provincial cities of southern France. There, young men from the local elite participated in violent clashes between rival bands.[65] Pacification of the elites characterized the Dutch Republic from an early date. Its urban patriciates, certainly in the province of Holland, were not accustomed to engaging in violence. Dueling had never been very common among them.[66] In Amsterdam around 1700, the notion that one's honor had to be defended violently was largely restricted to lower strata. By that time the Dutch elites and middle classes were pacified to a large extent. For the patrician judges it was self-evident, even without a written rule to that effect, that anyone who was attacked had to retreat first, before he could legitimately defend himself.

In the New World this was altogether different. The duty to retreat, inherited from British legal tradition, was gradually turned into its opposite in American law. That is the subject of Richard Maxwell Brown's recent book. Although the larger argument he builds upon his legal-historical exposition has been heavily criticized, this exposition itself has not been questioned.[67] In a similar vein as Brown's critics, I am arguing that the law did not simply shape behavioral norms. The development that finally enthroned no-duty-to-retreat resulted from a complex interaction of ideological pressures, legal and administrative structures, and local circumstances. If a particular state was early in changing the law so as to do away with the British tradition, this does not necessarily mean that the body-associated concept of honor was particularly strong in that state. The overall trend toward no-duty-to-retreat, on the other hand, was certainly related to the peculiarly American trajectory of state formation processes. Monopolization of violence by a central authority was something first achieved in the Northeast toward the end of the eighteenth century. Before the Civil War this process hardly reached the Old South. Courts and juries routinely acquitted those accused of homicide; it was an act of self-defense to shoot your enemy when you saw him, because he might shoot you the next time. The fact that the antebellum South was an honor-and-shame society was related to the relative absence of a central monopoly on violence.[68] Although dueling was imported there as a novel custom, the white elite adopted this custom in the context of an uninterrupted tradition of violent defense of their honor. By contrast, spiritualized concepts of honor, called gentility or dignity by historians, spread in the North in the course of the nineteenth century. A greater degree of pacification was a precondition for this. Still, in America as a whole the process of monopolization of violence remained a partial one in comparison with Europe. Tolerance of private violence was and is greater in American than in European society.[69] This explains the widespread acceptance of the no-duty-to-retreat principle.

A View on the Present

According to Ayers, after the Civil War a version of the old code of honor found its way to the South's black population. "Manhood came to be equated with the extralegal defense of one's honor, a manhood made manifest in control of one's woman and in unquestioning respect from one's peers."[70] The code included a refusal to seek redress through the law, in case of conflicts within their own community, as whites had done earlier, but for different reasons. The antebellum white elite considered themselves above the law; all postwar black people knew they were outside the law. Ayers goes on to suggest, while not stating this explicitly, that the attitude of extralegal defense found its way to the North in the twentieth century, taking hold in urban lower-class neighborhoods irrespective of race or ethnicity. It should be added that the South-North trajectory probably was not the only one. Immigrants from southern Europe, for example, may have acted as cultural mediators in their turn.

Very likely, then, the ancient code of honor and its accompanying culture of violence have not disappeared entirely. This would be in accordance with Elias's theoretical approach. Elias always warned against any kind of teleological concept of long-term developments. They have no endpoint. Elements of earlier phases are observable in the present, though often in a transformed manner. This raises the question to what extent and in what manner "traditional" notions of honor and ritual live on in present-day street violence. A recent book attempts to make precisely this link, tracing the history of one family from the late nineteenth-century South to the urban ghetto of the late twentieth century.[71] It would be a worthwhile undertaking to study modern violent groups, in Europe and America, against the background of the evidence presented in this volume. It is my conviction that our understanding of today's gang cultures can be enhanced by the study of the culture of violence and honor in distant societies in the past.

Notes

1. See, among others, Amussen 1988, Kloek 1990, Perry 1990, Wiesner 1993, Wunder 1992.

2. Of the authors listed above, Wiesner (1993, 5) acknowledges this in her introduction, but the rest of her book is, as her title suggests, only about women and femininity. See, however, her earlier article (Wiesner 1991), which focuses on masculinity.

3. Peter Stearns (1979) must certainly be called a pioneer. On changing concepts of masculinity in nineteenth- and twentieth-century America see Carnes and Griffen 1990 and Rotundo 1993. On men in the Middle Ages see Lees 1994; the apologetic tone of the preface and the introduction to Lees's volume attest to the subject's novelty. The works of two contributors to the current volume, Frevert (1991) and Nye (1993), must also be mentioned here.

4. Important studies include Blok 1980; Bourdieu 1972; Dinges 1994; Muir 1993; Peristiany and Pitt-Rivers 1992; Schreiner and Schwerhoff 1995; and Wyatt-Brown 1982. See also Bennassar 1975, 167–84; and Spierenburg 1991a, 197–200.

5. See Shilling 1993 for a carefully argued assessment of the literature on the relationship between the body and society.

6. This tripartite scheme, in various wordings, is recurrent in the literature on honor. See, however, Stewart 1994, who argues that honor must be viewed primarily as a right.

7. Stewart 1994 (esp. 142). The word *contemporary* is essential, since Stewart presents no historical data for the Bedouins, as he does for Europe.

8. Velzen 1982.

9. Cf. Ikegami 1995.

10. Blok 1980. See also Bourdieu 1980, esp. 111–34.

11. C. W. Bynum 1991; Cadden 1993; and, though less with reference to gender, Pouchelle 1983. See also C. W. Bynum 1987 and Camporesi 1988.

12. "Medieval" mainly stands for the period since about 1100. In fact, the ambiguity about sex and gender may have arisen with the increased emphasis on clerical celibacy in the early twelfth century. Cf. McNamara's contribution to Lees 1994.

13. Cadden 1993, 201–2.

14. C. W. Bynum 1991, 102–14.

15. Laqueur 1990. See also Laqueur's and Londa Schiebinger's contributions to Gallagher and Laqueur 1987. Laqueur's approach differs from that of Foucault (1976) to the extent that the former is concerned with views of what it is to be a man or a woman, rather than with sexuality and the discourse about it. For long-term perspectives on the history of the body generally, see Feher, Naddaff, and Tazi 1989 and Culianu 1991. It is intriguing to realize that the medieval view, that not all bodies can be classified as either male or female, is closer to modern biological knowledge than the view originating in the eighteenth century. Cf. Shilling 1993, 52–53.

16. Cohen and Cohen (1993, 24) consider women's role as slightly more active than other scholars do: "by her beauty, clothing, industry, wit, modesty and social grace, a woman could win honour for herself and for her menfolk." On different conceptions of male and female honor, see also Koorn 1987 and Cavallo and Cerutti 1990.

17. See, among others, Ingram 1987, 125–67.

18. Herlihy (1985, 62) stresses that the Church advocated monogamy and sexual restraint from an early date and claims that the Church had some success in this already in the Middle Ages. However, in the milieu of laymen the double standard continued to operate for a long time.

19. Nye 1993, esp. p. 13.

20. This physical concept of honor and respect remained prevalent for a long time in several social situations. It was a reality for German landlords and serfs around 1700 (Luebke 1993). It still prevailed around 1900 among Sicilian local elites (Blok 1974).

21. Muchembled 1989, esp. pp. 260–68. See also Gauvard 1991, 724–26; Sabean 1984, 144–73.

22. Farr 1988, 180.

23. Cf. Spierenburg 1991b, 44–45 and the literature referred to there.

24. See Simon Stevenson, "The international decline of violence, 1860–1930: If there was one, did it come from a new masculinity?" Paper presented at the nineteenth meeting of the Social Science History Association, Atlanta 1994.

25. E. Cohen 1992, 617–19; T. Cohen 1992, 864. On notions of honor in sixteenth- and seventeenth-century Italy, see also Burke 1987.

26. Valentin Groebner in Schreiner and Schwerhoff 1995, 361–80.

27. Gowing 1994, 32. The other cases discussed in this article contain no references to such a close analogy of honor and the body.

28. Farr 1991.

29. Mohrmann 1977, 237–38, 278n. 55.

30. Andrew 1980; K. Brown 1986, 184–207; Chauchadis 1984; my contribution to this volume.

31. Cf. McGowen 1987. On the body in eighteenth-century England, see also Porter 1991, a programmatic article about the history of the body, in which the subject of honor is strangely absent.

32. Wiesner 1991, 776.

33. Cf. Billacois 1986. Other recent works on dueling, not mentioned already, include Kiernan 1988 and McAleer 1994. Kiernan, however, presents a very outdated, value-laden approach, which seriously hampers his analysis. McAleer's work, largely based on literary

sources, deals with Wilhelmine Germany. While Frevert (note 51 of her contribution) is very critical of it, Nye (note 12 of his contribution) finds it a splendid history.

34. Spierenburg 1984, 189–90.

35. Simpson 1988, 110.

36. Frevert 1991, 196–214 (esp. 202).

37. Brüdermann 1991.

38. See the drawing by Jossot on the cover of Nye 1993.

39. Spierenburg 1994 and 1996.

40. See R. C. Davis 1994.

41. Waardt 1996, 20. See also Marsilje et al. 1990, and De Waardt's contribution to Schreiner and Schwerhoff 1995, 303–19.

42. Muir 1993 (case in Villach on pp. 220–21). Among the English aristocracy, a parallel transition from attack with superior numbers to the duel occurred in the early seventeenth century. See Stone 1965, 225–27, 242–50, 770. Clearly, the exact timing of the change cannot be explained in terms of "modern" vs. "backward" regions; the Friulian chronology must be related to the fact that the duel originated in Italy.

43. In France this was still true for the provincial elites in the early eighteenth century and the lower middle classes in the early nineteenth. Cf. Daumas 1987 and Reddy 1993.

44. Muir (1993) explains the transition from the vendetta to the duel in Friuli along similar lines. By the eighteenth century, at least in England, even suicide was sometimes considered honorable. See Macdonald and Murphy 1990, 182–87.

45. For these examples, see Fehr 1908, 25–26. Compare Stewart 1994, 130–31.

46. Ylikangas 1976, 83, 87–88, 91, 95.

47. Tapio Bergholm, "Violence and Masculinity on the Waterfront: Finland in the 1920s and 1930s," paper presented at the nineteenth meeting of the Social Science History Association, Atlanta 1994.

48. Cf. Weinstein 1994.

49. Mark Haller, "Loansharking in Philadelphia: The Collection of Illegal Debts," paper presented at the nineteenth meeting of the Social Science History Association, Atlanta 1994.

50. Butterfield 1995, 3–18.

51. Finnegan 1995.

52. There is an abundant literature on the family and marriage in early modern and nineteenth-century Europe focusing on emotional relations between spouses. For a synthetic overview, see Spierenburg 1991a, chap. 8. Comparable publications for the American South seem to be more scarce. V. E. Bynum 1992 makes a beginning, but she deals with the antebellum period and focuses on deviant women rather than on marital life among the majority of whites. Peter Bardaglio, *Reconstructing the Household: Families, Sex, and the Law in the Nineteenth-Century South* (Chapel Hill, 1995), came to my attention after I finished writing this introduction.

53. In their meticulous analysis of lynchings, Tolnay and Beck (1995) have no place for the gender dimension. They adopt a basically functionalist perspective, in which the relative frequency of lynching per county is the all-important variable.

54. With "classical honor-and-shame society" I mean that honor and shame played a large role in that society, not that a typological distinction can be made between shame and guilt cultures. Compare the introduction to Peristiany and Pitt-Rivers 1992.

55. Ayers 1984 and Wyatt-Brown 1982. See also Miller 1994.

56. Compare K. Greenberg 1990.

57. According to Wyatt-Brown, southern *men* were hardly influenced at all by (evangelical) religion. See, however, Ownby 1990, who disputes this claim (esp. 12–18).

58. Elias 1992, 61–158.

59. For the chronology of dueling in England, see Simpson 1988, 106–7 and passim.

60. Bruce 1979, 42–43.

61. Ayers 1984, 267–68, 270–71.

62. With respect to punishment, see Spierenburg 1987.

63. Elias 1969, 2:351–69.

64. On Scotland, see K. Brown 1986.

65. Hanlon 1985, 247–48, 251.

66. Van Weel (1977) suggests that the custom of dueling was largely restricted to some groups of students and to foreign soldiers.

67. R. M. Brown 1991. Critical reviews by Roger Lane (*Journal of Social History* 26 [fall 1992]: 211–13) and Eric Monkkonen (*Journal of American History* 79 [March 1993]: 1570–71).

68. Next to this, the type of relations between social classes influences notions of honor: as explained above, honor is exclusive by nature. The fact that the South was a slave society with a rigid hierarchy was an important factor, too.

69. Compare Tilly 1990, 69.

70. Ayers 1984, 234–35.

71. Butterfield 1995.

ONE

ELITE DUELING

THE DUEL is a custom situated at the crossroads of concepts of masculinity, experiences of violence, and codes of honor. The first part of this book deals with the official duel, practiced among elite groups in early modern and modern Europe. Each chapter focuses on a country with its own peculiar history of dueling. Whereas the essay on Germany traces the story back to the early seventeenth century, the contributions on Italy and France pick it up in a later, crucial phase. In fact, all three chapters pay particular attention to the fin de siècle and for obvious reasons. The half century from about 1860 to the First World War is now recognized as a period of the duel's revival. No longer was it the exclusive prerogative of the aristocracy. Many duelists had a bourgeois background, whereas the code of honor that they cherished, in all three countries, was interwoven with nationalism. Together, these three essays offer a comparative perspective on the duel in modern Europe.

Within this overall pattern there were differences of timing. In Germany the duel's history appears to have been characterized by greater continuity than in the other two countries. Hence, Ute Frevert refuses to speak of a revival, pointing to an unbroken line from the early modern period to the "bourgeois era." Steven Hughes, on the other hand, emphasizes the connection between Italian unification and the bourgeois duel, making a case for revival. These positions are not as antagonistic as they would seem at first. Hughes bases his argument primarily on numbers: in the second half of the nineteenth century more duels were fought in Italy than at any time since the sixteenth. Frevert primarily discusses the ideas of contemporary observers and practitioners; she deals with ideology rather than the frequency of dueling. It appears, then, that the ideology of dueling continued to be influential, whereas its actual incidence was subject to ups and downs. In most of Europe, the military formed the bridge between early modern and modern dueling. In France, for example, civilian nobles by 1700 had become less apt to challenge each other, but aristocratic army officers as well as common soldiers continued to resolve conflicts by way of a duel. The custom was carried over to the new national armies of the nineteenth century. Bourgeois officers and, subsequently, bourgeois civilians embraced the duel. To the extent that Germany witnessed a greater historical continuity, this can be explained by the greater impact of the military on its society. Although the Piedmontese military occupied a prominent position in post-unification Italy, the public life of the elites in that country was marked less by military influence than in Germany. In the French Third Republic, the army was hardly a public presence at all.

There were other national differences. The student duel, for example, was mainly a German phenomenon. Its origins probably lay in the aristocratization of German universities in the seventeenth century. The social compulsion to duel, though clearly present everywhere, was particularly strong in Germany. Severe sanctions, including social ostracism, awaited "cowards" who refused to issue a challenge to someone who had insulted them. With respect to the duel's association with nationalism, Italy comes out at the extreme end. Italians sometimes challenged a foreigner to a duel if they felt he had insulted, not them personally, but their country. There are no such examples in the essays on Germany or France. Hughes links the Italians' sensitivity to his overall argument that dueling helped the rising elites of a liberal state handle new freedoms of public speech: a "normal" process inherent to the early stage of a parliamentary system. Significantly, injurious articles in the press were the main cause of duels in Italy, rather than insults face to face.

A crucial difference lay in the attitude of the modern state. In the French penal code (and until 1871 in Rhenish and Bavarian law) dueling was no longer a criminal matter of its own. Duelists were to be sentenced according to the laws of physical injury and manslaughter. Prussian law, which became binding for the whole German Reich in 1871, maintained special legislation for duelists. In 1844 the Prussian minister of justice justified this with the statement that legislators ought to follow public sentiment by refusing to impose a dishonorable punishment for an action that usually stemmed from love of honor and courage. The phrase *dishonorable punishment* is crucial. As a corollary to notions of honor, Germans also had strong feelings about infamy. Particularly infamous were the executioner's touch and punishment generally. So it was felt that doing something for honor's sake, however illegal it might be, could never lead to being subjected to infamy. This vision of dueling as absolute contrast to a state of infamy helps to explain the duel's wide appeal in Germany. Yet the difference in attitudes among the various states should not be exaggerated. In France and Italy, not the law but actual judicial practice was discriminatory. The courts tended to be lenient toward honorable duelists. In fact, duelists received lighter sentences than men engaging in "ordinary violence" in all three countries.

A final difference concerns the end of dueling. This time, Germany and France resemble each other: Frevert and Robert Nye agree that the First World War dealt the final blow. Nye says it most explicitly: what killed the duel was the gulf that separated the peacetime pretensions of courage based on the harmless dueling practices of the day and the real, deadly terrors of the trenches. Moreover, the myth that upper-class men had more courage than ordinary souls had lost credibility, now that simple peasants had shown more valor than the gentlemen who sat out the war in their Parisian bureaus. In Italy, by contrast, the duel reemerged after 1918 and remained prominent until about 1925. Were Italians less shocked by wartime experience than the French and Germans? In any case, the war did not have such a devastating effect on the duel in Italy as it had in the other two countries. This may be explained with reference to the stronger association of the duel with nationalism in Italy and the fact that public speech was the duel's principal arena. Italian dueling took place in a context of nationalism and free speech rather than in tales of courage. So the practice could easily be resumed until the fascist regime finally ended it. The fascists not only suppressed the duel outright but they destroyed its infrastructure by curbing the possibilities for public expression.

1

The Taming of the Noble Ruffian:
Male Violence and Dueling in Early Modern
and Modern Germany

UTE FREVERT

Men's identification with violence is hardly a new topic and was certainly not the creation of feminists in the 1970s. It has long been assumed that men have a special tendency to exercise force, to carry out disputes aggressively, and to advance their interests through violence. But opinions differ widely as to whether this behavior is an anthropological constant and unalterable fact attributable to genes or hormones (e.g., too much testosterone) or not. Much evidence, however, favors social and cultural factors as decisive in how often and how far aggressive tendencies (which are innate in both genders) are manifested. Some societies strictly forbid men violent conduct, whereas others highly reward brash and dashing behavior as well as a readiness to use force.[1] Some societies differentiate male aggressiveness according to age group or class, and some provide reserved areas such as the army or sports where men can practice violent activities in a controlled and authorized setting.

One such setting was the duel: a ritualized act of force between two men for the purpose of reciprocal preservation of honor. Here I will examine dueling as a phenomenon that sheds light on how Central European societies dealt with male violence and how and why they accepted it as long as it was practiced by the social elites according to certain rules. I will also analyze for what reasons violence was individually acted out and what functions it performed across time. Quite obviously, the duel was subject to change, both in its forms and in its performers. In this, it clearly reflected the transition from aristocratic to bourgeois society. Throughout the early modern and modern periods, however, it exemplified masculine values par excellence, values which were and remained closely tied to the exhibition of violent behavior.

Violent Men and the Point d'Honneur in the Early Modern Period

As a new form of single combat between males, the duel established itself in the sixteenth century, first in Spain, Italy, and France, and then in the German territories after the Thirty Years' War. Unlike the chivalrous tournament of the late Middle Ages, the early modern duel was not a fighting game but a serious armed confrontation in which the life of both combatants was at stake. While the tournament was an officially arranged courtly ceremony with hundreds of knights participating, a duel never took place without a specific personal cause. In this it was similar to the feud, but it differed from the feud in its adherence to certain rules and the fact that it generally did not extend to third parties. Such had also been the case for the judicial single combat of the Middle Ages, although the duel was an unofficial rather than an official conflict and thus did not have any legal bearing.

The conflict was generally triggered by an insult or an offense to one's honor, the definition of which might depend on the individual involved. The early modern period was marked by extreme sensitivity in the perception of such offenses and a constant readiness to injure the moral and physical integrity of an opponent. This combined with a generally pugnacious culture, and the period abounded with single combats of a wide variety, including surprise attacks, spontaneous clashes, and carefully arranged duels. Consequently, the borderline between a duel and a mere scrap was not always clear, although the deciding trademark of a duel was that it involved the use of potentially deadly weapons such as sabres, rapiers, or pistols. Thus fistfights or fights with sticks were not regarded as duels but as "scraps" or "scuffles." Furthermore, the duel included a formal ritual; it had to be preceded by a challenge, and seconds had to be involved. Seconds arranged the place and conditions of the duel and were present when it was carried out.

The purpose of such rules was to elevate the single combat of honor above ordinary quarrels and to give it a certain outward dignity. They formed part of a program of controlling emotions and compulsive actions that accompanied what Norbert Elias has called the "process of civilization." This program—if one can call it that—did not put violence in the pillory of public virtue and political morality. Rather, violence was considered necessary and indispensable to solve certain conflicts and to demonstrate power. However, this violence needed to be predictable, calculable, and limited. It had to be rationalized and disciplined, objectives which were accomplished by the duel—or at least *supposedly* accomplished by the duel. Many cases from the early modern period show how difficult it was for contemporaries to obey the rules. In France, the historian François Billacois even sees a deregulation of the duel emerging around the turn of the seventeenth century. Contrary to the duels of the 1550s, which were still carried out in the tradition of judicial combats and chivalrous tournaments and which took place in a highly official and controlled setting—the king himself decided whether a duel was legitimate, set the time and place, and was personally present during the fight—duels in the following decades took on increasingly chaotic and violent traits.

Ironically, this growing violence seems to have been prompted by efforts to control the duel. To the same extent that the secular authorities, following the example of the church, began to forbid and punish the duel, public control and regulation dropped. The threat of punishment by the state led to secrecy, and even though certain forms of the previous ritual were maintained, they did not suffice to prevent the transformation of the duel into a murderous hand-to-hand fight full of thirst for vengeance. Armor was used less and less, and the swift and agile rapier gradually replaced the heavy sword. The fight was carried out in an aggressive manner; its aim was the death or at least the injury of the opponent.

Even the introduction of seconds could not fundamentally "civilize" the single combat of the early modern period. They did not just enforce the rules and ensure the fairness of the fight, as later became the custom. On the contrary, the seconds of the sixteenth and seventeenth centuries understood themselves to be allies and protectors of their clients, and they actively intervened in the encounter. Sometimes each duelist brought

along three or four seconds, who at first fought each other and then joined
their respective principals. These customs also are a reminder of the medieval feud, which focused on two opponents but also included their fol-
lowers. Only gradually did the rule gain acceptance that each opponent
was allowed a single armed second, who could only intervene in the fight
when he saw a serious breach of the rules that posed a threat to his client.[2]

The increasing regulation and civilization of the duel served not only
to contain and control violence. They also had the function of separating
the rituals of violence of the nobility from the kind of encounters found
among the lower social orders. Discipline and rationalization were to be
or become the distinctive traits of the aristocracy. This message was often
disregarded by the nobles themselves and by the men of other classes in
the early modern period. Around the middle of the seventeenth century
there were an increasing number of cases in Hamburg in which "people of
ordinary ranks, following the example of the upper classes" sent out challenges and fought duels.[3] In 1699 there was a duel in Werl between a
member of the renowned *Erbsälzer* guild and an officer in the service of
Denmark during which the guild member was killed. Artisans of the seventeenth century also carried rapiers, allowing them to carry out conflicts
according to the noble example in a "passage at arms."

However, this was not at all in the interest of the sovereign ruler, as
the reaction of the *Kurfürst* to the duel in Werl proved: he forbade the *Erbsälzer* guild to carry rapiers. The guild protested against this prohibition
by arguing that frequently "among people both of the higher and lower
ranks two have a clash with their rapiers"—and in those cases the other
members of their class were not ordered afterwards to "lay down the
rapier."[4] Without a doubt, the availability of deadly weapons increased
the potential for violence at the time. In this regard, the efforts by the authorities to prohibit the use of such weapons are understandable. The nobility itself remained unaffected by this. Sabre, rapier, and sword were the
insignia of its class, and it could not do without them. This not only
counted for active military officers but also for that part of the nobility
that served at court or pursued other forms of civil life. Even the new nobility did not exclude itself. On the contrary, to prove their equality and to
compensate for differences in position, new nobles were even more prepared to adopt aristocratic practices.

Thus, for example, in 1709, the thirty-year-old Johann Hektor von
Klettenberg, whose father had been ennobled by the emperor as a Frank-

furt burgomaster and who did not feel accepted by the other patrician families of the city, deliberately provoked a duel with a member of the rich and renowned von Stallburg family. During a reception he bragged about his heroic deeds so much that one of the von Stallburgs felt compelled to remark that he too stood his ground. Klettenberg demanded proof and announced that the following morning he would bring a set of pistols. Even though Stallburg did not take the matter seriously and some common acquaintances sought to mediate, Klettenberg insisted on his challenge, and the duel took place. After the pistols had failed several times, Stallburg wanted to end the duel, but Klettenberg insisted on a continuation. Consequently, they drew their rapiers, and in the course of the fight Stallburg was so badly wounded that he died on the field. Before expiring he exclaimed: "Brother, I am hit." His opponent had then approached him and responded: "Brother, forgive me." A handshake cemented their reconciliation — and the fraternal bond that had been created through the fight. Such encounters thus traversed the social tensions between the not very wealthy social climbers of recent nobility and the rich patricians of long-standing pedigree.[5]

What is striking here is the readiness with which Stallburg accepted Klettenberg's challenge even though he did not see cause for conflict or a duel. Had he refused, it would have been regarded as cowardice, and Frankfurt society would have blamed him for not accepting the challenge and thus breaking the nobility's unwritten code of honor. To be regarded as a coward for avoiding a duel equaled expulsion from society, a social death sentence, to which possible death in a duel was obviously preferable. This social compulsion to duel was highlighted by the Prussian edict on dueling of 1713, according to which "officers and soldiers who had been insulted or provoked were held despicable and almost unworthy of commerce or company of other people of honor and reputation, if they avoided confrontation with their offenders out of mere fear or out of consideration of the severe punishment required by the edict." The same law also mentioned that among students there were many who consciously provoked a comrade, who was insulted but not prepared to challenge the offender to a duel, to do so after all. They would not only take to task the offended party verbally, by repeating the insult to him "in a very rude way," but also "exclude him from their company, at the table and in conversation, by turning the plates upside down, not offering him a drink, or other humiliating acts and gestures."[6]

It was common knowledge in the early modern era that students were particularly apt to act aggressively and use extreme force. A victim of a typical student "scrap" was Heinrich Platen, a student of noble extraction, killed in 1620. In his funeral address, the Wittenberg superintendent Balduin sharply castigated the extreme violence in the student milieu. Instead of mediating irrelevant arguments with a "joy of peace," they preferred to "fight them out with ferocity." Revenge was a constant motif, and there was a fine line between gaining honor and preserving it. According to the superintendent, "many seek to find great honor in scrapping," while others argued that "one cannot maintain an honorable name in any other way."[7]

Concern over the growth of student dueling was exemplified in a 1686 critique by A. Fritschius, a civil servant from Rudolstadt. He noted that some duels, especially among students from the nobility, arose from a "false opinion of the Point of Honor," according to which an insult demanded "satisfaction." But as a rule most duels were fought "for completely low and irrelevant causes." They arose, he continued, from conflicts rooted in "nightly walks in the streets, so common nowadays, accompanied by barbaric screams, and in feasts and drinking bouts at tavern tables and in private rooms and the consequent excessive drunkenness." Such behavior, common in the student youth culture, apparently led increasingly to conflicts that became more violent because of the growing dissemination of the rapier. Fritschius quoted an old professor as saying, "In my day there were students that carried coats, but nowadays they all look like soldiers." The "coat," the monks' dress that was reminiscent of the ecclesiastical tradition of university life, was replaced in the seventeenth century by aristocratic dress that included the rapier, as universities came more under the influence of the nobility. Each university that wished to attract a noble clientele had to supply a fencing runway and employ a competent fencing master who could instruct the students in the art of crossing swords. According to Fritschius, if the universities had not complied with the needs of their students or had forbidden them to carry rapiers, "such strictness would be followed by the universities' ruin, and the students would be caused to desert the academies entirely."

Nevertheless, there was increasing concern toward the end of the seventeenth century on how "duels and scraps of the students in the academies could be controlled with more vigour." Fritschius, who had sent his work to princes and town magistrates before publication, received positive reactions without exception. Some universities forbade dueling but to little effect. In 1701, the duke of Saxonia, Friedrich, wrote to his noble colleagues that in his opinion "the harmful ill of dueling has caught on both at the courts and among other nobles, as well as in particular at the universities of the Holy Roman Empire in such a way that measures applied against it and repeated sharp orders generally have been to no effect."[8] Like the Saxonian, the duke of Württemberg thought that united action of all princes was necessary to "emphatically oppose this ill that has caught on too much." He remarked that the University of Tübingen turned away "malicious and quasi-habitual duelers." However, gathering from the extensive correspondence between the university and the government, this evidently had not solved the problem.[9]

Despite isolated attempts, there was no success in bringing together all German or even all European rulers, as Friedrich II proposed, for a united initiative against student and nonstudent duels. Many princes did issue edicts "against self-revenge, injuries, disturbances of the peace, and duels" (Prussian mandate of 1713), which were written "with blood" and prescribed the death penalty for duelists who had killed their opponents.[10] But it was exactly such draconian punishments that kept the edicts from ever being applied. Even if a case legitimately came to court, the duelist seldom received his sentence, and he was as a rule reprieved by the prince.

Contemporaries were well aware of this contradiction. Even legal scholars were unable to clear it up. They pleaded for a ban on dueling and strict criminal prosecution, yet they often awarded the duel positive functions. The main reason why it was seen as reprehensible was that it constituted "an intrusion on the sovereignty of the state."[11] The absolutist state was offended by the obvious usurpation of authoritarian power, which undermined the orderly conduct of its jurisdiction. It could not tolerate the fact that its subjects wanted to "administer justice themselves" and that they fell back on violent means of conflict.[12] Such behavior, as the influential jurist Carl Gottlieb Svarez explained to the Prussian crown prince in the early 1790s, violated "the first basic law of civil society according to which its members are obliged not to decide their disputes through private violence, but rather to reach a decision in accordance with the laws of the state through its appointed judges."[13] Karl Reinhold, a professor from Kiel, argued in 1796 that such private adjudication "breaks the treaty that makes the citizen a citizen and makes the state a state."[14]

It was not so much the violence itself of dueling that bothered the princes, but rather the fact that duelists took the law into their own hands. Thus, the mandates against dueling of the late seventeenth and early eighteenth centuries were aimed not so much at the so-called *rencontres,* or spontaneous clashes in which disputes were immediately settled by force and without further preparation. Rulers tended to judge such clashes mildly because they derived from "first and sudden agitation, against which there is no resistance."[15] In contrast, formal duels that were planned without "sudden agitation" were regarded as violating the "high-courtly office" entrusted to the sovereign.[16] Thus, the edict issued by the electoral prince of Jülich, Kleve, and Berg in 1692 instructed the inquiring authorities to investigate meticulously whether alleged *rencontres* were not in fact "real duels" that had been arranged "verbally, or by correspondence, secret messengers, servants or others."[17] Only such an arrangement made private single combat between two subjects a serious problem, a usurpation of "the preserved rights of the sovereign," and hence a crime against the state.[18]

At the same time, though, it was obvious that the state opposed this crime far less strictly in practice than in theory. Immanuel Kant complained in 1798 that the duel "receives leniency from the government, and it is made a matter of so-called honor in the army to take action against insults into one's own hands. In such cases the head of the army does not get involved; without, however, making them publicly legal."[19] Svarez, too, pointed out these political inconsistencies to the future Friedrich Wilhelm III of Prussia when he was still crown prince. On the one hand, the monarch forbade his subjects any initiative toward self-help; on the other, he tolerated it with the nobility and even agreed to dismiss officers who had obeyed the ban on dueling and rejected a challenge: "The officer who fights is taken in. Who doesn't fight is also taken in."[20]

Svarez's colleague Ernst Ferdinand Klein, who worked on a new codification of the dueling laws, came to the conclusion that governments were not really interested in emphasizing the legal ban on dueling. This lack of interest stemmed from the fact that dueling was "too deeply woven into our constitution and our customs." In addition, dueling was practiced almost exclusively by the higher strata of society, which were especially important to the state. There even seemed to be "something solemn and respectable in duels," which as such made them valuable and dear to the authorities. Society was not served "if the total eradication of duels was linked to the extinction of the longing for honor," and Klein further worried that "the violent suffocation even of a false and misguided longing for honor could at the same time easily suffocate the longing for real honor." A state that cared for the moral integrity of its elites must not take such a risk "because with the evil, if it could ever be destroyed, at the same time something very good would be eradicated."[21]

What was this "very solemn and respectable good"? Klein found it in the longing for honor and in the readiness to defend one's honor with life and limb. A similar argument was brought forward by Goethe's brother-in-law, Johann Georg Schlosser. In his opinion it was easier and more forgivable that someone "would let his life be taken without resistance, than his honor, however imagined it may be. As long as we must live with people, we must maintain a position among them. Who lets himself be pushed down, who is kicked in contempt, is worse off than the dead."[22] Bavarian law professor Martin Aschenbrenner conceded that there was "a certain honor of life without which the most upright and talented man could not assert himself; for honor consists in the public opinion of a man who is held to know ways of maintaining his independence."[23]

According to "public opinion," this self-assertion, as a proof of honor, had to be carried out in a courageous, energetic, and decisive manner, so that the duel presented itself as a "vehicle of courage and determination."[24] It was preferable to other ways of securing respect because it mastered violence and passion and only allowed them an ordered, controlled form. In the same sense, Osnabrück civil servant Justus Möser praised the duel in 1786 because it prevented wild outbreaks of self-revenge and "restricted it to a solemn and formal encounter." Thus "nature kept its right," but took on a civilized guise.[25] Six years later the popular philosopher Christian Garve from Breslau honored the duel as cultural progress: "What has been caused by the inadequacy of social institutions, and has had its roots in the independence of passions, has in its consequences helped to give society true advantages and to master these same passions."[26] And in 1827, Goethe saw in the "principle of the point of honor a certain guarantee against raw violence." For that reason he wished it could be "kept alive" by all means.[27]

But a duel did not only seem more civilized and cultivated than a normal scrap; it was also more communicative and entailed a distinctive element of reconciliation and consensus. By agreeing to a fight with the same weapons, chances, and risks, the challenger abstained from any form of revenge or retaliation. Instead, he conveyed the message to his opponent that he accepted him as an equal with whom he would struggle for self-assertion on equal terms. Thus, although an enemy, he could also be a potential friend with the transformation taking place through the fight. In the proximity of death, both combatants underwent a sort of ritual cleansing in which all feelings of hatred were cast away. In the moment of greatest danger each recognized the opponent as his alter ego, who subjected himself to this danger in the same loneliness and freedom. A new connection was thereby established; brotherhood and lifelong friendship could follow such an encounter.[28]

A duel thus separated men less strongly and less permanently than alternative strategies of solving conflicts such as, for example, suing for libel. This was also the opinion of Ernst Ferdinand Klein. For him, the duel was a generally accepted form "under which the divided could approach each other again." This made it extremely useful for social peace.[29] However, like many of his contemporaries, Klein wanted to reserve the duel for serious and grave conflicts. For this reason he wanted duels to be punished by the authorities (even though they were useful). The aim of punishment was not to take revenge or to generally deter duelists. Instead, the measures were to prevent duels from being misused for anything other than solemn and respectable causes. If the duel went unpunished on principle it would quickly degenerate into "dangerous foolishness," and this would seriously damage the philosophy of the duel and its supposedly noble character.[30]

From the perspective of the late eighteenth and early nineteenth centuries, such foolishness, mischief, and passion had already been toned down and had virtually disappeared from the practice of dueling. The demilitarization of the nobility had contributed to this development as well as its growing accommodation to the concentration and representation of power at court.[31] Whereas the duel of the sixteenth century could hardly be told apart from a "scrap" or a "tussle," the duel of the eighteenth century had consistently developed into a highly ritualized single combat of honor, whose formal restrictions reflected the stiff ceremony of the noble courts.

The duelist of the eighteenth century still had to show physical bravery if he did not want to lose the respect of the other members of his class. At the same time, however, he did not use the duel to increase his honor or to win new honor by overcoming his opponent. It was not the victory itself but the willingness to risk his own life that constituted the honorableness of a duelist. Courage and bravery served not to punish the opponent but to protect oneself from disrespect. The forms of the duel also became more civilized and detached. This was supported by the increasing use of firearms, which prevented physical close fighting and allowed the duelists a more measured and disciplined conduct. The seconds acted more and more exclusively as public supervisors who made sure that the duel did not degenerate into an emotional act of revenge.

According to observers, even the willingness to get into a duel had diminished significantly in comparison with earlier times. "It is true," an anonymous author wrote in 1757, "one isn't as anxious any more to put one's honor into provoked quarrels."[32] Likewise, according to Christoph Meiners, a professor from Göttingen, professional ruffians were no longer tolerated in the enlightened society of his time. Only serious insults that were irredeemable by "either the judgment of a court or the revocation and declaration of honor by the offender" could spark a duel that was "if not publicly allowed, at least quietly tolerated or excused."[33]

Whether duels really took place less frequently in the eighteenth century than in the seventeenth or sixteenth is beyond our knowledge. There was no official record of duels. Furthermore, publicity was avoided if possible in an effort not to draw the attention of the courts even if they did not look too closely into these matters. Most duels took place secretly or became known only to a chosen few whose discretion could be trusted. Contemporary opinions and assumptions thus have to be dealt with carefully. Too often they formed part of politically biased strategies of argumentation. Thus authors who felt committed to a middle-class, "enlightened" creed in progress generally tended to note a diminishing tendency to duel, whereas contemporaries who were more skeptical or pessimistic about progress (or who demanded political intervention) were more likely to announce an increase in fights of honor. Thus baron Adolph von Knigge noted in 1785 that duels were becoming "more and more rare."[34] On the other hand, in 1819 Bavarian parliamentarians, asking the king for a stricter law on dueling, complained that the "prejudice" was anything but abating. On the contrary, it was constantly taking in wider circles and had, "so to speak, become a fashion."[35] In the same year, the author of a philosophical treatise on dueling estimated "at least two thousand duels taking place in Germany every year"—a number that can be neither verified nor falsified.[36]

The Duel in the Age of Bourgeois Society

We do have reliable information, though, for the late nineteenth and early twentieth centuries. The German Reich began keeping criminal statistics in 1882 and between that year and 1912 they reveal 2,111 criminal cases against dueling. Altogether, 3,466 men were *convicted* between 1882 and 1914 for offenses related to dueling. This, however, was only the tip of the iceberg, and jurists agreed that the criminal statistics did not give "a true picture of the actual frequency of the duel in Germany."[37] Only a fraction of all duels ever came before a court. As a rule, all those involved remained silent. Because a duel was based on the agreement of both sides, there was generally no legal plaintiff. In this it differed from other crimes such as physical injury or theft. But even if information leaked and rumors spread, it was never certain that there would be a police inquiry or that the public prosecutor would raise charges.

In view of this situation it is hardly possible to say that dueling no longer had a place in the age of bourgeois society.[38] On the contrary, the single combat of honor was able to maintain its position in the nineteenth century in most European states including France, Russia, Italy, Austria-Hungary, and Germany. Only England and the northern European countries provided an exception.[39] Evidently, the duel and its underlying principles were able to survive in bourgeois societies and did not lose their appeal. At first sight, this may seem surprising. After all, bourgeois society, as it began to develop from the ancien régime at the end of the eighteenth century, saw itself as a firmly civic community. At least in theory, violence was a highly suspicious way of solving conflicts. That citizens sought to settle their disputes or conflicts of interests by use of force did not seem to fit into the concept of bourgeois society acting in a rational and disciplined manner. Political theorists accepted that war was often unavoidable for protection against outside threats, but within society they wanted to avoid when possible the "small-format war." For example, in 1843 the representatives of the Rhenish provincial parliament argued, "Our time of spiritual maturity can no longer accept intrusions of violence and self-help and can only embrace legality."[40]

This message was only partly received by the citizens, though. Neither men from the provincial and urban lower classes nor those belonging to the better-off circles of society could bring themselves to completely renounce physical force. Whereas journeymen, day laborers, and factory workers sought to decide their quarrels with fistfights or knives, military officers and those with a university background held onto the practice of dueling. However, unlike men of the lower classes, potential and actual duelists tried to justify their actions politically and morally by bringing them into accord with the principles of civil society.

Thus the famous law professor Rudolf von Ihering left no doubt in 1872 that he considered the "courageous fight" to be a "duty of moral and physical self-preservation." He saw duels, like wars and revolutions, as "scenes of the same drama: the fight for justice." That the use of direct force played an indispensable role was evidently a matter of course for Ihering and did not need to be questioned any further. Just as he, like most of his contemporaries, accepted war as a legitimate form of international conflict management, Ihering also recognized the violence in a duel as justified and necessary.[41]

As long as one could not do without war, so the argument ran again and again, the duel also had to be tolerated because it was based on the same "law of nature."[42] It was no coincidence that in the midst of World War I, when "raw violence alone now rules the earthly existence of men," the writer Hermann Bahr gave this "law of nature" some thought. As "an old duelist, though retired now for many years," he understood the duel as an expression of "the last earthly truth," according to which "justice, conscience, spirit, mind, or whatever else we might call the presumed powers of the human community, are only a pretext, shiny façades, mild illusions, but hidden inside is the lord of life himself: raw violence."[43]

In the case of the duel, however, this violence did not break into civilized "civil life" in a "raw" or "blunt" manner but slipped on a "dignified and aesthetic" garment.[44] According to Jena professor of philosophy Jakob Friedrich Fries, this was thanks to "fighting regulations," which "granted each man the right to the same advantages in the fight." Thus the duel of honor strictly speaking was "something in between war, in which all violence and trickery are allowed, and peace, in which only the law prevails."[45] In the duel, to take up a phrase of 1805, violence was forced to "be just."[46] This was supported by binding rules that steered, controlled, and limited the use of force. Without these rules a duel was no longer a duel, a fact which state legislation also took into account by only regarding those fights carried out in accordance with the regulations as legally privileged duels. Fights without strict rules fell under the regular laws for physical injury, manslaughter, or murder.

With this limited definition of a "legal" duel, legislators were making a clear social distinction. It was assumed that the duel's elaborate code of rules could only be learned and applied by members of the upper classes. Only among such people, a high civil servant of the Prussian ministry of justice argued in 1833, "was found the respect for custom, as well as the cast of mind and moderation, which contain the only guarantee against the most dangerous consequences of the duel." The scuffles of the "lower popular classes," on the other hand, were "disorderly scraps," in contrast to which the duel stood out positively as a demonstration of "honor and morals."[47]

Thus, the reformed legal system of the nineteenth century also assigned the duel a special elevated position. Whereas French law (and under its influence Rhenish and Bavarian law) had erased dueling as a criminal matter of its own, Prussian law, which became binding for the whole German Reich in 1871, maintained special legislation for duelists. They should not, as was designated by the French model, be sentenced according to the laws of physical injury and manslaughter, but rather according to those regulations designed specifically regarding the practice. After all, duelists were not "raw, criminal, or foolish and unreasonable people," but "common members of classes in which honor and obedience of the law are held highest, who stand closest to the monarch." Even though their action was illegal, it was done for the most respectable motives and fulfilled "what public opinion honored and demanded."[48] The Prussian minister of justice Friedrich von Savigny also agreed with this concept. In 1844 he justified the duel's special status by saying that the legislator "must not stand in direct opposition to public sentiment, and so must not pronounce himself in favour of a dishonorable punishment for an action which, as a rule, stems from love of honor and courage."[49]

Love of honor and courage—these politically desirable virtues distinguished not only the nobility in the nineteenth century but also large parts of the middle class. When the *Allgemeines Landrecht für die Preußischen Staaten* came into force in 1794, it had still excluded them from the dueling society. At the time, the law had not accepted fights among nonnobles as duels; instead, it had classified them as attempted murder.[50] The Prussian criminal law enacted in 1851, however, repealed the privileges of the exclusive "dueling classes." Thus it took into account a social and economic development by which the middle or "educated" classes had risen into the circle of society capable of giving satisfaction. In the nineteenth century,

in fact, duels were no longer confined to the nobility but increasingly occurred among members of the middle classes. Of the 232 Prussian duelists
whose encounters took place between 1800 and 1869 and could be reconstructed from the records, at least 101, or some 44 percent, were of noble
birth. In contrast, of the 303 duelists who found their way into Prussian
judiciary, ministry, and cabinet documents between 1870 and 1914, nobles
accounted for no more than 19 percent.

Thus, within a century, a model of behavior, which had its roots in
early modern noble culture and had until then been jealously guarded by
the aristocracy, had been passed down to the middle classes. But what exactly persuaded middle-class men to take up the duel and the code of
honor connected to it? Did they merely "copy the aristocracy's manners,"
as Social Democratic Party leader August Bebel suspected in 1896 and as
some historians keep on arguing? [51] Or were there other more "bourgeois"
motives? In answer, a distinction needs to be made between internal and
external motives, that is, between individual tendencies and social pressures. On the one hand, middle-class men were influenced increasingly by
institutions that obeyed the *point d'honneur* strictly and kept it alive. The
most important of these institutions was the military, in which up to
World War I (and after) the compulsion to duel was semiofficially in force
and was approved by the king and *kaiser*. In 1858, the Bavarian minister
of war Wilhelm von Manz saw the duel "closely connected to the honor of
noblemen which was the main support of the warrior-class." [52] In 1912 his
successor still characterized dueling as a "basic pillar of the army." Its
main function was to prevent "the dangers of the loss of habit of belligerent virtues" that arose during long periods of peace. For this reason both
the officer corps and the state were interested in preserving the duel as a
demonstration of "belligerent courage and self-sacrifice." Thus, the com-
mander-in-chief must maintain "the undisputed right to dispel weak elements that cannot meet these requirements." [53]

To the same extent that middle-class men became military officers — in
1860, 35 percent of the Prussian officer corps had middle-class back-
grounds, increasing to 70 percent by 1913 — they also became accustomed
to the social pressure that demanded dueling for honor. [54] This was true
even of those men who did not want to become professional officers. During their year of obligatory service, middle-class recruits became familiar
with honor as defined by the military; if they strove for the rank of an officer in the reserve, they had to arrange their civil lives in strict accordance

with it. Again and again it was impressed upon them from the highest places that they "had to remember their position as an officer while working in a business." Even as civilians, they were always under the obligation to care for "the preservation of their honor as members of the officer corps."[55] Evidently these admonitions proved successful. According to the Ministry of War, officers of the reserve were more frequently involved in duels at the end of the nineteenth and at the beginning of the twentieth century than active officers. A representative to the Imperial Diet critically commented on these figures, saying that officers of the reserve apparently tended "to be even more eager than the active officers to show a certain vigour and to put an exaggerated amount of emphasis on the point of honor."[56]

Such exaggeration could be related to the fact that reserve officers were under a double social obligation to duel. After all, the army was not the only institution in which the *point d'honneur* was at home. It was also practiced at the universities. By the end of the nineteenth century, half of all German students belonged to special societies, and two-thirds of these gave — as the jargon of the time called it — "satisfaction." Even the newly founded gymnastics, choral, scientific, and regional societies, which were often critical rivals of the established student corps and fraternities, very quickly adopted the code of honor of the traditional associations.

This code, which increasingly began to appear in print after the late eighteenth century, obligated students to react to insults with a challenge to a duel. Among themselves, as well as in their dealings with officers, nobles, and men with university degrees, conflicts of honor had to be settled by an armed encounter. Thus, the student body, which had been predominantly middle class as early as the eighteenth century, claimed a concept of honor equal to that of the nobility and officers. It understood itself as "a separate class, isolated from the other citizens," which competed with nobles and officers for high social standing.[57]

Among students, equality was to prevail; the "advantage of birth" lost its validity.[58] Noble and middle-class students were united, as the physician Adolf Kußmaul wrote remembering his Heidelberg student days, in "a student knighthood, in which princes and barons, sons of civil servants and farmers honored each other as free and equal society members."[59] The code of honor and the practice of dueling were considered positive influences on "suppressing a stupid pride of ancestry and [creating] an equality of nobles and the bourgeoisie." Whereas at the end of the eighteenth century no nobleman outside the university would have degraded himself to duel with a commoner, it evidently became no longer "advisable among students to turn down a duel under the pretext of aristocracy and inequality of class."[60] Such a refusal would have been read as a sign of cowardice and would have lastingly excluded the person concerned from the social respect of his fellow students.

That students in particular cultivated a concept of honor connected to the demonstration of courage and violence had much to do with their age structure and the specific demands of adolescence. Just like the journeymen, with whom they frequently quarreled — especially in the eighteenth century — and who cultivated a raw and aggressive disposition, students also sought to overcome their insecurities of age and status by a deliberately vigorous and dashing *"comment."* They wanted to "show themselves manly in all circumstances"; they wanted to be seen as adults.[61] For this purpose they invented a model of behavior that stressed discipline, comradeship, bravery, and unconditional loyalty, as well as the ability to hold one's drink. Within this ethos, the duel played an essential role. As proof of courage, determination, aggression, and the acceptance of violence, it gave youthful students a manly dignity that masked the actual dependence of their position. The duel, according to Friedrich Schleiermacher in 1808, embodied the students' interest in "gaining the highest dignity," and he recommended it as an "indispensable instrument of male character formation."[62]

The students' longing for self-assertion and initiation was indeed very strong. This was especially obvious in a new form of ritualized single combat, which was adopted at the universities in the course of the nineteenth century and which originally had little in common with the classic duel of honor. In these so-called fencing bouts, the particular clothing, weapons, and methods generally ruled out serious injuries. Reasons for such bouts also differed significantly from those of the duel, because they were based on "stylized insults," which had been invented by the student societies and which were exchanged between their members.[63] From the middle of the nineteenth century even these imitated insults were completely given up, and fencing bouts were arranged by "assignment." Any personal motive had disappeared from such encounters; the only point was to try one's strength, show courage, demonstrate steadfastness, and make one's mark as a worthy society member. More than three-fourths of the annual eight thousand sabre duels that took place at German universities in the 1890s were fencing bouts arranged by assignment and constituted little more than fighting games. Just under a quarter were light duels of honor that were contracted independently of the regular rituals of fencing bouts.[64] Thus, the duel had not disappeared from the student environment but was restrained in everyday university life.

For this reason, fencing bouts had a double function. On the one hand, they helped to maintain a certain aggressiveness and a preparedness to use force in the way that students behaved, but without posing a serious threat to life and limb. On the other hand, they kept up the memory of the classic duel of honor and even habituated students to its precepts. When, in the 1850s, the young fraternity member Heinrich von Treitschke was insulted by a corps student "in the most vulgar way," he challenged him to a pistol duel. To his father he justified himself by saying, "I did not want to fight out a matter of honor with such a silly thing as a sabre bout."[65]

The societies themselves took scrupulous care that their members acted in accordance with the *comment* (the societies' rules of correct behavior) and reacted to serious insults in an appropriate fashion, that is, by a challenge to a duel. Refusals to act accordingly were punished with exclusion. In this way the student societies maintained a strong compulsion to duel among their members, similar to that of the officer corps. More important and more successful than the threat of severe sanctions, however, was the habitus that the societies inculcated in their members. It remained influential long after the student had left the university and had become a graduate member of a fraternity. Civil servants, lawyers, doctors, philologists, technicians, and engineers who had belonged to student societies were likely to take the laws of honor seriously in their later lives and act according to them.

The lawyer Ernst Meyer, for instance, had long passed thirty when he fought a duel with a Prussian officer named von Donop in 1839. Even though his student days were a decade behind him, in his encounter with von Donop he instinctively fell back upon the forms and habits practiced at the university. When the officer called him a "silly boy," the old pattern of escalation kicked in: "Blushing, I must admit it," Meyer wrote in his defense statement, "that at the moment the long-forgotten student-*comment* intruded into my mind." It induced him to respond that von Donop was "a most miserable cur," an insult that had to be followed by an immediate challenge to a duel.[66] If his memory had failed him, he might have been reminded of his duties by his former student society. This happened in 1885 to the Berlin architect Bornemann, who, having been slapped by a colleague named Krause, at first "took no further action." Thereupon, Krause reported the case to Bornemann's old student dueling society, which instructed its former member to issue a challenge. Bornemann subsequently agreed to do so. A married man in his late twenties, Krause had evidently internalized the rules of the academic *comment* better than Bornemann and did not need any official admonition.[67]

The social institutions that embraced the dueling code — student societies as well as the army — surely did not exercise complete control over the actions of their members. There were repeated cases of men who successfully sought to evade the compulsion to duel. But there was no massive opposition to the duel in imperial Germany; rather, the practice was generally accepted. This loyalty to the code cannot simply be explained as the result of the institutional support that dueling found in the army and universities. Without being convinced of the individual "meaning" of a single combat, thousands of men would not have put their lives at stake, written farewell letters to their closest relatives, and suffered both the fear and reality of death. Social pressure alone could not have promoted such sacrifice. It had to be augmented by what dueling supporters had internalized and what they called its "idealistic side."

Masculinity and Violence in the Duel

This idealistic side was closely connected to the proof of manliness shown in the duel. A highly acclaimed masculine nature could be expressed and validated through dueling, which simultaneously provided the opportunity to distinguish certain male gender characteristics purely and clearly from the female and to relate them to each other. It was taken for granted in nineteenth-century gender discourse that a man should embody a certain wildness and roughness. According to an encyclopedia of 1806, the term *male* carried "the connotation of strength and bravery," whereas for another of 1824, being a man was associated with courage, power, and "bursting passion." It continued that "from man loud desire rages" compared with woman, in whom "quiet longing is at home." And further on: "The male must gain, the female seeks to preserve; the male by use of force, the female with kindness — or cunning."[68]

Another encyclopedia, this time from 1835, affirmed that the basis of force and violence was located in the male body: "Physically the male is indicated by larger size, stronger bones, coarser muscles; mentally, however, by more courage based on a greater feeling of strength and thus a greater ability to perform the strenuous deeds of life; at the same time [he has] a strong compulsion to assert himself in life with his powers and his will as the more able sex in general; for this reason, war, hunting, taming of animals, and the larger part of those deeds demanding physical strength are for the most part done by men, just as in creating and destroying it is the male character that mainly proves itself."[69] Violence and destruction belonged to the "male character" as much as the impulse to build and the traits of fatherly protection. One set could not come without the other.

Such ideas endured deep into the twentieth century. A Catholic reference book noted as late as 1933: "To real manliness belong strength, bravery, . . . readiness for life's emergencies and commitment in case of danger. Participation in public affairs, to fight for the community's goals, lies within the nature of the male. Belligerence and the task of safeguarding his community, authority, discipline, leadership and power, the male regards as his natural prerogative. Man moulds the state, its hardness corresponding to his nature; he carries out the historical clashes, and fights the wars." However, to this positive characterization the dictionary added a warning not to overemphasize "wildness, rawness, and violence." Instead, the object was to work toward a "limitation and check on the concepts of honor and war" and to tone down the destructive and aggressive potential of masculinity.[70] Without a doubt, this appeal referred to the extreme aggressive militant cult of masculinity brought about by the end of the Weimar Republic and the National Socialists' marching hordes. In the brawls and streetfights of the early 1930s, the destructive element of "manhood" surfaced unvarnished and without restraint. In the end, violence became a frenzy, a medium in which virility and power could be experienced.[71]

Compared with this, the nineteenth century gave male violence a significantly more disciplined form. Except for the army and the police, which were authorized by the state to exercise force, there were no associations whose principles of organization included instrumental violence. The vigorous, expressive use of force was also strictly regulated. Only in the "society of those capable of giving satisfaction" and in student fencing bouts were men allowed to let off steam, and then only in a well-ordered, predictable, and controlled form. It was exactly this form which made such violence acceptable to the civil society of the bourgeois age. Under the condition that violence was bounded and restricted, it could be integrated into the character of the male gender and even perform important educational functions. These achievements were expressed clearly in the self-descriptions of duelists.

The duels by assignment, for example, were supposed to "toughen up and increase the student's personal courage and to train him to become aware of his strength and manliness." The duelist had to prove this manliness by entering the fencing ground without a sign of fear and also giving no indication that might be read as weakness or cowardice. For instance, the *comments* of the early nineteenth century labeled those who retreated during a duel beyond the boundary of the fencing runway as cowards. In the second half of the nineteenth century such strictures increased. "The first requirement" of a good fencing bout, the fraternity member Georg Pusch reported, "is now to 'stand.' We are no longer satisfied if a student merely steps up to fence wearing the colours of his society, but we demand that he takes the blows he cannot parry without even flinching."[72]

The style of fencing also changed: instead of priding themselves on the aesthetics of fencing, with equal emphasis on offense and defense, the duelists of the 1880s struck at each other simultaneously and without restraint. The Prussian minister of justice remarked disapprovingly that they "regarded the observance of skillful rules of defense as stemming from cowardice."[73] What must have seemed to fencing masters as a mockery of their art, the students took as an expression of the highest vigor and of a dashing character. They were not bothered by the serious injuries it caused; they did not care that many a society member reminded contemporaries "vividly of a beef steak."[74] On the contrary, dueling scars on the face were proof of special courage and bravery.

Even the new rules were lopsided in their emphasis. Evidently, more important than the ability to strike out bravely was the ability to take the opponent's blows without a flicker of fear or pain. This was thought to be an essential "aid for the education of character," which was at least equally important for later life as demonstrating courageous aggressiveness. Thus one tract of the 1880s preached: "Once you have looked the opponent in the eye a couple of times when the swords cross, and do not flinch when one blow after the other hits home and warm blood runs down the body, then it will also be easier in difficult situations in life to maintain one's composure, and not only to bear physical, but also emotional pain more easily."[75]

In 1912 the dueling societies proclaimed in unison that the idea of the

fencing bout was by no means "to injure the opponent as gravely as possible. Of course, any duelist can be joyous of a victory. But this question is
never central in the evaluation of a fencing bout. Here the only matter is
whether the duelist has 'stood well,' that he has shown no fear of the blow,
the gashing wound, and that the pain has not brought about any sound.
Truly, the fencing bout is merely an aid for the education of manly
courage, self-control, the decent treatment of a fellow student even if he
is the opponent, and the responsibility of everything one does."[76] In imperial Germany this argument found the highest validation. Kaiser Wilhelm II emphasized in 1891 that fencing bouts "toughen up the courage
and strength of a man, and that basis of steadfastness is won that becomes
important later in life."[77] In parliament both liberal and conservative representatives praised the positive educational effect of such armed encounters. "The German man," the Württemberg parliamentarian and university chancellor Carl Heinrich von Weizsäcker said in 1897, "should be
able to defend himself in every sense and be educated in this way."[78] Likewise, according to the *Hamburger Nachrichen* on April 25, 1896: "No other
physical exercise has such a positive effect on the development of personality, strength of character and courage as exercise with the sword." After
all, "when evaluating the student fencing bout, one has to assume that at
the university the young student is not only to be educated in his subject
but also should receive the basis for his whole future destiny. It can only
help his manner as a man to become accustomed to arranging his behavior
according to his duties and personal responsibilities."

The student duel thus conveyed an education toward manliness — a
manliness combining strength, power, self-control, and aggressiveness.
This manliness was in turn expressed perfectly in the duel. Here too, "the
central element was to *face* the opponent," whereas the actual outcome of
the combat became secondary or even "completely irrelevant."[79] This
sharply distinguished the duel of the nineteenth century from its predecessors of the sixteenth and seventeenth centuries, which had emphasized
the result, that is, who won and who lost, as being of primary importance.
This shows how much the image of manliness had changed over time. In
the first half of the eighteenth century a man could play out passion and
"intense emotions," whereas a century and half later, one had to keep
a cool head and exhibit absolute "calm and sangfroid."[80] For the "educated," the duel thus became a means to "protect themselves against an excessive amount of their own passion."[81]

The duel served therefore to enable a man to act out his strength, power, and violence in a disciplined and controlled form. To forbid him this behavior was, according to von Ihering, an expression of "unmanliness" and "moral castration."[82] Conversely, people of the "better society" regarded a man who evaded a duel as a coward and a weakling. Even the German Anti-Dueling League, founded in 1902, expressly refused to impose a formal promise on its members not to fight duels under any circumstances. Even they had to maintain the liberty to "show that we are not what we are thought to be — namely cowards."[83]

That they were neither cowardly nor treacherous, duelists demonstrated by facing each other as equals. They acted under the same conditions and with the same weapons, just as they shared the same chances and risks. The violence they practiced was mutual and hence "just." Nobody was cheated. Each used force actively and suffered it at the same time. Consequently, the duel was an act of violence based on reciprocal consent: a treaty that allowed the mutual acceptance of physical aggression within a set frame of rules.

It was a matter of course that such a treaty could only be concluded by men within the better circles of society. Men of the lower social classes were not seen as having the necessary rationality, control of emotions, and self-discipline. Equally unthinkable was a duel between a man and a woman. Women, so it was believed, were just as incapable as men of the lower classes of behaving in a disciplined, calm, and cool-headed manner during a conflict. Besides, it was considered contrary to their womanly character — the main traits of which were thought to be gentleness, love, weakness, and fearfulness — to get involved in a violent fight.[84] Contemporaries of the nineteenth century were convinced with few exceptions that nature had arranged it that way: "The whole moral existence of the female was based on demureness and chastity, while that of the male rested on courage and strength."[85] That is why, as the liberal Carl Welcker noted, "for the female, an offence against womanly modesty and chasteness, and for the male, unmanly cowardice, lead to the loss of honor and respect."[86]

In conclusion, men of the middle class and nobility used the duel during the nineteenth century to prove that they were neither unmanly nor cowardly. Thus they also earned the reputation with women of being "quite piquant and interesting."[87] At the same time, the male code of honor put enormous pressure on women. Not all but many duels were fought over the issue of adultery. As the Prussian minister of justice Beseler explained with sympathy in 1907, a husband whose virility was under attack sought to "restore his questioned manliness through a duel."[88] Challenging his rival with sword or pistol, he saved his male honor, and if he suffered injury or death, it was his wife's fault. A married woman of a noble or a middle-class family thus did well to scrupulously control her sexuality and to avoid unfaithfulness, if possible. But a young, unmarried woman was also obliged to guard her honor, which meant her chastity.[89] If she did not, it could happen that her father or brother would challenge her "seducer" to a duel. By doing this, he did not save the honor of his daughter or sister, which was lost once and for all, but rather his own.

Of course, the dueling code put pressure not only on women but also on men. As the Prussian minister of war von Falkenhayn stated in 1914, it forced a distinctly belligerent behavior upon men that was supposed to suppress any doubt about their "manliness and their ability to defend themselves."[90] It demanded actions from them, the violence of which endangered their own and other men's existence. Nevertheless, they held on to the duel up until World War I—despite the criticism of Social Democrats, leftist liberals, Catholics, and feminists. It was only due to the experience of unrestricted violence in an industrialized mass war and a series of social changes that the duel lost its ground as a reserved area of controlled violence after 1918.[91]

Notes

1. See D. Gilmore 1990, esp. chap. 9.
2. Billacois 1986; Kiernan 1988.
3. "Mandat, daß niemand zu Duellen ausfordern, noch sich dazu ausfordern lassen soll" [Edict stating that nobody shall give or accept a challenge to a duel] (29 February 1660), in *Sammlung der von E. Hochedlen Rate der Stadt Hamburg sowohl zur Handhabung der Gesetze und Verfassungen als bei besonderen Ereignissen in Bürger—und kirchlichen, auch Kammer-Handlungs—und übrigen Polizei-Angelegenheiten und Geschäften vom Anfange des 17. Jahrhunderts bis auf die itzige Zeit ausgegangenen allgemeinen Mandate, bestimmten Befehle und Bescheide, auch beliebten Aufträgen und verkündigten Anordnungen* (Hamburg, 1763), 1:170–71.
4. Preising 1959.
5. Weber 1857, 109–10.
6. *Sr. Königl. Majestät in Preussen, und Churfürstl. Durchl. zu Brandenburg Erklärtes und*

erneuertes Mandat, wider die Selbst-Rache, Injurien, Friedens-Stöhrungen, und Duelle (Berlin, 1713), 3, 15.

7. Balduin 1621, n.p.

8. Hauptstaatsarchiv Stuttgart, A 202 Bü 2534 (letter dating from 11 November 1701).

9. Hauptstaatsarchiv Stuttgart, A 202 Bü 2534 (reply dating from 30 March 1702); A 274 Bü 64.

10. See Prokowsky 1965.

11. Schlözer 1786, 3.

12. Bavarian dueling mandate (1779), in Meyr 1784, 137–45.

13. Svarez 1960, 411.

14. Reinhold 1796, 130ff.

15. Scotti 1821, 218 (quotation from a 1692 edict).

16. Bavarian dueling mandate (1773), in Meyr 1784, 81–85.

17. Scotti 1821, 207–21.

18. Svarez 1960, 412 (quotation); Aschenbrenner 1804, 19ff.; Roßhirt 1819, 465.

19. Kant 1968, 259.

20. Svarez 1960, 415.

21. Geheimes Staatsarchiv Berlin-Dahlem, Rep. 84 a, no. 8034 (17 August 1809).

22. "S.R." [= J. G. Schlosser]: Schlosser 1776, 1129–30.

23. Aschenbrenner 1804, 29.

24. Leo 1787, 20.

25. Möser n.d., 117.

26. Garve 1974, 623–24.

27. Müller 1982, 162.

28. Loen 1751, 447; *Von den in Deutschland gewöhnlichen Gebräuchen bei Duellen und über die Mittel die Duelle abzustellen* (Leipzig, 1804), 109–10. See also the Klettenberg case, discussed above.

29. Klein 1805, 144.

30. Geheimes Staatsarchiv Berlin-Dahlem, Rep. 84 a, no. 8034 (17 August 1809).

31. See Elias 1983, esp. chap. 5; Guttandin 1993.

32. "Historisch-moralische Abhandlung von den Zweykämpfen der Deutschen und anderer Völker in den mittlern Zeiten," *Nützliche Sammlungen* 65 (1757): 1030.

33. Meiners 1788, 678.

34. Knigge 1978, 108.

35. *Verhandlungen der Zweiten Kammer der Ständeversammlung des Königreichs Baiern* (Munich, 1819), 3:60.

36. Penzenkuffer 1819, 4.

37. Kohlrausch, Zweikampf, in *Vergleichende Darstellung des deutschen und ausländischen Strafrechts* (Berlin, 1906), 3:146.

38. Billacois calls nineteenth-century duels a mere "echo," and Kiernan suggests a rebirth of dueling in this period, which rests on the (false) assertion that dueling had died out before.

39. For France, see Nye 1993; for Austria: Deák 1992, chap. 6; for Germany: Elias 1989, 61–158; Frevert 1995a; McAleer 1994; for Britain, Frevert 1993.

40. *Verhandlungen des 7. Rheinischen Provinziallandtags 1843* (Koblenz 1843), 77–78.

41. Ihering 1872, 21, 35, 99.

42. Bartunek 1912, 8.

43. Bahr 1918, 228–29.

44. *Das Duell in seiner moralischen und gesellschaftlichen Berechtigung* (Leipzig, 1871), 5.

45. Fries 1818, 337.

46. "Einige Bemerkungen über die Dienstverhältnisse im Militair," *Neues militairisches Journal* 13 (1805): 52.

47. *Motive zum revidirten Entwurf des Strafgesetzbuchs für die Preußischen Staaten* (Berlin, 1833), 1:162, 156, 154.

48. Ibid., 1:103, 115.

49. Geheimes Staatsarchiv Berlin-Dahlem, Rep. 84 a, no. 8035 (18 September 1844).

50. *Allgemeines Landrecht* 1970, 694.

51. *Stenographische Berichte über die Verhandlungen des Reichstags, 9. Legislaturperiode, IV. Session 1895/97* (Berlin 1896), 3:1809 (Bebel quote). McAleer's (1994) interpretation has been heavily criticized by Richard Evans (*Times Literary Supplement*, 16 December 1994), David Blackbourn (*London Review of Books*, 9 February 1995), and Ute Frevert (*Journal of Modern History*, 1996).

52. Bayerisches Hauptstaatsarchiv, Munich, Abt. IV, A XIII 3, Fasz. 4a (9 August 1858).

53. Bayerisches Hauptstaatsarchiv, Munich, Abt. IV, M Kr no. 11097 (29 December 1912).

54. Cited figures in Demeter 1965, 29.

55. Quote ibid., 288; Bundesarchiv-Militärarchiv, Freiburg, RM 3/v.10118 (18 January 1913).

56. *Verhandlungen des Reichstags, Stenographische Berichte* 285 (1912): 1931.

57. Bayerisches Hauptstaatsarchiv, Munich, Abt. II, MInn no. 72423 (19 September 1821).

58. Einundzwanzig der ältesten Constitutionen der Corps und ihrer Vorläufer bis zum Jahre 1810, *Einst und Jetzt* (1981 special issue): 75.

59. Kußmaul 1899, 125–26.

60. Michaelis 1973, 383–84.

61. Einundzwanzig der ältesten Constitutionen der Corps und ihrer Vorläufer bis zum Jahre 1810, *Einst und Jetzt* (1981 special issue): 32.

62. Schleiermacher 1846, 614.

63. Ernsthausen 1894, 40–41, 49ff.

64. Salvisberg 1896, 25.

65. Treitschke 1912, 264.

66. Staatsarchiv Detmold, L 86, no. 1739.

67. Deutsches Zentralarchiv Merseburg, Hist. Abt. II, 2.2.1. no. 17836 (8 January 1887).

68. Krünitz 1806, 723 (first quote); *Allgemeine deutsche Real-Encyclopädie für die gebildeten Stände*, 6th ed. (Leipzig, 1824), 4:182 (other quotes).

69. Pierer 1835, 162.

70. *Der Große Herder,* 4th ed. (Freiburg, 1933), 7:1545–46.

71. On vitalistic vs. instrumental forms of male violence, see the contributions by Eve Rosenhaft and Peter H. Merkl to Mommsen and Hirschfeld 1982.

72. Pusch 1887, 11, 23.

73. Deutsches Zentralarchiv Merseburg, Hist. Abt. II, 2.2.1. no. 17834 (6 October 1880).

74. Flach 1887, 17.

75. Karus 1888, 12–13.

76. Geheimes Staatsarchiv Berlin-Dahlem, Rep. 84a, no. 8037.

77. Quoted in Fabricius 1898, 355–56.

78. *Verhandlungen der Württembergischen Kammer der Abgeordneten auf dem 33. Landtag in den Jahren 1895/97* (Stuttgart, 1897), 4:2185.

79. Düsterlohe 1896; Graeser 1902, 39.

80. First quote: Zedler 1750, 1330–31, 1337. Second quote: Medem 1890, 40; Czeipek 1899, 12.

81. *Kirche, Freimaurerei nebst einem Anhange: Über Wohlthätigkeit. Ein wahres Wort auf die Angriffe gegen Duell und Freimaurerei,* 3rd ed. (Berlin, 1858), 16.

82. Ihering 1872, 95–96.

83. *Compte Rendu du Premier Congrès International contre le Duel* (Budapest, 1908), 102–3, 108.

84. See Frevert 1995b, 37ff.; Hausen 1976.

85. Greveniz 1808, 66.

86. Welcker 1838, 641.

87. *Verhandlungen der 50. Generalversammlung der Katholiken Deutschlands* (Cologne, 1903), 193.

88. *Stenographische Berichte über die Verhandlungen des Preußischen Herrenhauses in der Session 1907* (Berlin, 1907), 173.

89. See Frevert 1995b, 194ff.

90. Geheimes Staatsarchiv Berlin-Dahlem, Rep. 84a, no. 8037 (22 April 1914).

91. See Frevert 1995a, chap. 6.

2

Men of Steel: Dueling, Honor, and Politics in Liberal Italy

STEVEN HUGHES

In 1869, Captain Giuseppe Scaglione, a prosecuting attorney in the Italian army, defined dueling as a "cancerous, incurable plague of society."[1] His diagnosis was echoed by other observers who felt that post-unification Italy was caught in the throes of some kind of dueling mania, and the considerable controversy raised by such widespread ritualized violence would continue even into the early fascist period. Indeed, between 1860 and 1930, Italian men would fight thousands of duels which, by definition, had to continue until one or both of the participants had somehow been injured. Such routine bloodletting was tolerated — and even encouraged — as long as the combatants could be considered "gentlemen" (a loose term involving both social status and personal character) and as long as they followed the code of honor — a set of rules governing behavior before, during, and after a duel.

The present article seeks to understand this unprecedented increase in dueling after 1860 and the role it played in Italian society. In order to do so, it evaluates and utilizes the many statistics gathered by Iacopo Gelli, a journalist who systematically studied dueling during the period and eventually became Italy's primary authority on the practice.[2] From his data and other sources one can determine that dueling was not simply an atavistic, middle-class aping of a once powerful aristocracy; rather, it performed a variety of political and social functions that were inherent to the arrival of a liberal, constitutional regime on the peninsula. Free speech, parliamentary debate, and relatively relaxed press laws created new forms of interchange with which Italians had little social or legal experience. Considering as well Piedmont's takeover of Italy's military and the general desire to maintain the heroic energy of the Risorgimento, one can appreciate how dueling aided in the creation, legitimization, and empowerment of a new political elite: an elite that self-consciously set itself apart from the masses by using exclusive concepts of honor and its defense. Even more interesting, perhaps, the article ends with a brief comparative note that shows how dueling played a similar role in other countries making the shift to liberal government and how such rituals of violence — bound by codes of honor — may in fact be viewed as a "normal" process inherent to nascent parliamentary systems.

Dueling, of course, was hardly new to Italy. Both the theory and practice of the "point of honor" and its bloody resolution had originated in Italy during the Renaissance and then spread through France to the rest of Europe. After the unequivocal denunciation of the duel by the Council of Trent and the onset of the Counter Reformation, dueling appears to have diminished substantially on the peninsula, although there is some evidence that Piedmont, with its growing military ethos and its proximity to France, provided an exception to this general rule.[3] The practice appears to have rebounded somewhat during the Napoleonic intervention and the subsequent restoration, both of which witnessed a number of well-known duels. Among these was a famous encounter in Florence in 1826 between the Neapolitan general Gabriele Pepe and the French poet and diplomat Alphonse de Lamartine over a poem published by the latter impugning the weak and servile nature of contemporary Italy. Much to Italian delight, Lamartine received a deep wound in his right arm: "Thus was punished the hand that had written."[4] Dueling had become common enough in Lombardy during the late 1850s that Count Visconti Venosta — later the perennial foreign minister of liberal Italy — could recount how he and other noble patriots, as part of a scheme to prevent elite fraternization that might dull the region's Risorgimento élan, were able to force a challenge on anyone willing to socialize at the court of the Austrian governor.[5]

Despite such incidents, however, there is no mistaking the widespread and rapid increase in dueling that came with Italian unification between 1859 and 1870. Paolo Fambri, who was famous as a Risorgimento hero, hydraulic engineer, practical philosopher, and theoretical mathematician, to say nothing of avid duelist, affirmed that some three thousand duels had occurred in the first seven years of the country's existence.[6] Other commentators estimated that in the 1860s Italy saw at least one duel a day, which would actually amount to a surprisingly accurate confirmation of Fambri's assertion.[7] Challenges and swords continued to fly through the 1870s. Finally, in 1879 Luigi Bodio, head of Italy's statistics office, felt that the time had come to study the problem in a scientific fashion. He thus requested that Iacopo Gelli, a journalist highly regarded as an authority on matters of chivalry and fencing, begin to gather statistics on dueling throughout Italy. Gelli started his study in May 1879 and continued to collect data at least up through 1921, and his results provide a numerical portrait of Italian dueling through much of the liberal period.

Gelli's Statistics

But how good are Gelli's statistics? Naturally they are limited by the automatic problems attending the quantification of illicit activities, particularly the "dark figure" of unreported crime that always haunts the cliometrician. Moreover, dueling provides special difficulties in that the perpetrators were often the elites of the land whose power and position would tend to discourage the authorities from prosecution. Gelli himself was aware of the problem of underreporting and in particular pointed out that military duels were hard to track down because the officers involved preferred to keep the matter out of the public eye.[8] Likewise, as Robert Nye has suggested for France, those duels dealing with highly personal family matters or the honor of women were often surrounded in secrecy so as to protect the privacy of the principals.[9] Indeed, Nye would suggest that, given such problems, duels in France were seriously underreported, and although an "expert" such as the French criminologist Gabriel Tarde could only find about sixty duels a year in the 1880s, the real number probably ranged between two and three hundred. In sum, as with most crime one must accept that, even at their very best, statistics can only reflect the visibility rather than the reality of dueling.

But there are reasons to believe that Gelli's statistics do at least offer a consistent portrait of that visibility. First, he approached their collection with a certain amount of methodological rigor. Either he or one of his associates would systematically scan Italy's major newspapers for evidence of duels, and upon finding such evidence he would send off a printed questionnaire to a contact in the area to be completed and returned. Since many of Italy's post-unitary duels were semipublic affairs, or even fought for the sake of public consumption, it is reasonable to assume that such a technique would cover a good deal of the practice. Also, those duels based on sexual impropriety, which were most likely to be kept secret, were also considered more serious and thus likely to result in a dangerous injury or a death, which would come before both the law and the press. In addition, Gelli was well placed to undertake the task. As a recognized expert on the duel (his bibliography on the topic, written with Baron Giovanni Levi, remains unparalleled and his dueling code eventually became the standard for all of Italy) he regularly corresponded on questions arising over affairs of honor. Given his network of contacts among fencing masters, other journalists, and "chivalrous" elites sitting on various juries and courts of honor, he was in a unique position to ferret out information on duels throughout the country, no matter how clandestine.[10] Finally, Gelli recognized many of the pitfalls of data collection and was on guard to take note of changing laws and jurisdictions that might create reporting errors.[11]

All in all, such was the quality of Gelli's statistics that Bodio felt it safe to include them in Italy's official *Statistica delle cause delle morti* published by his office in 1891. Unfortunately, whatever rigor Gelli may have used to collect his statistics, their publication can only be called erratic, a result perhaps of his economic need as a journalist to spread his material across a variety of articles rather than produce a single definitive piece. Also, he published his findings more or less as they changed from year to year, often appending them to other publications about dueling. Consequently, one has to deal with different sets of data, which although usually consistent do not always cover all variables for the entire period. Finally, Gelli made simple mistakes in calculation, and occasionally his published figures simply do not add up the way they should. In sum, Gelli's statistics are hardly perfect, nor given the dark figure could they be, but they do open a number of quantitative windows that allow us to look at the causes, participants, and outcomes of most reported duels, and thus they provide some insights into why dueling found such a comfortable niche in the political and social ethos of liberal Italy.

In his best run of material, Gelli analyzed 3,513 duels that occurred between 1879 and 1894.[12] As revealed in Gelli's *Statistiche del duello*, most of these duels took place in the 1880s, which averaged 269 reported duels a year (see appendix A).[13] Although this figure falls somewhat short of the "duel a day" claims of observers in the 1860s and 1870s, it still seems very high, and if for fun one were to apply Robert Nye's formula from France, it would suggest that Italy actually saw about nine hundred duels a year, which really would have constituted an epidemic.[14] Whatever the case, even if Gelli's numbers are closer to the truth than those of his French counterparts, it is easy to see why people considered dueling a very real problem, especially if one considers that, for every duel fought, a number were avoided through various forms of mediation. It would have been difficult for a "gentleman" to ignore the possibility that he too might some-day be caught up in one of these chivalric disputes, or *vertenze*, and re-quired to defend his honor.

Journalism and Politics

But why so many vertenze and hence so many duels? Gelli's statistics sug-gest that the advent of liberal politics and a free press had a lot to do with it. Breaking his reported duels down by motive (appendix B), he found that journalistic polemics constituted by far the largest single catalyst of duels, and politics followed in third place, with unspecified oral arguments falling in between.[15] This obvious overlap between pen and sword might be explained in part by the dramatic nature of dueling itself. Newspapers could and did use duels as a means of gaining attention, creating excite-ment, and increasing readership. Another important factor was Italy's lack of libel laws, a result perhaps of the country's long history of strict press controls. Under the absolutist regimes there had been little need to adju-dicate printed insult or calumny because virtually nothing reached the public without first passing through the finely knit filter of the govern-ment censor. Likewise, Italian journalists had little experience, especially in the 1860s and 1870s, in dealing with their newfound freedom, and it was always easier to err on the side of sensation rather than caution. What-ever the reason, dueling became a critical part of Italy's early print cul-ture, and some editors felt that a newspaper had not really "arrived" until it was "baptized in blood" by a duel.[16] Such was the extent of this conflict that the Press Association of Rome was created in 1877 with the specific goal of creating a jury of honor capable of adjudicating vertenze among its members and thus reducing the number of duels between them.[17]

Similar arguments might apply to politics as well. Certainly the publicity that attended a duel could benefit a deputy by affirming both his position as a man of honor and the strength of his convictions, to say nothing of gaining easy access to the press. It became expected for deputies to duel, and Felice Cavallotti, head of the parliamentary "historic left," died in 1898 fighting in his thirty-third such encounter.[18] Such was the strength of the tradition that one Italian historian, Emilia Morelli, told me that when her father was elected to the Chamber in the 1920s he felt compelled to take fencing lessons. But the roots of political dueling went deeper than press reports or photo opportunities; rather, they were imbedded in the evolution of the liberal regime itself. Before unification, few Italian elites had had much experience with parliamentary politics, and except for Piedmont the idea of a "loyal opposition" had been tantamount to treason under the old regimes. Especially in a public forum, urbane discourse and polite disagreement are social skills that evolve, and Italy's early *Camera dei deputati* was known for its rough-and-tumble debates during which the president occasionally had to clear the galleries and halt proceedings. The division between the political and the personal had scarcely developed in Italy, and the lines were blurred even more by the very nature of the Risorgimento itself, which had been carried out by a tiny number of elites led by such romantic personalities as Mazzini, Cavour, and Garibaldi. Then again, the heroic exploits of 1859 and 1860 had given way to acrimonious and violent confrontation over how to complete the unification process, the final solution of which made Rome the new capital in 1870 but also threw large numbers of elites (and especially the ultra-Catholic nobility) into intransigent opposition. Italian politics consisted of a muddy middle of powerful personages with extremists on both the left and the right who fundamentally disagreed with the system itself. This was hardly fertile ground for consensus, and the duel reflected in its stylized violence the heat of Italy's early political discord.

It also continued, albeit in an individual way, the drama and heroism of the Risorgimento itself. As Italian politicians settled into the banal business of running a large country, the duel offered an exciting though temporary return to the dash and élan of the revolutionary period. This was not too different from how Visconti Venosta had seen the duel just before unification when he claimed, "The thought of duels kept our youthful fantasies burning. Dueling with Austrian officers seemed a patriotic duty; it was individual combat substituted for the war we were unable to fight; and it was certainly a means of keeping alive that continual tension of soul and that moral battle which were our force."[19] In a similar vein Luigi Dossena, a contemporary critic of the duel, would blame its post-unitary popularity on the martial courage that had been released during the drive for unity, which had then been confused with ideas of personal honor.[20]

One might go even further and suggest that as Italy remained a small fish in the big pond of European diplomacy, and as its military failed to function efficiently, much less gloriously, the duel offered an individual antidote to possible accusations of a lack of martial spirit or courage at the national level. Nowhere would this indirect patriotic function become clearer than after Italy's disastrous defeat by the Ethiopians at Adua in 1895, when France's prince of Orleans published an article in *Le Figaro* chastising the Italians for allowing Africans to triumph over a European army. He was soon answered by a challenge from the count of Turin, a prince of Italy's ruling family, to whose sword he eventually fell with a serious wound in the abdomen during a duel in the Bois de Boulogne.[21] Needless to say, Italy's newspapers rejoiced in this "triumph," which not only avenged the country's honor but helped take some of the sting out of Adua as well. This ran parallel to dueling's function in France, where Robert Nye has found that it was particularly important in rebuilding the country's martial confidence after defeat to Germany in 1870.

The Military

The prominence of the Piedmontese military in Italy also helps explain the proliferation of dueling after unification. As mentioned before, Piedmont seems to have maintained a longer continuous tradition of dueling than the other pre-unitary states, and the Risorgimento brought the various armies of the peninsula together under its officers. Significantly, the first national dueling code would be compiled by Achille Angelini, a Piedmontese general and aide-de-camp to Victor Emmanuel II. Moreover, the *relative* importance of the military in Piedmontese society was reflected in Italian society as well, especially as the new country spent more and more of its resources trying to keep up with its powerful neighbors to the north. The military was prominent in its relationship to the monarchy and the nobility, both of which continued to play a major role in Italy's social life.

Whatever the case, the importance of the duel to the Italian military becomes immediately obvious if one looks at a sample taken by Gelli of who participated in the practice between 1888 and 1895, the results of which appear in appendix C.[22] Out of 2,069 duelists, 702 (34%) belonged to some branch of the military. This figure was confirmed by another sample taken between 1890 and 1899 in which Gelli found that out of 1,065 duels, 289 (25%) occurred between soldiers, 153 (13%) included both soldiers and civilians, and another 623 (54%) involved just civilians.[23] Despite the preponderance of civilians in the raw numbers, Gelli rightly pointed out that because there were only about 18,000 men in Italy's officer corps at the time, the per capita proportion of military men in duels was consequently extremely high—especially if one considers that military duels were the ones most likely to remain secret.[24] This higher frequency is understandable in that many people simply expected officers to duel. Even opponents of the practice often exempted the military from their criticisms because such displays of physical prowess were natural to the profession, while defenders of the duel would argue that it actually kept the officers on their toes. So clear was this logic that in Italy as elsewhere in Europe tradition came to dictate that an officer had to accept a challenge to his honor or lose his commission, despite the harsh provisions of the military code against participating in duels.

One might almost argue that dueling provided a stepping stone to advancement or at least a rite of passage in that the vast majority of duelists were in the lower echelons. In a sample of 491 soldiers who fought duels between 1890 and 1894 (see appendix D), Gelli found that 420 ranked as lieutenant or below. One could blame such an imbalance on either youthful exuberance or demographic distribution, but one could also suggest that a duel was a means of "making one's bones" in the military—a proof of both courage and honor that would aid a young officer's career. This would run parallel to one of the functions of dueling in civilian life, which allowed new elites to test their metal, both literal and figurative, in the semipublic arena of the duel and thus signal their arrival as "gentlemen." As we have seen, dueling could directly enhance the career of a journalist or politician, but it could also indirectly legitimize their social status as being on a level with princes and generals. Thus Robert Nye has suggested that in France, "fencing and the duel helped promote equality because no man could refuse to cross swords with a legitimate opponent at the risk of personal shame and public ridicule. A world that recognized, at least in theory, no social boundaries in an activity once reserved for a narrow elite was a male social universe full of perfect individualism and equality."[25] This "perfect equality" was probably best demonstrated in Gelli's statistics by his punctilious refusal to categorize differences of birth as opposed to profession. "Noble" did not appear among his participants nor did he bother to set the aristocracy apart when distinguishing between military and bourgeois duels. This made perfect sense for Gelli, the son of a copper-smith who made his living by writing, but it also reflected the democratic function of the duel in Italian society.[26] Nor could the nobility do much about it, trapped as they were by their own sense of honor. As one mar-quis wrote in his memoirs, "One fought among the '*signori,*' that is, among recognized and accredited members of the only social category which then 'counted': officers and people living off rents. Sometimes, however, it was necessary to fight with professionals or politicians [who were] obvi-ously not *signori;* or even with deputies [*parlamentari*] of the left."[27] Those who refused to fight such social inferiors, he continued, would be accused of cowardice and hence socially disqualified. According to these rules, be-ing a "gentleman" became a matter of auto-definition, dependent on one's willingness to protect one's honor at the point of a sword.

At the same time, however, a heightened sense of honor for which one might risk life and limb over the most trivial offenses (e.g., staring too long into someone's eyes or reading their newspaper without permission) not only defined a man's entrance into a higher social realm but also created a psychological gulf between him and the plebeian masses. Although Italy's experts on honor might be willing to grant a certain *cavalleria rusticana* to the working classes (e.g., mitigating penalties for "crimes of passion"), they generally regarded the duel as a responsibility and a prerogative of "civil" society. A gentleman, according to Gelli, was a person of "refined moral sensibility" who found the laws of the state inadequate to the de-fense of his honor and who followed the rules of chivalry.[28] Such a defini-tion did not automatically exclude any groups or classes in society, but it did imply education, etiquette, and social contacts beyond the reach of most Italian males. In short, a gentleman was a man willing to fight a duel over personal honor according to the regulations laid out by other gentle-men. There was a certain egalitarianism in this, but it worked primarily for the rising middle classes and had its obvious limits.

The social functions, both direct and indirect, of dueling in Italy were enhanced by the fact that men of honor actually faced little real danger from either the law or the sword. The Piedmontese criminal code, which was eventually adopted throughout Italy, was far more lenient with regard to the duel than those of the other pre-unitary regimes, some of which still prescribed the death penalty for the very act of dueling. Even in the case of a death or serious injury, the Piedmontese code greatly mitigated the penalties if they occurred in a "legal" duel. Yet even these cases were rare, because Italian duels simply were not very dangerous. According to Gelli, in the 3,918 duels that occurred between 1879 and 1899, only 20 actually ended in death.[29] Likewise, of the 5,090 wounds received in these duels, only 1,475 were considered grave or worse. The others were judged as light (2,026) or very light (1,589). These results were encouraged by a variety of mechanisms. First was the choice of weapons. Gelli's statistics, as demonstrated in appendix E, show that almost 90 percent of Italian duels were fought with sabres, the sharpened blade of which caused lighter wounds more quickly than the single, more lethal point of an épée. Second, there were the many rules surrounding the conflict, which were designed to keep the duelists at absolute parity in terms of position and stamina and which purposefully worked to keep the opponents from getting seriously hurt. Should a duelist fall, trip, or drop his sword, the action was suspended so as to let him regain both balance and composure. Because it did not generally matter who won the duel, but only that both men's honor be "washed clean by blood," there was seldom a need to go beyond "first blood" to satisfy either society or the participants. In fact, the perfect Italian duel was probably typified by the frontispiece of C. A. Blengini-di-San-Grato's 1868 dueling code in which two men are shown shaking hands while one has his left arm bandaged by the attending physician. This is not to belittle the courage of men who risked their appendages if not their lives in the pursuit of honor, but it does make their willingness to take on a duel over seemingly trivial matters more understandable. In short, the prestige, position, and publicity to be gained from a duel greatly outweighed its risks, whereas to refuse a challenge could ruin a man's social and even professional life.

The Twentieth Century

Given the many factors militating in the duel's defense and its importance for the ruling elites of liberal Italy, it is hardly surprising that the practice, although falling off somewhat after 1890, survived well into the twentieth

century. This is clearly evident from Gelli's last major set of statistics, illustrated in appendix F, which offered a series of annual averages for duels occurring between 1879 and 1925. They show a consistent decline in
reported duels up through World War I, during which dueling virtually
disappeared, and then a significant increase in the postwar period.[30] Gelli
attributed the dramatic drop after 1890 to a number of factors, including a
new sense of self-worth based on honesty and hard work in Italy's growing urban areas, the spread of socialist ideas that condemned the duel, the
increased use of new dueling manuals (his own being the most successful), which helped adjudicate more disputes without steel, and especially
the new Zanardelli Law Code, which went into effect in that year. The
new code not only set higher penalties for duelists and their seconds but
also put teeth in the laws regarding personal defamation. This had led to a
tripling or quadrupling of cases of defamation: cases that previously might
have inspired duels.[31] Gelli warned, however, that only about half of
the decrease was real and that the greater penalties of the new code had
simply led more people to try to hide their duels. Using the 1890s as a
baseline of visibility, then, one could suggest that the diminution that followed over the next fifteen years probably mirrored reality pretty well, especially given the relative political calm of the Giolittian period after the
turn of the century.[32]

As for the extraordinary decline of the duel during the First World
War, the single largest factor was the Italian high command's decision
in 1914 to order the postponement of all military affairs of honor until
the war ended. Other gentlemen may have followed the army's example,
putting off their personal grievances while the country was in danger, although the stringent press controls of the period may have been as important in that they perhaps limited both insulting debate between journalists
and the public announcement of duels.

All of these factors would in turn help explain the apparent recrudescence of the duel after the war. The military had a large backlog of
vertenze to work out, while the press, free of its wartime trammels, entered into the most politically volatile period of united Italy's history. In
parliament, in newspapers, and in the streets, fascists, liberals, and socialists literally fought for control of the country, and many were the challenges exchanged and the duels fought as insult and aggression became
the norm of public life. Ironically, the eventual triumph of the fascists,
many of whom prided themselves on having fought various duels before

their assumption of power, would prove the beginning of the end for dueling in Italy. Although the regime based its rhetoric on conflict, energy, and national honor, the ideology of state power, hierarchy, and discipline quickly came to dominate and found dueling too individualistic and too blatant in its flaunting of the government's monopoly over coercion. Likewise, when fascism destroyed liberalism and its freedom of discourse in parliament and press alike, it restricted the public debate that could lead to duels and the publicity that often made them worth fighting. The latter issue eventually came to the fore when Alfredo Rocco, who oversaw the creation of the fascist law code, determined that all public references to duels had to be prohibited in order to stop feeding the vanity of duelists.[33] Sure enough, after 1927 one searches the Italian newspapers in vain for news about dueling. This, of course, does not mean that dueling came to a screeching halt with the consolidation of the fascist dictatorship. A number of duels still occurred in the 1930s, but there was a general recognition even as early as 1928 that they were becoming the exception rather than the rule.[34]

In conclusion, the final waning of the duel under the axe of fascism only highlighted its connections to the liberal phase of Italian politics, during which it served any number of sociological and political functions. Although the frontispieces of various dueling manuals virtually dripped with medieval symbols of heraldry and chivalry, the new interest in dueling clearly transcended the old parameters of aristocratic honor and was tied to the new public nature of political discourse and the rise of a hybrid class of elites who could legitimize their position as gentlemen through their willingness to risk their lives for their honor. Thus as Bertram Wyatt-Brown has suggested for the southern United States, "The duel was not an aristocratic custom that was learned at 'mother's knee.'. . . Instead, dueling was a means to demonstrate status and manliness among those calling themselves gentlemen, whether born of noble blood or not."[35] But Wyatt-Brown's statement draws attention as well to the international nature of dueling and the parallels to be drawn to other countries. As mentioned before, Robert Nye has shown that dueling also had a major recrudescence in France after 1870, because after the humiliating defeat of the Franco-Prussian War and the fall of Louis Napoleon's empire, it became a rallying point of bourgeois Republicanism that stressed patriotic "virility," personal civility, and individual honor. Developmental timing seems to be important in all of this, for dueling flourished in the

United States between the Revolution and the Civil War and in England during the period of the Reform Bill, both periods in which new elites came to power using the rhetoric and the devices of liberal government, free speech, and individual achievement. Can one postulate a period of "liberal" development in which up-and-coming elites "learned" how to handle their new freedoms and used dueling as a means of both setting limits on behavior and legitimizing their own status in society?

Such an idea gains considerable credence from the work of Joanne Freeman. In examining the famous duel between Alexander Hamilton and Aaron Burr, she argues that honor and dueling were intrinsic to the personal nature of politics in postrevolutionary America: "Without the anonymity and formal alliances offered by membership in an institutionalized party, political interaction revolved around the identities and aspirations of individual politicians. Factional alliances and personal friendships were often indistinguishable. An attack on a political measure was an attack on an individual, and an attack on an individual demanded a personal defense. A politician's private identity and his public office were thus inseparably linked." She suggests that studying affairs of honor in America "reveals the dynamics and disposition of politics in an age predating the emergence of permanent national political parties. It uncovers a ritualized, honor-bound, public-minded, yet personal level of political interaction—a grammar of political combat that politicians recognized and manipulated as a means of conducting politics in the early republic." This "grammar of political combat" would have been familiar to the elites of united Italy, where the weakness of formal parties and the dominance of key personalities were prominent features of parliamentary life all the way up to the advent of fascism.[36]

At the same time, Freeman's ideas suggest the extraordinary flexibility of dueling and honor as social mechanisms that could serve different countries across time. This becomes even more striking when one goes beyond liberalism to consider the importance of dueling in more authoritarian cultures such as those of Germany, Austria-Hungary, or Russia. What seemingly universal values (at least within a European context) could allow dueling to function effectively under such diverse social and political circumstances? Answering that question may well help to shed more light on the larger problem of men and violence.

Appendix A: Reported duels in Italy between 1880 and 1894

1879	203 *	1888	269
1880	282	1889	132 †
1881	271	1890	177
1882	268	1891	138
1883	259	1892	122
1884	287	1893	146
1885	261	1894	98
1886	249	1895	73 *
1887	278		

* Represents only six months.
† Represents only five months.

Appendix B: Duels in Italy between 1879 and 1895, arranged by motive

Journalism	1,125
Oral dispute without specific cause	875
Politics	431
Insults and scuffles	392
Matters of intimacy	279
Unknown causes	242
Physical aggression	184
Gambling	36
Religion	31
Private interests (money?)	14
Hunting	1

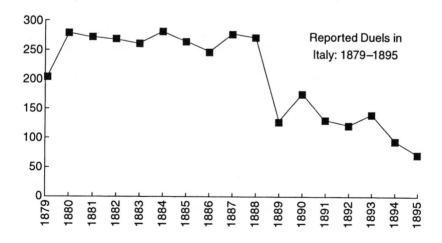

Reported Duels in Italy: 1879–1895

Appendix C: Participants in duels between 1888 and 1895, arranged by profession

Members of the military	702
Journalists	425
Lawyers and notaries	246
Profession unknown	133
Students	117
Capitalists and the independently wealthy	110
Politicians (not counting senators)	107
Engineers	34
Professors	32
Merchants	29
Medical doctors	27
Fencing masters	24
Clerks in public administration	19
Bankers	18
Judges	8
Actors	6
Diplomats	5
Industrialists	4
Workers	4
Music teachers	3
Private clerks	3
Accountants	3
Senators	2
Pensioners	2
Other	6
Total	2,069

Appendix D: Military participants in duels between 1890 and 1894, arranged by rank

Undetermined	2
Soldier	2
Cadet	4
Sotto-ufficiale (non-com?)	134
Sotto-tenente	73
Lieutenant	205
Captain	61
Majors & colonel	9
General	1

Appendix E: Duels between 1879 and 1899, arranged by weapon

Sabre	3,501
Pistol	244
Sword	159
"Inappropriate" or "all'americana"	14

Appendix F: Yearly averages of duels in Italy between 1879 and 1925

1879–89	276
1890–1900	116
1901–10	65
1911–15	45
1916–18	2.5
1919–25	74

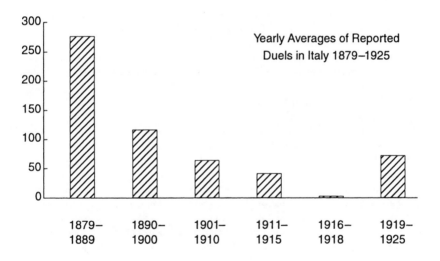

Yearly Averages of Reported Duels in Italy 1879–1925

Notes

1. Scaglione 1869, 5.

2. For more information on Gelli's expertise see Steven Hughes, "Honor in Modern Italy and the *Codice cavalleresco* of Iacopo Gelli," a paper given at the American Historical Association meeting in San Francisco, 6 January 1994.

3. On the decline in dueling see Billacois 1986 (English translation: *The duel: Its rise and fall in early modern France* [New Haven: Yale University Press, 1990], 42–43). As for the

Piedmontese, one eighteenth-century chronicler, Giuseppe Baretti, reported, "They are withal so punctilious and so ready to draw the sword, that more duels are fought in Piedmont than in the rest of Italy taken together." Quoted in Broers 1990, 787.

4. Jannone 1912, 56.

5. Venosta 1906, 395–96. On Austrian officers as another tempting target see 336–37.

6. Fambri 1869, 13.

7. For instance see Dossena 1861, 5–6; Scaglione 1869, 5.

8. Gelli 1901, 4.

9. Nye 1993, 185.

10. It is indicative of his position within the dueling world that between 1890 and 1899, Gelli (1901, 9) claimed that some 3,186 affairs of honor, or *vertenze*, had come to his attention and of these only 1,155 had ended in actual duels. By 1926 Gelli could brag to a friend that he had personally intervened in over 7,000 affairs of honor, primarily in his role first as secretary and later as president of Florence's prestigious Court of Honor. See Gastone Banti, preface to Gelli 1926, xii.

11. For example, Gelli 1901, 4–6.

12. This set of data can be found in Gelli n.d. The same material was also apparently appended to the 1896 edition of his famous *Codice cavalleresco*. Gelli's attempts to be systematic could lead him into trouble, as when he published only five months of 1889's duels so as to make up for the fact that he started his study in June 1879, but he then went on to count ten years and a month, the month being to compensate for problems he encountered in the first few months of his study. His data from 1880 to 1888, however, and from 1890 to 1894 are all based on twelve-month periods.

13. Appendix A from Gelli n.d., 9.

14. It is indicative, although hardly conclusive, that Gelli's first six months of collecting data, which was for 1879, yielded 203 duels, which would result in an annual rate of about four hundred duels a year and which would easily fit the "duel a day" description of contemporaries.

15. It is perhaps superfluous to add that such disputes might well have contained elements of either politics or journalism, but we will never know how many. As Gelli was quick to point out, he listed some ninety-seven more causes than duels because in some cases he felt it necessary to place a single incident into two categories. Although hardly scientific by today's standards, given the total numbers I do not feel that this methodological largess overly influences his results.

16. Cesana 1874, 141–60. Another editor, Gaston Banti, later claimed that he paid his journalists for defending the paper in duels and that there seemed to be an increase in duels toward the end of the month when their salaries began to run thin. This was the same Gaston Banti who put a fencing gymnasium in his newspaper offices to keep his men fit for duty. See Santini and Nadi 1989, 22, 25. Conversation with Santini revealed that this information was related to him directly by Banti, who had been his mentor in the newspaper business.

17. *Atti costitutivi dell' Associazione della Stampa Periodica in Italia* (Rome: Popolo Romano, 1877), 3.

18. Gelli 1928, 332.

19. Venosta 1906, 337.

20. Dossena 1861, 5–6. Others, such as the Piedmontese general Achille Angelini, felt

more cynically that unification had allowed a lot of unscrupulous characters an opportunity to duel for fun and profit. Angelini wrote in this spirit to the Garibaldean general Nino Bixio. Quoted in Paolo Fambri, "Il codice cavalleresco," *La Venezia,* 5 December 1889, p. 1.

21. A very pro-Italian version of the episode can be found in Gelli 1928, 89–92.

22. Gelli n.d., 19. For some unexplained reason Gelli only included the first six months of 1893 and 1895.

23. Gelli 1901, 10. Working out the percentages of the participants indicates again that soldiers account for some 34 percent of all duelists. In his article, Gelli says that there were actually 1,155 duels in the period, which would leave him 90 duels short. This is one of his odd miscalculations. However, it almost exactly mirrors an error he made in a previous calculation for the same variable. Thus, in his *Statistica del duello,* he showed that for 1890 there were 24 duels between soldiers, 46 between civilians, and 16 between soldiers and civilians, for a total of 86 duels. But in his overall statistics he showed 177 duels for that year, creating an error of 91 duels. Because this is the only year for which he made such a mistake, and because he consistently made it with regard to the same variable, I would argue that he probably started his calculations of civilian vs. military duels sometime during 1890 and hence the discrepancy.

24. Ironically, Gelli (1901, 10) also reported that in the 153 "mixed" duels the civilians came out on top 99 times versus 39 times for the soldiers and 15 times in which both parties were wounded.

25. Nye 1933, 167.

26. For more on this issue see Hughes, "Honor in Modern Italy and the *Codice cavalleresco* of Iacopo Gelli."

27. Marchese Mario Incisa della Rocchetta, *Impressioni e ricordi di 'altri tempi* (typescript in possession of the family). Thanks to Anthony Cardoza for sharing this document from a private family archive with me.

28. Gelli 1926, 1.

29. Gelli 1901, 11.

30. Gelli 1928, 17n. One must keep in mind, of course, that Italy's population continued to grow, so in per capita terms the decline in reported duels was even more dramatic.

31. Gelli 1901, 5–7. He further mentioned the recent frequency of deaths from duels, a reference perhaps to the six dueling fatalities that occurred between 1895 and 1898.

32. Moreover, in 1908, the Italian military put forth a new code on dueling, which forced all officers to place their vertenze before a court of honor before any combat.

33. See, for instance, the arguments of the court of appeals in Bologna in Fusco 1930, 3–4. Also see *Lavori preparatori del codice penale e del codice di procedura penale* (Rome: Mantellate, 1929), 5(1):185–86; and *Atti della Commissione Parlamentare chiamata a dare il proprio parere sul progetto di un nuovo codice penale* (Rome: Senato, 1930), 6:246.

34. On duels in the 1930s: I interviewed one fencing master, Maestro Enzo Musumeci Greco, of the Accademia d'Armi Aurelio Greco in Rome, who trained seven men to fight duels in the 1930s. Maestro Greco is still teaching fencing! On duels becoming exceptional by 1928 see Ettore 1928, v. Given the blanket blackout on dueling news, perhaps the best indication that duels were still taking place was the fact that people still felt it necessary to write articles against the practice, e.g., Lovati 1939; Molinini 1934.

35. Wyatt-Brown 1982, 355.

36. Freeman 1996, 296, 293.

3

The End of the Modern French Duel

ROBERT NYE

Why did the duel in France die out? Was it "ridicule," as V. G. Kiernan suggests: the accretion of incidents imposing risible conditions and little danger, motivated less by outrage than by the thirst for publicity, living on in a national myth cut off from social reality? The duelist of the fin de siècle, writes Kiernan in a pungent metaphor, "was coming to resemble a dog scratching a street pavement with its hind paws."[1]

There is certainly some truth in this judgment, which I will acknowledge in what follows, but the principal reason for the abrupt disappearance of the duel was not the consequence of a long history of decline rooted in social or cultural evolution, or the emergence of growing moral disapproval of the sort that culminated in the outlawing of slavery, torture, or, in recent times, capital punishment. The duel was still in robust health in 1914; a final attempt to outlaw the duel in the parliament of 1921 failed as miserably as the previous ones of 1819, 1829, 1848, 1851, 1877, 1888, 1892, and 1895. What killed the duel, I will argue, was not its vestigial inefficacy but its pretention, not its failure to enlist devotees loyal to the ancient code of honor but its claim to be the only remaining civil rite in which modern men could face death squarely and measure their courage against peers.

Together with a million and a half Frenchmen, the duel perished in the bloody trenches of the western front. Although the legal right to duel was spared by a parliament of war veterans and seasoned politicians, many of whom had defended their personal honor in the golden years of the pre-war dueling craze, only a handful of duels were consummated after November 1918. The last of these took place, incredibly, in 1967 between Gaston Deferre and a Gaullist parliamentary deputy named René Ribière.[2] Press coverage was respectful of this travesty in the time-honored tradition of such reportage, but formal duels had long since fallen into the category of curiosities in which no one imagined anything more than *amour-propre* to be at stake. The duel had received its true *coup de grâce* in the Great War from the dramatic contrast between the glorious metaphysics of courage and death invoked by prewar duelists and the cruel wages of courage exacted on the killing fields of the war.

The Persistence of Dueling

For many centuries the duel was one of the few civil rites to escape the state's growing monopoly on violence. No amount of official disapproval or repression, including exile or death, could deter duelists from what they regarded as a natural right; death brought by the sword of the king's executioner or by a noble peer was infinitely preferable to a life lived in the shame of a just challenge dishonorably evaded.[3] State-building monarchs were justly concerned that well-armed vassals might challenge their dearly won authority, but their truculent nobles stood to lose far more by surrendering their cherished duel: their identity as a privileged class, to be sure, but also as men. The cream of the French nobility—perhaps ten thousand men—perished in duels in the last decade of the sixteenth and first decade of the seventeenth centuries.

The blood that coursed through a nobleman's veins was the sign and guarantee of his superiority as a *natural* being, distinguishing him from the low-born and the vile. But to retain that distinction for himself and his heirs he was obliged to shed that blood negligently in war or in personal combat. Though noblemen were born with a set of unique virtues, these had to be actualized in deeds so that the myth of nobility as a *vocation*

could be maintained.[4] Thus the courage that a man displayed in the violent moments incidental to his rank was both merited and natural, a personal quality that was nonetheless in constant danger of forfeit. A nobleman in early modern France who avoided the duties of his rank could
therefore suffer a total derogation, not only of his social status but of his
very existence as a social being, experiencing a kind of "civil death."[5] This
obliteration encompassed his whole identity as a man: in his capacity as a
noble warrior, born to exercise a soldier's vocation, and as a progenitor,
whose "noble" qualities were passed through his blood to his heirs.

As I have argued elsewhere, the personal qualities prized by early
modern noblemen — courage, loyalty, frankness — were first imitated and
later adopted by wealthy commoners who entertained some hope of gaining access to power and joining the highest ranks of society.[6] It was ordinary for the men of this new elite to lay claim to the quality of personal
honor possessed "naturally" by nobles and to defend it at the same risk of
derogation, although in the course of the eighteenth century, while this
process of assimilation was taking place, affairs of honor were far less frequent than in the reign of Louis XIII.

Historians now appreciate that the duel continued to play an important role in the social, political, and cultural life of several European countries throughout the eighteenth and nineteenth centuries and up to and in
some places beyond the First World War. Until recently, however, the
memory of the duel was kept alive largely in the writing and collections of
antiquarians, armorers, and eccentrics. It was treated as an anomaly by
mainstream historians and explained as an absurd atavism sustained by an
aristocracy in its death throes. Even recently, when dueling has been acknowledged by historians, which has seldom been the case, the favored
explanation has been that it was because the European nobility had managed to survive in a few institutional domains where they took shelter
from the instrumentalism and pacifism of bourgeois society, and where
dueling operated to remind them and their social inferiors of the supremacy of those whose forbears exercised the military arts and for whom
gallantry came naturally.[7]

In point of fact, however, by the end of the eighteenth century, the old
nobility no longer had a monopoly on the use of the sword; indeed, virtually everywhere in the West the duel was an engine for the integration
of bourgeois and aristocrat. Members of the upper middle classes intermarried with old nobles, laid claim to equal political and social status, and

marked out new barriers to guarantee the exclusiveness of this new alliance of notables.[8] The duel was one of many ways this exclusiveness
could be preserved; men without the leisure to practice weapons or learn
the etiquette of the *point d'honneur* could not hope to rub shoulders with the
elite. In the striking image of Edmond Goblot, however, behind the ramparts of class a level democratic "plain" ensured the solidarity and sense of
distinctiveness of the well-born and the well-endowed, for whom the duel
served as the warrant and symbol of their superiority, both socially and
as *men*.[9]

Within the ranks of this composite elite, the *point d'honneur* was not a
thing apart, a set piece of rules governing combat; it was wholly integrated into a code of honor that regulated relations between upper-class
males throughout the public sphere. The duel was the capstone and final
court of appeal, so to speak, in a system of etiquette whose chief aim was
the modest goal of not giving offense, whether in matters of salon *politesse*,
in parliamentary decorum, or in the growing domain of publicity and letters. Men used the duel to test the integrity and sincerity of others, to display their own, and to distinguish between inadvertent and intended
offenses to their personal and family honor. In effect, a ritual that had
been in early modern times a monopoly of men of noble birth became in
the modern class system a rite of social standing.

But the duel was still, as it had always been, an occasion to publicly
demonstrate the personal courage that testified to the qualities of a man.
By giving or accepting challenge, a man not born to the military vocation
could unambiguously display his masculinity in a moment of (admittedly
risky) action that it might otherwise take a lifetime of resolute but peaceable activity to attain. Virtually everywhere in nineteenth-century European society, as Ute Frevert has written about the German example, "the
duel was the embodiment of bravery, courage, strength, skill, toughness,
consistency, and self-discipline — virtues that were considered to belong to
the inventory of every man's personality."[10] Indeed, for men engaged in
the hurly-burly of public life in the first decades of the century, the duel
established a framework and the limits for personal interaction in a new
public sphere that had not yet constructed its own rules and traditions and
for which the rule of law was still a relative historical novelty.[11]

I have argued that France was the country where the civilian duel
flourished as nowhere else. In the German lands, Italy, Austria-Hungary,
and even England, the duel was closely linked to military milieus, so that

access to its mysteries often took place in the regimental reserves where aristocratic and bourgeois officers submitted alike to a common ethos, military usages, and the weapons unique to soldiers: the saber and the pistol.[12] Thus, though the Italian duel was similar socially to the French in terms of its largely bourgeois participation, duelers favored the battlefield panache of the saber, and German duelers preferred the sidearms worn by officers. In nineteenth-century France a national myth gradually emerged which emphasized the anteriority, the historicity, and the universality of the French duel, and which favored the épée, the weapon of good King Louis's musketeers. Although the officer corps was dominated by aristocrats in France as elsewhere, the duel did not flourish there but in civil society, where the sword as an instrument of justice and the duel as a mode of social advancement ensured its enduring popularity.

Over the course of the century, the number of men whose social station qualified them to send and receive dueling challenges increased, particularly in Paris, but also in most towns with rapidly growing middle classes. Fencing also experienced a revival in popularity after midcentury, for a mixture of social, aesthetic, and hygienic reasons, and served, as it had always done, as a preparatory school for would-be duelers. Because dueling was not banned in the criminal code, it is difficult to know for certain how many duels took place in a typical year during the first two-thirds of the century, but it was probably not more than one hundred. A duel usually reached the courts only in capital cases or where the acknowledged rules governing the point of honor had been breached.[13]

The Third Republic

Beginning in the mid-1860s, however, the latent social potential that the duel had been slowly accumulating was effectively exploited by Napoleon's Republican opposition. Politicians and journalists were quick to take up pistols or, more commonly, swords in defense of person and cause, and fencing halls became popular Republican venues. This gallant temerity lent a certain force to Republican political rhetoric, but it also served to dramatize and symbolically represent the basic elements in Republican ideology—individual liberty and equality—and help set the foundations for the civic value system of the Third Republic. In principle, any man, no matter what his origins, could cultivate the art of fencing and engage in duels, because a Republican man was a free agent responsible for his actions. A social universe of free agents was also a universe of equality, because no man could refuse to cross swords with a legitimate opponent at the risk of personal shame and public ridicule.[14] There were still obvious limits to the democratization of the duel that confined its practice to the middle and upper reaches of the urban bourgeoisie, politicians, journalists, and men of letters, but by 1875 or so the duel was aligned firmly with generally progressive political forces in the new Republic.

An important collateral development to the democratization of the duel was the roughly contemporary elaboration in scientific and medical milieus of a standard anatomical and physiological model of masculinity. While it would be an overstatement to claim that doctors and biologists somehow invented masculinity in the course of the nineteenth century, they did identify what they believed to be its characteristic morphological, developmental, and functional features; these were regularly expressed as "hygienic" norms and eventually percolated through all the nation's social strata. Experts did this in the course of working out a modern notion of sex difference in which masculinity and femininity became virtual binary opposites in a hegemonic system of heterosexuality.[15]

Inexorably, though at a glacial pace, a cultural concept of a "natural" and universal "male" emerged to replace the social, political, and cultural distinctions which had historically categorized men by class, birth, or geography as ontologically different (and unequal) beings. This development ensured that by the end of the nineteenth century a more or less standard cultural ideal of masculinity had emerged that was common to all men and was rooted in male sex and in the masculine behavior appropriate to it. Together with a number of cognitive elements that distinguished "rational" males from "emotional" females, the characteristic feature of modern masculinity was personal courage, which was believed, in the evolutionary schemata of the day, to have ensured the survival of individuals and societies alike.[16] The duel lagged behind the creation of a "universal" masculinity, however, in admitting to its practice only the upper-class men who had mastered its elaborate ceremonies, and this, in effect, excluded the overwhelming majority from participation.

This "standard" masculinity took form, however, in a particular and contingent historical context. The circumstances which gave birth to the modern Republican movement meant that the progressive and democratic elements in dueling rhetoric were joined together with a vitriolic patriotism for which revenge against Germany was an inescapable theme for the subsequent forty years. The shock of defeat in the war of 1870 produced ruminations of all kinds about the viability of French institutions, the quality of French honor, and the capacities of French men.[17] There eventually developed a groundswell of idealized nostalgia for a heroic and chivalrous past in which Frenchmen had faced danger willingly for the "national" ideals of justice, frankness, and generosity, which was contrasted with the unmediated brutality, utilitarianism, and egoism of German "honor" and, willy-nilly, the lesser honor of other nations.[18]

The genius of the French, it emerged, lay in a sense of honor that welcomed—indeed, courted—death in the defense of a set of civilizing ideals that ennobled and purified its champions. This paradoxical combination of bravado and spirituality circulated for the next half century in the form of rhetorical formulas celebrating the duel as a paradigmatic institution in civil life. In the absence of national wars, the duel was often characterized as a moral equivalent of combat, even as the very condition of civilization itself.[19] As Anatole France wrote in 1886, the sword was "the first tool of civilization, the only means man has found to reconcile his brutal instincts and his ideal of justice."[20] Edmond de Rostand, who gave the fin de siècle its most enduring dramatic hero, the swashbuckling poet Cyrano de Bergerac, spoke to the Academie Française in 1912 about the glories of French "panache," which he called the "modesty of heroism," "in which to make jokes in the face of danger is the supreme act of politeness, a delicate refusal to yield to the tragic."[21]

In part encouraged by this atmosphere of uplifting manliness, duels increased dramatically in number as did the social diversity of their participants. By the founding of the Third Republic the duel was a thoroughly accepted device at private law for regulating differences between gentlemen, and because affairs of honor began to receive an unprecedented degree of publicity from the printing of their official *procès verbaux* in the mass press, they are easier to trace and to count. I have estimated that between 1875 and 1900 there were at least two hundred duels each year, perhaps three hundred in certain years, and in periods of unusual political effervescence—as in the Boulanger and Dreyfus affairs—dozens of duels a week for weeks on end.[22]

Fatalities were rare. Although there were scores of dangerous abdominal wounds, severed tendons, and damaged eyes, there were probably no more than two dozen deaths in duels in this era. Nevertheless, the risk of death haunted each duel; men were said to put their affairs in order and settle gambling debts before an encounter. According to the journalist Félicien Pascal, a review of the fin de siècle dueling craze demonstrated that when the outcome of a duel goes against them, "The gentlemen and simple bourgeois of France know how to die correctly, gallantly, and without complaining."[23] In the sporting and fencing press, death was a veritable school for character: when two men, "steel in hand," have risked their lives, the memory of these moments of danger provides a salutary steadiness for them in each crisis they face in later years.[24] Thus, everyone was born with an instinctive horror of death, but a man could endure life only by exposing himself to danger, educating his nerves, and developing his sangfroid.[25] As Adolphe Tavernier wrote in his dueling manual in 1885, the disagreeable emotion a men feels before a duel is "a concession we make to nature," the "beast" within us reacting against a danger that must be "conquered" by the will.[26]

The numerous apologists for the duel denied it was a brutal and brutalizing ritual. The modern duel, they claimed, civilizes its participants in two fundamental ways. First, by giving men confidence in their personal force, the duel promotes mutual regard and "pacifies" relations between men.[27] Second, fencing and the duel are disciplines of self-mastery and etiquette; they teach a man the forms to observe in his interactions with others and increase his stock of urbanity and wit. Unlike the rowdy quarrelers of yesteryear, it was precisely those men whose personal courage and skill with weapons was most developed who were the *least* likely to issue or provoke dueling challenges.[28] According to an editorial of 1887 in *Le Temps*, France's leading opinion daily, the democratization of arms and the promotion of their skillful use that was taking place in the fin de siècle was a "work of humanity" that would lead to fewer, not more, bloody duels.[29]

There were, however, some strains in the effort to portray the less dangerous modern duel as superior to its bloody ancestor. Looking back at the outmoded manners of the old regime, the journalist Hughes LeRoux wondered in 1888 if the turn of the nineteenth century might not bring "a few smiles at our expense."[30] There were, to be sure, a lamentable number of duels that came off in inelegant fashion: gentlemen foiling their swords in their flowing chemises, getting entangled in one other's buttonhooks, falling unceremoniously in the mud after ungainly lunges, or, more seriously, committing breaches of etiquette in which seconds or principals had resort to underhanded methods or plebeian violence. The merciless army of fin de siècle cartoonists had ample opportunity to ridicule the less dignified aspects of dueling.[31] It is clear enough that dueling numbers dropped off a bit after 1900 to perhaps a hundred or so a year; it also seemed to some contemporaries that publicity had become the major if not the sole basis for challenges. Photographs began to appear in the papers, and an actor named Le Bargy, apparently hoping to land the lead role in a new production of *Cyrano de Bergerac*, provoked duels on successive days with critics unappreciative of his talents.[32]

It was perhaps the echo of mocking laughter in their heads that moved the authors of dueling apologetics to indicate the continuity in early modern and modern duels and to regularly link the duel with skill at arms and war. As one dueling enthusiast wrote, "If they do not pretend to equal, much less surpass the mad audacity and heroic valiance of men at arms, gallant knights, gentlemen of noble race and proud aspect, with their hot blood and impatient alacrity, whose deeds illuminate each page of our history, our end-of-the-century bourgeois have by compensation reason to think that in the matter of the point of honor they are superior to their ancestors in courtesy, correction, and probity."[33] One could also contrast the honor of rival nations invidiously with the French variant. German honor was notoriously brutal and given to ruse, the *point d'honneur* in Austria and Spain rewarded bullying and provocation, and the British, to their eternal shame, loved their vulgar pugilism and blood sport and had transformed matters of honor into sordid calculations of pecuniary interest.[34]

However, the most convincing way to bring credibility to the duel in this era of nationalism was to link it directly to war. Thus we hear, "The battlefield is like the dueling ground, war like the duel, in the sense that all the courage in the world will shatter against ramparts built on twenty solid years in a fencing hall."[35] The encouragement that the duel provided for expertise in arms and for the cultivation of the personal qualities of temerity and sangfroid were regarded as strong advantages indeed. Should war come, the discipline of the point of honor will "remind the soldier that he is a man, not just a cog in the great military machine, that he has not only to spill his blood for the fatherland, but also for his own dignity and personal honor."[36] These themes were taught systematically in the schools of the Third Republic, with the aim of breeding a taste for heroism and self-sacrifice in the future warriors of France.[37] In both its historic and modern forms, the duel played no small role in this educative process by serving as an exemplar of the courage required in personal combat.

However, the modern duel entered the first decades of the twentieth century with an increasingly unmanageable number of ideological contradictions. It civilized and pacified its practitioners, but embraced a metaphysics of death. It proclaimed a democracy of male courage and virtue, but based much of its appeal on its aristocratic history and social connections. It trusted the deterrent effects of personal and national strength, but invoked the certainty of war. The tension in these contradictions were in delicate equilibrium, as the writer Jules Claretie understood. One must resist making a question of honor out of every conflict that arises, he warned, for "the day the last shred of chivalry is torn away from the duel, we will see it for what it is in reality: a butchery that is occasionally heroic and nearly always stupid, but perhaps inevitable, like war."[38]

The First World War

When war finally came it brought less glory than gore, a savage conclusion to gallantry, and the eclipse of hopes that national strength and audacity alone might prolong Europe's long season of peace. On the very eve of the war, Georges Breittmayer, a Parisian socialite and fencer, was putting the finishing touches on what was destined to be the last dueling manual published in France. The manuscript gathered dust until Breittmayer's own military obligations permitted him to return to his work in the winter of 1917–18, but so much had changed that in order to rehabilitate the duel, which had languished during the war, he was obliged to completely recast his book. He knew that after the sacrifices and horror of the war, the duel must be serious or forfeit its right to arbitrate differences between men, so he adopted as his motto, "Lutter jusqu'au bout" [struggle to the end].[39]

From now on, sword duels would be conducted with gauntlets to prevent the scratches on hand and wrist that had ended many prewar duels. The extent of the terrain would be severely limited to exclude elaborate defensive parades, and a man had to be seriously disabled before any thought could be given to stopping. In the case of pistol duels, four balls must be exchanged (two were sufficient before 1914); if this brought no result, the duel must continue with swords until blood flowed. The war introduced two new weapons to the French duel once regarded as alien or unthinkable: the revolver, which had been the side arm of wartime officers, and the bayonet, which Breittmayer called the new "French arm par excellence."[40]

To cut down on the pages of legalistic procedural detail common in prewar manuals, Breittmayer tried to keep his to a minimum. He forbade publicity, honor juries, and all but the most perfunctory arbitration in the interests of making affairs of honor private, abrupt, and final. Unbidden, neither the director of combat nor the doctor could intervene on the dueling ground, he wrote, because "war has leveled those utopias." Men must fight until they choose to fight no longer.

Much space had been devoted in prewar manuals to who was qualified to duel with whom, who was "indigne" and therefore an unsuitable opponent to anyone, and how one recognized such distinctions.[41] Breittmayer cut through all the talk of certain men's "nervous sensibilities" and keen "susceptibility" to offense. He decreed that anyone of draft age, which was then nineteen, could duel. The only disqualification applied to men who had avoided war service or engaged in dishonorable wartime activity.[42] Breittmayer thus acknowledged in his new code what emerged as the most important distinction among men in the postwar era. As a writer for one of the frontline trench newspapers put it in August 1918, "France will find among us men tested by war, soldiers who, having learned how to die, will know how to live and who will break with the past. The future is ours. We must seize it from the cowards, from the fainthearts, from the traitors and shirkers, from people who don't know what war means."[43] In effect, the social distinctiveness of the duel, which had marked the whole of its history from medieval times, had finally evolved to a point where it was isomorphic with all mankind, at least those able-bodied enough to serve in an army of mass conscription. There is a certain irony in the fact that the duel lost the last shreds of its appeal at the precise moment that all men qualified to participate.

The war did not teach to the veterans who survived it many positive lessons on which they could agree. Some concluded for pacifism, others for eternal military readiness. Some wanted their suffering in the war memorialized for all time; others wanted to erase its memory in the forgetfulness of civilian life. But the war did teach these men a certain "modest pride" in what they were *not*. Antoine Prost has summarized this sentiment: "It was an entirely personal feeling, something intimate, an inner confidence, an esteem which one could bestow on oneself. Veterans knew now that they were not cowards. They did not think of themselves as heroes, and they would have gladly been spared the ordeal; but, after all, they had had this unique experience and had not failed to rise to it."[44]

Breittmayer's new code probably went as far as it could to eliminate the frivolous aspects of the duel, but the twenty-five paces separating men holding single-shot dueling pistols made a ludicrous contrast with the deadly terrors of no-man's land; the spectacle of an unpolished *poilu* brandishing his army-issue bayonet eliminated the aristocratic cachet of the ritual; and Breittmayer's decree of silence banned a host of motives that had once inspired men to seek a reputation for bravery in personal combat. There is also the matter of the heightened danger of Breittmayer's duels. The men who had fought in the war had proven their courage in the face of far greater dangers, and those who had avoided service, or were too young to fight, could not hope to equal their ordeals in dueling-ground heroics.

In the course of the war a new standard of masculine courage surfaced that made the courage required in a duel — even Breittmayer's "reformed" duel — into a Tinkertoy version of the real article. A duel in the years after 1918 might have gained some notoriety for the men who engaged in it, but it could no longer sustain a reputation for bravery or rehabilitate sullied honor. This does not mean that personal honor and its particular exigencies disappeared altogether in the postwar world, but men of honor lost the desire, or perhaps the right, to arrogate to themselves the violence of personal combat to protect it. Though it would have happened soon enough anyway, the outbreak of the First World War transformed the duel in a matter of days, unequivocally and forever, from a magnificent gesture to a forlorn imposture. Considerations of personal honor did not suddenly disappear from social life after 1918, but took new forms consistent with the conditions of modern life. Legal recourse to offenses against family and personal honor became more acceptable, as had been the case in England and North America for half a century.[45] The ideal of the amateur athlete subsumed part of the ethos of the duel in the figure of the modern Olympic competitor who cares less about winning (or losing) than in how he plays the game.[46] Perhaps most important, the demonstration of courage took both more exotic and more institutionalized forms. Aviators, explorers, and mountain climbers became icons of modern masculinity for certain rare individuals, while frontline service in war provided a set of credentials that confirmed the manliness of those who survived it and haunted the generations of men who were too old, too young, or too infirm to fight. Finally, honor and its rhetoric continue to express the struggles of religious, racial, and sexual minorities in the West in their quest for legal and civil equality.[47] Honor has outlived the ritual that was once its last and proudest expression.

Notes

1. Kiernan 1988, 261–70.

2. On this duel see Billacois 1986, 309–10. An earlier duel, with only aesthetic issues at stake, was consummated in 1958 between the dancer Serge Lifar and the marquis de Cuevas. Ibid., 314.

3. See Schneider 1984; Cuénin 1982.

4. On the "myths" that surrounded noble race in the early modern era see Jouanna 1977; on the noble "vocation" see Schalk 1986; on the symbolism of blood in dueling see Billacois 1986, 332–37.

5. Billacois 1986, 346.

6. Nye 1993, 31–46.

7. See, in this vein, Gay 1993, 9–33; Kiernan 1988; Mayer 1981.

8. Mosse 1993.

9. Goblot 1925. See also Nye 1993, 31–46, 127–37.

10. Frevert 1993, 229.

11. On the duel and the public honor of journalists in this era see Reddy 1994.

12. There is now a splendid history of the duel in imperial Germany: McAleer 1994. On dueling in nineteenth-century Italy, see the forthcoming work of Steven Hughes.

13. Occasionally the papers from the period report on duels, but duels were often private affairs about matters that both principals wished to hide from public scrutiny. I explain my reasons for arriving at the number of one hundred duels per year in Nye 1993, 136–37.

14. I have discussed these developments at length in Nye 1993, 164–69. On the desire of Republicans to shape a new "republican" man, trained in arms, protective of family and fatherland, and energetic in his own defense see Auspitz 1982.

15. I have discussed these developments for France in Nye 1993, 72–126.

16. Nye 1993, 216–28.

17. The importance of these cultural debates is well known. They are summarized brilliantly in Digeon 1959. The most important postwar document of this kind was Ernest Renan's (1871) *La Réforme intellectuelle et morale.*

18. See the editorials in the mass circulation *Le Petit Journal* of 1 January 1871, where these invidious comparisons were made for perhaps the first time, and also Nye 1993, 154–60, for evidence of the postwar interest in the culture of chivalry.

19. The formula of the critic and journalist Jules Janin, dating from the 1830s, was repeated ad nauseam in the fin de siècle, to wit, "The duel makes of each of us a strong and independent power; it makes of each life the life of the whole of society; it takes up the cause of justice the moment the law abandons it. . . . We are still a civilized people today because we have conserved the duel." See the discussion in Nye 1993, 146.

20. Anatole France, *Le Temps*, 18 July 1886.

21. As quoted in Halkin 1949, 443.

22. I have consulted a number of well-known dueling inventories to arrive at these figures, notably Desjardins 1891; Tarde 1892; Thimm 1896. I have supplemented these inventories with copious selections from the mass press. See Nye 1993, 182–87.

23. Félicien Pascal, "Les Duels d'autrefois," *La Libre Parole*, 28 August 1892.

24. Carles des Perrières, "Duels d'autrefois," *L'Escrime*, 27 November 1881, 119.

25. Dr. Watrin, "Physiologie," *L'Escrime*, 2 December 1881, 136–37.

26. Tavernier 1885, 73–74.

27. Laborie 1906, 17; Villeneuve 1894, 26.

28. Louis de Caters, "Autrefois et aujourd'hui," *Annuaire des maitres d'armes français, 1889–90* (Paris: Bureau de l'escrime français, 1889), 48. See also Nye 1993, 160–64.

29. *Le Temps*, 3 February 1887; see also the editorial of 26 June 1887 insisting that the duel was not an "atavism" of barbarian times but a promoter of "exalted sentiments."

30. Hughes LeRoux, "La Vie à Paris," *Le Temps*, 7 January 1888.

31. See the illustrations in Nye 1993 and my discussion of the "futile" duel, 210–15. Kevin McAleer (1994, 188–92) draws particular attention to French duels of this kind, in contrast with the more dangerous German duel.

32. *Le Journal*, 8 and 9 November 1911. For photographs from contemporary newspapers see McAleer 1994, 190–93.

33. Cloutier 1896, 74.

34. Anonymous, "L'Offense en France et à l'étranger," *L'Escrime*, 25 December 1881, 163–66; "Nouvelles et Echos," *Gil Blas*, 18 July 1889; Jean Frollo, "Les règles du duel," *Le Petit Parisien*, 6 August 1887; Laborie 1906, 31.

35. Adolphe Corthey, "Français et allemands: Armes blanches et armes à feu," *Le Moniteur officiel de la gymnastique et de l'escrime*, 20 November 1886, 5–6.

36. E. Cardeillac, "Duel au regiment," *L'Escrime français*, 20 August 1890. See also Nye 1993, 164.

37. See Gerbod 1982. Stéphane Audoin-Rouzeau has pointed out that the huge increase in school propaganda for the young in the years 1914–18 simply developed the models set in place in the 1880s. See Audoin-Rouzeau 1993, 154–56.

38. Jules Claretie, "La Vie à Paris," *Le Temps*, 31 March 1885.

39. Breittmayer 1918, 6. To do less, he wrote, would be ridiculous (5).

40. Ibid., 13–16, 57, 75, 82.

41. See esp. Laborie 1906, 6–17; Croabbon 1894, 11–27.

42. Breittmayer 1918, 9.

43. Audoin-Rouzeau 1992, 124.

44. Prost 1992, 15.

45. See Frevert 1993, 219–27; Simpson 1988.

46. On this development see Macaloon 1981.

47. See Harris 1992.

TWO

POPULAR DUELS

PART 2 shifts the focus from the official duel to its unofficial popular counterpart and to plebeian culture generally. Did men — and women — from the lower and lower middle classes have their own particular concepts of honor? This question has been on the historical agenda for some years, but historians' interest has hardly extended to the culture of (male) violence and its rituals and codes. The essays that follow, dealing with the Netherlands, Italy, and the United States, discuss precisely this issue. It is revealed that a popular form of dueling existed, which, though resembling the elite duel, had peculiar features of its own. Dying out in the northern city of Amsterdam in the course of the eighteenth century, the popular duel was still alive in the southern European city of Rome by 1900. In both towns its classic manifestation was a knife fight between individual men. The entire range of plebeian fighting rituals was broader, extending to the collective level. A good example of this is the group violence of volunteer firemen in antebellum America. Rather than upholding their individual honor, the firemen fought for the honor of their company. Since one company always stood opposed to another, the "riots" they started can be seen as popular duels, too.

The subjects of the three essays are truly novel. Until now, the popular knife-duel has hardly been noticed by historians. Possibly it originated in imitation of the elite duel. Although collective fistfights have been dealt with in the literature on popular culture in preindustrial Europe, they have been less frequently studied by American historians, and insofar as collective fights in America have been made a subject of study, the perspective was that of ethnic conflict rather than traditional notions of honor. The subject's novelty is intriguing, because the types of sources used are hardly novel. Greenberg bases her story on newspaper reports. Boschi and Spierenburg are using court records as their principal source. In particular, they use homicide trials.

Homicide is present in all three essays. Even the firemen riots sometimes resulted in deaths. As a rule, however, the firemen fought without lethal weapons, so homicide was not a typical result. The clashes between fire companies had no significant influence on the homicide rate. This was different in Amsterdam and Rome. A substantial number, though probably still a minority, of popular knife-duels ended in the death of a protagonist. In both towns, the homicide rates are known for the period studied. At first they were relatively high, and knife fights made a significant contribution to the figures. In both towns the rates declined during the period studied. Whereas in Amsterdam the decline of the homicide rate closely paralleled the disappearance of knife fighting, in Rome the popular duel continued to be practiced into the 1910s, when the homicide rate had already declined. Possibly, Roman popular duelists learned to fight without lethal consequences.

The homicide figures confirm that violent crime was preponderantly a male activity. This was especially striking in Rome: between 1870 and 1914 the share of men was over 90 percent, not only among the offenders but also among the victims. The close association of male popular violence with the world of the tavern also is a constant feature, equally characteristic of Amsterdam around 1700 and Rome around 1900. In the case of the American firemen, the intimate relationship between their riots and their duties precluded an association with tavern culture. However, the riots resembled knife fights in another important aspect: because women were not recruited into volunteer fire companies, the male character of violence was underlined in their case.

The three cases discussed differ in the extent to which the popular duel was echoed in contemporary literature. In the Netherlands a few picaresque novels and a number of crime pamphlets were published, but they hardly contained references to knife-fighting rituals. The latter had a greater resonance in late nineteenth-century Italy. The "fair" popular duel appeared in Italian literature as well as in Roman court records. This leads Boschi to entertain a residue of doubts regarding the authenticity of the stories his defendants told to the court. Spierenburg, on the other hand, is confident that the basic structure of the responses in the Amsterdam interrogation protocols represents reality. In contrast to the mere literary comment on knife fighting, the American volunteer firemen drew the attention of the press. The firemen were more visible as a group and, consequently, there was a greater public concern over their behavior. Still, the press was not the only medium paying attention to riots at fires.

With the figure of "Fighting Mose," firemen violence also made it into literature. Some degree of fiction and mythmaking, then, was superimposed on all three groups of fighters — the least so in the Netherlands, due to the modest literary production of the period. The American firemen stood at the other side of the spectrum: they even acquired a national reputation, because of Mose and no less as a result of sensationalized press reports. In their case, the myth broke loose from reality, becoming relatively independent from actual firemen violence.

The evidence of the essays in part 2 can be confronted with that contained in part 1. This allows us to compare developments in elite and popular violence. A number of things are striking. First, honor was as important in the popular duel as it was in the elite duel. Although not every Amsterdam or Roman knife fight was fought with a code of fairness in mind, practically all fights touched on matters of personal honor. Collective honor was a conspicuous issue in the firemen's riots. A significant difference between the popular duel and the elite duel lies in the former's greater directness. Rituals there were, but they were attuned to an instantaneous settlement once a conflict had arisen. Certainly, popular duelists never issued written challenges. Although they may have viewed their own behavior as akin to that of elite duelists, the latter hardly acknowledged the popular duel as real. Indeed, the elites denied a sense of honor to persons from the lower and lower middle classes. The lack of intergroup recognition of honor may have been greatest in antebellum America. Many of the middle-class people who condemned the "riots" (their definition anyway) among volunteer firemen probably would have approved of a duel within their own milieu. An intriguing point of comparison, finally, lies in the student fencing bouts of imperial Germany: they became increasingly fierce, in accordance with the imperative to control one's emotion and pain. This led German students to take pride in their scars, just as Dutch lower-class knife fighters had done earlier. The heyday of the German student fencing bout came after knife fighting had disappeared in the Netherlands. Here we have an example of a higher social group holding on longer to an "uncivilized" attitude than a lower social group.

4

Knife Fighting and Popular Codes of Honor in Early Modern Amsterdam

PIETER SPIERENBURG

Abram Janse Smit died of his wounds late in the night of 19 December 1690. Earlier that night, he had been fatally stabbed by a man he had never met before. It was all because of his sister-in-law, a woman known as *Molenaars Jets* (Miller's Jets). She must have been notorious, but for what we don't know. Once in a tavern, a group of sailors who had just come ashore asked whether anyone knew where Miller's Jets lived, and a man promptly showed them the way.[1] That night in the winter of 1690, Jets was in a cellar-bar on the Verwers Canal (cheap drinking places were often located in the basements of houses). For unstated reasons, she got into a quarrel with a certain Claas Abrams, who threw three pieces of a tobacco pipe at her face on purpose. She called him a *gauwdief* (sneaky petty thief) and then left with another woman. When Claas rose to pursue her, a man stopped him at the door. That man and other male customers held him in the cellar for a quarter of an hour and finally let him go when he promised to do Jets no harm. Quickly forgetting his promise, Claas spotted Jets at Rusland Street and followed her, without further harassing her yet. At the Lommers bridge

Jets was lucky to meet her brother-in-law, Abram. He was in the company of Freek Spanjaart, a famous knife fighter. Despite his fame, during the incident about to follow in which his friend lost his life, Freek was to be an inactive spectator.

As we would expect, Jets complained to her brother-in-law about Claas's earlier harassment and the fact that he continued to pursue her. Turning to him, Abram drew his knife. But then he announced that he had no inclination to fight, and he walked on. Claas did not trust his words. Moreover, Claas found it unacceptable that someone should draw a knife on him without any reaction on his part. So he went after Abram with his own knife in his hand. Then Abram asked Claas twice whether he intended to harm Jets. When he received no reply, a knife fight ensued. During the combat Freek Spanjaart and Jets just watched. In the middle of it Abram's knife broke. He requested the knife of his friend Freek and got it. Apparently, his adversary granted him a timeout for the exchange. It did not help Abram. He was dangerously stabbed and taken to the "bandage house." Claas left the scene. Later that night, upon his request, it was Jets who went to the bandage house to see the victim. At that moment Claas was hiding in a cellar where his child was nursed. Jets returned after midnight, reporting that Abram had died. Thereupon, Claas fled the town. However, he returned and was caught a few weeks later, which resulted in his decapitation in January of the next year.[2]

In certain respects this case is illustrative not only of "honorific" violence but of all homicides tried by the Amsterdam court in the seventeenth and eighteenth centuries. For example, the encounter took place in a lower-class milieu, which is equally true for the great majority of homicidal incidents. Like Claas Abrams, most killers were men. In cases of lethal knife fights, not only the killer but the victim, too, was male without exception. In such incidents, just the outcome determined who became a corpse and who a potential fugitive. Knife fights in particular have great potential for a study of the social context and cultural meaning of violence. Such fights, and the tavern quarrels often preceding them, can be analyzed in terms of ritual, honor, and male culture just as much as the official duel. Earlier historians usually passed over tavern brawls, considering them as indicative of the hot passions of previous centuries. They merely saw a heap of senseless violence. Although passions certainly were involved, there is more to say about these incidents. Again, what matters is the sociocultural context. The historical anthropologist Anton Blok states that as we go into greater detail with our analysis, what seems senseless violence at first sight becomes meaningful violence instead (which implies that we understand it better, not that we should approve of it).[3] Often, a man acted violently because he felt there was no other possibility; he just had to do it.

This is precisely what Claas Abrams himself said: he had to react in some way when Abram Janse Smit drew a knife on him. Necessity also obliged Freek Spanjaart, the famous fighter, to refrain from helping his friend. Had he intervened, it would have become a vulgar brawl or at least an unequal and therefore infamous fight of two men against one. Intervention was thought honorable only if the purpose was to separate the combatants. With two against one, Abram's reputation as well as Freek's would have suffered. For the latter to lend his knife to his friend was all right, because it made the contest equal again. It was an inherent risk, far from inevitable, though, that a combat like this would result in the death of one of the protagonists. Freek judged Abram's and his honor more valuable than his friend's life. The killer, too, in the end lost his life due to the dictates of honor. He might have been spared the death penalty; after all, his adversary had been the first to draw a knife. It did not matter, the Amsterdam *schepenen* (judges) argued, because Claas had his chance to run away at the point when his adversary's knife broke.

Homicide in Amsterdam

Annual homicide rates are routinely used by historians as an indicator for the level of violence in a town, region, or country at a particular time. There is general agreement that these rates underwent a secular decline in Europe from the late Middle Ages until about 1970. This long-term trend has been established first for England, where homicide rates averaged about 20 per 100,000 inhabitants in the Middle Ages.[4] On the Continent, on the other hand, medieval rates might be as high as 50 or more. The figures for Amsterdam are based on body inspection reports (the best source for this). Homicide rates underwent a steep decline from about 47 per 100,000 in the fifteenth century, an average of 25 in the sixteenth century, to a low point of 3.25 (partly due to underreporting) in the 1660s and 1670s. There was a temporary rise to about 9 per 100,000 between 1693 and 1726. Thereafter the rates declined: they stood between 2 and 3 in the second half of the eighteenth century. They were lower still during the nineteenth and most of the twentieth century.[5] Knife fights were endemic in Amsterdam during the low-homicide decades after the middle of the seventeenth century as well as during the temporary peak in the last decade of that century and the first quarter of the eighteenth. They appear to have been particularly frequent, however, in the latter period.

Body inspection reports tell us little about the pattern of knife fighting or the sociocultural context of violence in early modern Amsterdam. For this, court records are a much better source. The evidence on knife fighters, their codes of honor, and their notions of masculinity is derived from a series of 143 homicide trials conducted between 1650 and 1810. It is supplemented by a preliminary analysis of trials for nonhomicidal violence in Amsterdam. In both series, the interrogation protocols are rich in documentation. A crucial question is whether any change occurred in the pattern of violence during the 160 years studied and, if so, how to explain it.

Before the presentation of the evidence, the quality of the sources must be assessed. On the whole, the Amsterdam court records are very informative. The court left witnesses and defendants ample room to speak for themselves. These depositions are rich in details and, more than once, the magistrates were obliged to inquire into the meaning of certain expressions, places, or events. It is a fashion among modern researchers to analyze protocols like these purely as "texts" or "language." Alternatively, defendants' stories are considered as just strategies to get away with it as best they could. Did defendants, and maybe witnesses as well, embellish their stories after the event? If they did, we might see more order in the culture of violence, a greater adherence to codes, than there actually was. Of course, researchers should always be on their guard, and strategies certainly played a part. However, evasive responses are easily recognizable for what they are, and as a rule they do not impose more cultural order or sense on the events. Many defendants started by denying the major allegations or turning threatening words into neutral ones. I am reassured by the magistrates' careful inquiries in serious cases. Almost always the court confronted the accused with several witnesses. The interrogation protocols regularly contain different versions of the defendant's confessions, from which it is possible to reconstruct the likely course of events. When it came to torture, the accused usually admitted what the principal witnesses had said. In most cases I am confident that I have the "real story," but with respect to certain contested events it was impossible to choose between two versions. Surely, not all the details are always right, but we do have an image of actual fights. There is no fiction in the archives here.

Although "honorific" knife fighting forms the principal concern of this article, to understand it better it must be contrasted with less honorable violence. One-on-one combats with equal weapons can be termed popular duels. They were a prominent feature of Amsterdam street life up until about 1720. The knife fight's fall from prominence marked a major shift in the character of violence in the city. By the second half of the eighteenth century, violence emanating from conflicts in intimate relationships comprised a much greater share of Amsterdam homicide, although this category remained fairly steady in absolute terms. Violence among partners or family members will be discussed only insofar as it sheds light on the central issues of ritual and honor and their interconnections with gender. Two contemporary terms, appearing frequently in the court records, are closely associated with these central issues. The word *voorvechter* denoted a man who had great skill in knife fighting and respected its rituals. Voorvechters used the term *eerlijk man* as a compliment to a fair fighter. Literally meaning "honorable man," the concept combined the issues of honor and gender.

The Knife-Fighting Culture: Ritual, Honor, Gender, and Social Boundaries

Who participated in the knife-fighting culture? It was not only a male preserve. It was also situated in a lower-class milieu. To be more precise, most fighters occupied a social position along the border of the "respectable" and the "disreputable" segment of the urban lower classes. This is true for the protagonists in popular duels as well as most other killers in the homicide series. The definition of respectability, of course, lay with those who claimed to possess it.

About half of the fighters also were petty thieves or they committed property crimes on an occasional basis. A group of five young men who walked the streets on a Wednesday night in July 1681 apparently lived off petty crime. When a quarrel arose, two of them tested their skill with knives and one died. The survivor, a boy of about fifteen, fled the town. Later he confessed to committing petty thefts in Leiden and Utrecht between the incident and his eventual arrest.[6] Lambert Bouman and Fredrick Lodewijckse probably counted as disreputable as well. The conflict in January 1696, in the course of which they challenged each other to a knife fight, had arisen over a prostitute.[7] Other fighters were ex-soldiers or sailors temporarily ashore. They might be on the "right" side of respectability. Still others had recently come to town in the hope of finding employment. The homes of these people, when mentioned, often were in the dark alleys running between the main streets. Several homes consisted of just a room in a house. Many fighters were "sleepers": people who stayed in someone's house for a while and paid for bed and board. The occupational and housing categories overlap. Between two voyages, sailors usually stayed in a "sleeping-house." Some of them were foreign sailors. A homicide case in 1729 resulted from a conflict between two Englishmen who ran boarding houses. In the end, a "sleeper" from one house, James Jackson, stabbed a "sleeper" from the other, William Bellet Young.[8]

Sailors received their final payment upon discharge. During their first few weeks ashore, they certainly had money to spend. Others might have obtained it by illegal means, but it is also possible that they saved it from their wages. Bordering on the disreputable did not necessarily mean being very poor. There were hardly any vagrants among the group of fighters. We know that most of them must have had some money available, because they liked so much to go out. They preferred to spend their pennies in public places.

The world of the tavern, suspect for the respectable segment of the city's population, was central to the knife-fighting culture. Fighters felt at home in various kinds of public places, from cheap cellar-bars to fancier establishments where music was played. Some particular bars were mentioned in more than one homicide protocol. A few notorious inns lay just outside the Haarlem gate. Taverns with music belonged to the culture of semirespectability just as much, which is illustrated by the name of the violin player in "the court of mice nests," Karel Scheetneus (Charlie Fartnose). The court clerk denoted one place bluntly as "Eva's whores and thieves' bar." When a man had been stabbed to death on her doorstep, Eva and a few male customers were arrested, primarily to be heard as witnesses.[9] Although there is talk of brothels and prostitutes in several homicide cases, most of the public places frequented by the fighters seem to have been just for drinking. Of course, drinking was often accompanied by gambling and chance games such as tik tak (a kind of backgammon). The killing of Arent Schinkel by Cornelis Timmerman, for example, resulted from a disagreement in a tavern in the late summer of 1706. Cornelis, a sheepskin seller, had lost two jars of wine to Arent, a tinsmith. Later he suggested to people who knew him that Arent was a swindler; in the same tavern he called Arent a rascal several times. On the night of 30 December Cornelis was looking for Arent along in Nes Street. He learned that his enemy sat in a neighboring bar, so Cornelis went outside to wait for him. When Arent finally left for the street, too, a fatal combat ensued.[10] Many more cases of violence punished by the Amsterdam court originated from disagreements over gambling debts or pretended false play. It is a tribute to the centrality of the world of the tavern that one homicide resulted from a "dispute" among four drunken companions over which bar they should visit next.[11]

Not every incident arising in a tavern was a fair fight. The homicide series contains a few cases in which the defendant had stabbed an unarmed innkeeper who refused to serve him. Those killers had simply lost control in a state of utter drunkenness. They were a minority; most drink-related acts of violence were combats of one against one. When they were particularly skilled, fighters enjoyed local fame in the world of the tavern. In fact, we know that Freek Spanjaart was a famous fighter, not from the trial of Claas Abrams, discussed earlier, but from a passage in the protocols of a trial a few months later. The defendant, Hermanus de Bruijn, was at least as famous. A female friend of his recalled a conversation, in his absence, at a place they often frequented. According to the innkeeper, nicknamed "the Baboon," Hermanus was a voorvechter no one could beat; the Baboon considered him even better than Harmen Hoedemaker or Freek Spanjaart.[12] Most likely, Freek's name did not ring a bell with the interrogators or the clerk who wrote it down. The court took note of this conversation as an additional incrimination. We learn from it that knife fights and their protagonists were discussed in taverns and that skilled fighters were probably admired.

One more type of unequal fight, that of stick vs. knife, reflects the social cleavages separating the culture of violence from the respectable segment of the urban population. Respectable people refused to become involved in knife fights. When they were threatened or challenged, they would try to ward off the danger by other means. A stick was the typical weapon of defense. With it, they would try to knock the knife from their attacker's hands or to hit him, or both. A quarrel over two fighting dogs between two neighbors, Willem van Busscherveld and Hendrik Westerman, in 1731 is an example. When Hendrik drew a knife and threatened to kill Willem's dog with it, Willem first withdrew into his house at his wife's insistence. But he returned, was challenged by Hendrik, and walked up to him with a broomstick in order to wrestle the knife from his hands.[13] Some people routinely carried sticks with them in the street, probably for use as walking sticks in more peaceful situations. In July 1706 Servaas van der Tas, having visited several bars, made a remark to three men he met in the street. They refused his company: "We don't speak to you, little friend." Thereupon Servaas drew his knife and attacked one of them, who warded him off with his stick.[14] In many respectable homes a stick stood behind the door, just as some shopkeepers today might have a baseball bat ready. It did not help Pieter Fontijn in 1711. He was a victim by accident. His attacker, Ambrosius Coertsz, first had been in the bar beneath Pieter's house. When he demanded another drink at 10:30 P.M., the landlord said he did not serve that late. A quarrel ensued, but the landlord managed to kick Ambrosius out. When the latter returned between 2 and 3 A.M., he knocked on the wrong door. Pieter opened and asked him whom he wanted to speak to. Ambrosius replied, "It is you I want," and immediately seized him. Escaping from the other man's grip, Pieter ran inside, came back with a stick, and swung in Ambrosius's direction. Then Ambrosius drew his knife. A struggle followed, and Pieter was stabbed twice in the chest.[15]

There are more cases like this. They exemplify the extent to which Amsterdam's inhabitants had to rely on their own resources to protect themselves and their property. Since a defense with a stick is referred to in the records on such a routine basis, we may suppose that it was an ordinary custom and often successful. When a man warded off his attacker in this way and there were no serious injuries, it was unlikely to be recorded. Cases of stick vs. knife in the homicide series are cases of unsuccessful defense; no stick-user was tried for homicide himself.

Stick vs. knife: for the historian it is an easy tool for distinguishing two groups and their cultures. The members of these groups were socially distinct, even though they might be neighbors. The people with knives belonged to the semirespectable segment of the lower classes. Characteristically, it was noted that Ambrosius Coertsz kept a concubine and had two children by her. The people with sticks belonged to the respectable segment or were lower middle class. Of course, the latter possessed knives, too. They might even carry one in their pocket, expecting to eat an apple somewhere, for example. But they were not ready to use it in a violent confrontation. It is unlikely that Pieter Fontijn had no knives at all, not even a sharp kitchen knife, in his house. He just did not want to become involved in a knife fight. Alternatively, it is possible that the people with sticks were such poor fighters that a knife simply would be useless to them. However, the sources convey the impression that the main reason for the way they acted was that they found it beneath their dignity to allow the other party to challenge them. They wished to keep aloof from the people with knives. In this urban community, the level of public security was such that most people had to be ready to defend themselves, but sociocultural differences played a major role in the choice of weapon.

Semirespectable though they were, the people with knives cherished the rules of their game. Combats of one man against another were not just indiscriminate clashes. Rituals and cultural codes partly dictated the course of knife fights. As I said before, they were popular duels. Respect for the rules was compatible with impulsive behavior and the unleashing of passions. The quarrels preceding a combat certainly were real, and the anger must have been deeply felt. The combination of ritual and sincerity is intriguing to our modern western minds. Fair fighters adhered to a few basic rules.

The first rule, already alluded to, was to ensure an equal combat. Everybody might be involved in the preliminaries, but when two men had actually started to fight, others normally stepped aside. This would seem wise when the bystanders were companions of both contestants: when the original quarrel had arisen within a group. In such cases, intervention only took the form of a third group member trying to convince the combatants to stop. However, there were also inactive bystanders who were companions of only one of the combatants. When Claes Hendricks Kraemer, called Smidje, met his old enemy, Jonker Bexe, at the Den Bosch fair in 1665, the latter was in the company of his cousin and two women. The enemies agreed to withdraw to a quiet place, but they became separated while trying to avoid the guard. A little later, Claes heard a voice say, "Smidje, where are you?" He answered and noticed that Bexe still was with his cousin. "There are two of you," protested Claes, whereupon Bexe's cousin said, "Go ahead. I won't interfere." It earned him a compliment from Claas: "You speak as an honorable fellow." The combat began. Bexe was to die from his wounds the next day, but by then Claes had already fled the town. He arrived in Amsterdam and found a job there, but two years later he was arrested and tried for Bexe's murder.[16] Upon a few other occasions, too, the Amsterdam *schepenen* dealt with far-away homicides. These cases suggest that the knife-fighting culture also flourished elsewhere in the Netherlands. An example of a noninterfering friend in Amsterdam was given at the beginning of the article. Another example concerns a tavern brawl in 1704. The course of events is not entirely clear from the records, but the defendant, named Jan, confessed this much: At a certain moment he, Jan, went outside followed by "Steentje" and "black Martin," who both drew their knives. Then Jan got a knife from a stranger. Steentje said to Jan, "Sta vast," and the combat began. Black Martin did not interfere.[17]

Another basic rule was to avoid embarrassing a landlord or landlady. When a conflict arose in a tavern and the participants sensed it was to be resolved through violence, they left for the street. The actual fight took place outside. Even to draw a knife indoors was not quite honorable. This course of events is so obvious from the records that it is unnecessary to document it with individual examples. Let me give a counterexample instead when, for once, a customer was stabbed inside a tavern. Cornelis Oudendijk and Willem van der Helm, sitting in Adam Beumer's cellar-bar on the afternoon of 29 November 1719, had words over an inheritance. Cornelis called Willem a scoundrel, and Willem replied that he should slap Cornelis's face for this insult. Then they were reconciled and had a drink together. A little later, however, when Willem sat on a bench near the fire, Cornelis stabbed him in the back without warning: treacherously, so the records say. Beumer immediately exclaimed, "How do you dare to perform such a *schelmstuk* [an act of roguery] in my cellar?" Cornelis just reacted by pulling the bloody knife out of Willem's back and putting it in his pocket.[18] Beumer's words speak for themselves; we can feel this landlord's astonishment and indignation. That Cornelis did not throw away his knife, a common device for hiding the evidence, suggests he was either simple or extremely drunk.

Knife fights resembled official duels in several respects. One party, at least, had to perceive an encroachment upon his honor. A disagreement accompanied by strong language or just a sudden insult often sparked the incident. For a combat to ensue, one party had to challenge the other. In line with the rule not to fight indoors, the challenge often consisted of an invitation to leave for the street together. During a tavern brawl, the words "Come, follow me outside" would not be misunderstood. In the street the fight did not necessarily start immediately. The quarrel might be continued verbally at first. The combatants might also agree to retire to some quiet area, a back street or a courtyard. Whatever they did, the yell "Sta vast" was the point of no return. When one party said this, both would draw their knives. From then on, the two were obliged, if not to attack, at least to defend themselves. If third parties were present, they served as witnesses. Their role was comparable to the seconds in the official duel, but their presence had not been arranged in advance.

The combat as such was a test of skill. In the cases of the homicide series it ended in death by definition, but it could also be over when one man had cut the other or obtained a clear advantage. Indeed, during their trial many killers confessed to having injured people on earlier occasions. A number of convicts themselves had scars. When the court inquired, they would routinely say something like: "I received this cut from a man at the Rose's Canal last Fall." The word *received* suggests a kind of acceptance, but it may actually be the court clerk's bureaucratic parlance rather than the fighters' own words.

This description of the ritual course of knife fights is a reconstruction from a number of cases. It is an ideal type. Individual duels might deviate in one way or another from the ideal course of events. Occasional details shed further light on the inherent codes. One December night two men, coming out of a cellar-bar arguing and drawing their knives, realized it was dark outside. "Come here, under the lantern," said one to the other, who followed him.[19] This small detail confirms that a duel started only upon mutual agreement. Lambert, a skilled fighter, had already cut his adversary on his left cheek when the latter inadvertently dropped his knife. Lambert allowed the other to pick it up again, then continued the fight and stabbed his adversary in the belly.[20] In another case the eventual victim, a sailor, had invited his adversary to leave the tavern with him. In the street the sailor made it clear that he only wanted a fistfight, but his adversary said, "I am not able to fight you with my fists." What exactly he meant by this is unclear. In any case, both men drew their knives, cut toward each other, were separated without injuries, looked for each other again a little later, and fought anew with fatal result for the sailor, who had been the original challenger.[21] In a homicide case in 1712 the killer, nicknamed Black Lou or Lou the German, did not care much for the victim, called Daniel Krijt, but both men respected the basic ritual. It began with a quarrel, for an undisclosed reason, in Daniel's room. Lou first went home to change clothes, putting on something more convenient. Back in Daniel's room, he drew his knife twice and then put it back into his pocket. Then he slapped Daniel's wife. The angered husband exclaimed, "Whoever hits my wife hits me." Lou immediately responded, "Sta vast," and he drew his knife again. Daniel said, "Vast it will be," and drew his knife, too. But soon he had been stabbed no less than eight times. As he lay on the floor motionless, his wife yelled, "Oy, my husband, he dies." Then Lou seized her and threw her on Daniel's body, exclaiming, "There, lie on your dead husband now; lie, so that the Devil may take you."[22] This case forms a clear example of the combination of deep anger and a respect for the basic ritual of the challenge.

A final example of a one-on-one combat shows that the ritual obligation to remain fair was not always fully respected. The four actors were Jan, Johannes, Dirk, and Frans. Incidentally, Jan had been to a funeral that day, presumably of someone who had died a natural death. In the evening the four men sat in a tavern at the Haarlemmerdijk, where Johannes and Frans started to quarrel with Dirk. All three went outside and drew their knives, but Jan followed them to hush them up. In particular, he tried to calm down Johannes, who was furious with Dirk. Then Dirk left the group. At Frans's insistence, the three of them went to a tavern at the Lindengracht to order another pot of beer. Along the way, Johannes, still angry because Jan had separated him and Dirk, twice drew his knife on Jan, who said he should wait until they had reached a place where he could remove his black coat, apparently meaning that he was unable to fight while wearing it. Jan got rid of it in the tavern at the Lindengracht, but a fight did not ensue immediately. A little later Johannes kicked Jan's dog, which caused the pot of beer, just ordered, to topple. Then Johannes issued the challenge, "Come, let's go," and went outside, followed by Jan. It was 4 A.M. Frans was no longer referred to in the story; he may or may not have been present during the combat. Jan soon got the upper hand. He stabbed Johannes in the belly. Johannes fell down, but managed to cut his attacker's thumb and to lodge his knife in Jan's right arm. Jan pulled it out, threw it away, and then stabbed Johannes in his right shoulder. Jan's knife stuck, too; he pulled it out of his adversary's shoulder just as a watchman apprehended him.[23] To stab an adversary after throwing away his knife certainly was a breach of the code of fair fighting. In this case, passions seem to have overtaken respect for ritual in the end.

Rituals of violence were supplemented by rituals of reconciliation. Be-

cause the interrogation protocols usually work toward a climax, the reconciliation they refer to was temporary, reached in the middle of a chain
of events. One ritual in particular stands out here. It is called *afdrinken:* the
men "drink the conflict away." Usually it goes like this: Two men have
an argument. They rise from their chairs, utter threatening words, and
maybe one slaps the other in the face. There is talk about settling the matter through a fight, but other men in the company hush it up and tempers
cool. At that point a bottle of wine or beer is ordered, and the whole company sits together and tries to forget the incident. But it is never entirely
forgotten. Passions may become hot again, and violence may or may not
flare up anew. In homicide cases, necessarily, reconciliation was unsuccessful in the end. It may be supposed, however, that hundreds of quarrels
and minor fights have really been "drunk away," without leaving a trace in
the court records. References to afdrinken are as numerous as they are
poor in details. The skilled Lambert, who allowed his adversary to pick up
his knife, had been reconciled to him earlier. It happened after the eventual victim, acting suddenly, had stabbed Lambert in his left arm. Accompanied by the tavern's landlord, Lambert visited a surgeon and returned to
drink the conflict away with his attacker.

The rituals discussed so far may be termed positive. Their basic aim
was to stylize violence, making it less naked and unrestrained, or to reduce its incidence. Negative rituals, on the other hand, were associated
with the repertoire of humiliation. Several historians have observed that
attackers followed cultural codes in deciding which part of their adversary's body to hit. In fifteenth- and sixteenth-century Artois, Muchembled
found that in many cases the victim's head had been hit, even though, in
order to kill him, it would have been more efficient to thrust a knife into
his belly. He concluded that the ritual disfiguration of an adversary's face
was meant to humiliate him.[24] Cohen and Cohen came to a similar conclusion for sixteenth-century Rome.[25] Yet, in the Amsterdam homicide series,
almost no victim died of head injuries. Victims were stabbed in the chest
or belly or elsewhere. A possible explanation is that popular duelists
around 1700 were not normally bent on killing each other. A knife fight
was a test of strength. Upon starting it, some combatants explicitly said
that the other "needed a cut" or "should have something." If a fight ended
in death, it was an "accident." In that case, for whatever reason, one combatant had become so furious that he disregarded the original purpose. At
that point, he did not intend to humiliate, just to attack.

The preliminary analysis of nonhomicidal violence, on the other hand, discloses several negative rituals. To manage to cut someone's face, for example, meant to show one's superiority over him. Some stabbings were clearly meant to humiliate. A peculiar act of degradation was to stab someone's buttock. In 1696, for example, two sailors saw their former helmsman, who had punished them while on ship, walking the streets with his wife. They decided to take revenge. They followed him to a narrow alley, where one of the sailors thrust his knife into the helmsman's right buttock.[26] A certain Co, nicknamed "Bale of Wool," who was tried for several acts of violence in 1711 when he was twenty, denied the charges. In his youth he had belonged to a group of boys hanging around at the Botermarkt, who habitually fought the boys from the orphanage. Two former orphanage boys accused Co of having stabbed one of their group in his buttock. Upon another occasion, also at the Botermarkt, Co was alleged to have thrown his knife into a girl's buttock. His mother had given the girl money to get bandaged.[27] In the nonhomicidal series, most victims of buttock stabbing were women. Negative rituals were practiced also by people who eventually became killers. Minor cuts and nondeadly stabbings turn up in the homicide series as additional charges against a number of defendants. Some had cut another on the cheek; others had stabbed a man in his arm. Several killers were accused of having stabbed a woman, their sweetheart or some other woman, in her buttock. Some denied this; others confessed.

Humiliation, shame, and honor: these themes played a role in most of the cases discussed. As knife fights were often begun in order to defend one's honor, insults often were the immediate cause. They included such common insults as *schelm* (rogue, scoundrel), thief, or whore. An incident in 1682 began when a passer-by thought that the killer was a Jew and called him *smous*.[28] A few young fighters felt insulted at being called a boy or "little brother." Not every insult was as blunt as the one Dirk Teunisse made to Gijsbert Jacobse. The two men met in a tavern. As if he wanted to frustrate later historians' attempts to determine killer-victim relationships, Gijsbert said to Dirk: "I know you, even though I haven't seen you for a long time." Dirk's reply must have been meant to indicate that he did not remember and didn't care, either: "Then you won't blow into my ass unacquainted." Gijsbert's interrogators recognized this as heavy language, for their next question was whether Dirk had also insulted him in other ways.[29]

Intriguingly, the "real" duel, arranged in advance and fought with swords or pistols, is almost absent from the Amsterdam court records. Duels with pistols, uncommon throughout Europe in this period, are not referred to at all. A few one-on-one combats were fought with swords, usually by (ex-)soldiers. Even then, an arrangement in advance was uncommon. In 1712 a group of night watchmen interrupted a rapier combat and pursued one of the protagonists, a naval officer. The officer pierced one of the watchmen with his rapier, was overpowered by the others, and was tried for homicide. The court showed no interest in the original fight.[30] Just one incident, in 1682, was unmistakably an official duel. The contestants were two French ex-soldiers, but in the eyes of their Third Republic compatriots the issue could hardly have appeared lofty. Our Frenchmen had a disagreement over the division of the spoils after they had snatched a farmer's purse at the city fair. They decided to settle the matter with swords. Two other soldiers promised to lend them their weapons for the occasion, which cost them twenty *stuivers*. They agreed to meet in a tavern the next day. All four eventually came. From the tavern they went to a wood-storage yard in the Jewish area. The duel was fought there, with the sword owners serving as witnesses. One combatant died and the other walked away, pursued by the victim's concubine until he reached the Muiden gate. He was arrested a few months later, after having killed a female friend.[31]

Gender was a factor in the knife culture in various ways. Evidently, the particular ritual repertoire and code of honor of these people belonged to a male world. The connection between masculinity and the code regulating the official duel has been noted already.[32] In making this code their own, the participants built up a self-image of a tough, noneffeminate man. This is equally true for the popular duel. No doubt, its participants felt that testing each other's fighting skill was testing each other's manhood, even though the sources contain few explicit references to this. We have to be content with indirect evidence. Chivalry may be taken as one piece of indirect evidence. A number of knife fights originated in the defense of a woman against a man by another man. Although it was common for men in this social milieu to beat women when they were angry at them, this did not always go unchallenged. Examples have been given already. Especially when a man harassed a woman in public, a regular feature of the tavern milieu, another man might interfere verbally: "You wouldn't dare to do that to a fellow," or "If she were my wife, I would beat you up." Sometimes such interventions led to a fight. Upon other occasions a man, crossing the streets in a bad mood and looking for trouble, said upon meeting a woman that she need not be afraid because he would never fight a woman. The implication, sometimes added, was that the next man passing by had better watch out.

In spite of such protestations, some women definitely were victims of male violence. The homicide series does contain female victims, and some of them had no intimate relationship to the killer. A homicide of a wife or concubine was usually committed at home. In taverns, it could happen that a man was so angry at a female acquaintance or a recent sweetheart that he stabbed her. Presumably, such an act fell outside the code of honor. Passions had taken the upper hand then. This observation can be formulated in a different manner: since women were not expected to participate in popular duels, they could not be formally challenged. There were no customary rules for combating women, and therefore they stood a greater risk of sudden attack.

These observations can be supplemented with cases from the nonhomicidal series. An ex-soldier from Zutphen, for example, was convicted in 1651 for injuring a woman's face with a broken glass. Having a wife in Zutphen, he had left that town in the company of a woman named Griet, and he had left her, too, for a woman with whom he lived in Amsterdam. The victim was yet another woman, whose relationship to him remained unrecorded.[33] The relationship between Claas Dorison and Annetie Borduur remained unrecorded as well. Claas went to get beer for her, had a quarrel with another man on his way, and came back without beer. When Annetie reproached him for this, he cut her in the neck and hand.[34] Extramarital relationships figured again in a trial in 1713. The defendant, Pieter Knoet, was married, but he had no idea whether his wife was still alive. Asked by *schepenen* if it was true that he lived with a woman with whom he had five or six children, he replied that he was only considered the father of the child of a certain Kee but that he did not believe it was his. In any case, Pieter was now living with Trijn Pieters, with whom he had quarreled in her home on a Saturday night. A woman living next door had interfered and said, "This is enough." Thereupon Pieter had beaten this woman and cut her face. He claimed she fell into his knife by accident.[35]

Cutting a woman's face could be an act of revenge by a jilted lover; such a custom is still reported in some countries nowadays. Thus, Jan Helt cut Margrietje Duijff's face from the eye to the mouth on Epiphany night 1698: without any reason, the court clerk wrote. He must have meant without an immediately preceding quarrel. Jan admitted that Margrietje was his former girlfriend.[36] An incident in 1711, we may suppose, arose because Magdalena Visser had rejected Adolf Gerrits. Adolf was sitting in a tavern with three women when Magdalena, who stayed with one of them, entered. This made "his blood change in his body." A little later, Adolf left the tavern, now in the company of four women. In the street, he started scolding Magdalena: "You thunder-whore! You beast! What do you do here? You have no business here." Then he stabbed her in her side. In court he admitted everything except calling Magdalena a whore.[37] The conflict behind Marten Elskamp's revenge, finally, remains unclear. He had been denied access to a family's home, in particular by the woman of the house. Earlier, he had often been welcome there, having returned from Indonesia with her son. On a September night in 1744 he knocked on the family's door. When the woman opened the door, Marten tried to cut her face, but she stepped back and received a cut in her arm instead. Under torture, Marten explained that this woman had "made him go astray" and "laughed at his sister."[38]

The relationships between violence and gender were multifaceted. Popular duels, as tests of manhood, were exclusively male affairs, but in various roles, women occupied a part of the stage.

Violence Changing: The Church and the State

Having analyzed the knife culture in a static fashion, I must now pose the question of change. And, following Elias, I must inquire into the interdependence of cultural change and other social developments. The knife culture may have had a long history; there is no reason to assume that the beginning of my series in 1650 was its starting point. Some information on earlier years comes from Roodenburg's work on the church discipline exercised by the Amsterdam Reformed consistory, 1578–1700. Disciplinary cases included acts of violence by church members. The consistory dealt with a number of serious injuries, some with knives, even a few homicides. Roodenburg gives no details about these cases, but he does present the total numbers of church members summoned for violence per decade. These numbers dropped to an insignificant level after 1630. He concludes that toward the middle of the seventeenth century the consistory's disciplinary drive had achieved success, as far as it concerned taming violence.[39] This finding is particularly significant, because the Reformed

community may be considered representative for the "respectable" segment of the city's lower and middle classes. Around 1600, apparently, being respectable did not preclude being involved in the culture of violence.
This leads to an intriguing conclusion: by the time when my series begins,
the division of the urban population into the people with knives and the
people with sticks had just come about.

The disappearance of the knife-fighting culture is revealed in the series itself. From its inception until about 1720, one-on-one combats were
conspicuously present. Homicide trials, to be sure, represent just a fraction of the total number of killings. As noted above, the actual homicide
rates peaked between 1690 and 1725, and this was mainly due to a heightened propensity for knife fights. It remains unknown what caused this
temporary upsurge. Did the knife culture gain strength just before it died
out? Whatever the interpretation, things had changed by the middle of
the eighteenth century. As revealed by the body inspection reports, the
absolute number of killings had substantially decreased then, and stabbings accounted for a smaller proportion of this diminished volume. In the
series of homicide trials, there were hardly any "honorable" knife fights
after 1720. Stabbings still were reported, but they were mostly unequal
struggles. They began as fistfights, for example, in which the eventual victim, taken by surprise, had not drawn a knife at all. Significantly, in the
second half of the eighteenth century, the only trial referring to a popular
duel—a knife fight complete with the yell "Sta vast" and all that—took
place in the relative marginality of the Jewish community.[40] The combined observations from the homicide series and the body inspection reports lead me to conclude that the incidence of popular duels must have
declined sharply in the second quarter of the eighteenth century.

My evidence and Roodenburg's data together point to the existence of
a medium-term cultural development: the process of marginalization of
the knife culture. The beginnings of this process date back to the late sixteenth century, when the Reformed consistory initiated its disciplinary
drive. Effective marginalization had been accomplished more or less in the
second half of the eighteenth century. This chronology concerns Amsterdam. Evidence suggests that the knife culture lived on longer in some
rural parts of the Netherlands. In a recent study of crime in the Groningen countryside, Sleebe notes that even in the early nineteenth century
many village fights started with a semiformal challenge. The challenger
invited his adversary outside, and the latter indicated his acceptance by

taking off his coat. Sleebe quotes a contemporary observer who remembered what dueling was like in the eighteenth century: Skilled fighters attempted to make long cuts in their opponent's faces, while they prided themselves on their own scars. A comparable attitude prevailed in Drente and Brabant around 1800. In the Groningen countryside, as far as can be ascertained from Sleebe's account, knives still dominated violent crime by the middle of the nineteenth century, but toward the end they became less common as a weapon.[41] Thus, the marginalization of the knife culture probably was a broader development, and its chronology varied with the region.

The evidence about this development supports my theory about long-term qualitative changes in the character of violence.[42] Notably, it points to change on the ritual-instrumental axis. The process of marginalization of the knife culture in Amsterdam meant, among other things, that ritual elements in violence lost importance during the eighteenth century. Admittedly, even modern violence may involve ritual of some kind, but a specific form of highly ritualized fighting disappeared. So what about the opposite pole, that of instrumental violence? The decline of knife fights did not mean that cases of homicide with a conspicuously instrumental character became more frequent in absolute terms. There was no positive breakthrough of instrumental violence. The share of homicides committed in relation to a property crime, for example, remained fairly steady between 1650 and 1810.[43] This still means that, on balance, Amsterdam violence moved a little closer to the instrumental pole of the axis.

Scholars influenced by Elias's historical sociology cannot be content with the sole description of a process, however long. Changes in the cultural meaning of violence must be linked to broader changes in Dutch society. Was the marginalization of the knife culture related to a process of state formation or, for that matter, economic developments? The present state of the evidence allows only a preliminary answer. This begins with an inquiry into the activities of the Church and the magistrates. The disciplinary drive by the Reformed consistory has been mentioned already. Although other Protestant churches have not been investigated in detail in this respect, we know that they, too, exercised moral discipline. Clearly, the godly thought all private violence sinful. We learn this from the tracts of several ministers, when they dealt with the sixth commandment. According to them, it referred not only to killing but to violence in general and the slightest quarrel that might lead to it. They routinely condemned

all sorts of violence, except such activities as executing criminals or wag-
ing war against Catholic Spaniards. Showing a vague knowledge of the
popular concept of honor, the ministers uncompromisingly disapproved
of it: true honor, they argued, originates from God alone.[44]

Additional evidence is provided by the resolutions taken at provincial
synods of the Reformed Church. Although such subjects as the regulation
of marriage and the suppression of practices considered superstitious received the greater share of the synods' attention, there was a steady flow
of resolutions concerning homicide and knife fighting. The Utrecht assembly of 1606, for example, heard complaints from the minister at Vee-
nendaal: no less than thirty people had been killed in the village since his
arrival there; unfortunately, we do not hear how long he was in office. In
the eastern provinces, between 1590 and 1610, a few preachers themselves were suspected of homicide.[45] In the 1630s the synod of South Holland spoke out against knife fighting several times. From the 1650s
onward, the efforts of the synods concentrated on dueling. They attributed this custom specifically to soldiers; apparently, they considered their
flock to be sufficiently pacified.[46]

This "civilization offensive" by the leaders of religious communities
was probably the main factor in the first phase of marginalization of the
knife culture: its fall from respectability. In the early Republic, the competition between several Protestant denominations extended from the doc-
trinal arena to the issue of the community's virtue in the eyes of outsiders.
Abstention from violence was one means of exhibiting virtue. The competition between denominations stimulated the drive to reform the behavior
of church members.[47] From them, knife fights were not tolerated and,
consequently, these fights became the habit of less respectable people.
From the end of the seventeenth century onward the consistories were
less active with regard to discipline. Moreover, the disrespectable "people
with knives" hardly cared about the consistories' concerns in the first
place. The disappearance of knife fighting after 1720, then, must be due
not so much to religious indoctrination as to repression by the state.

To some extent, church and state were intertwined. Apart from cor-
recting its members, the Church exerted pressure on the magistrates. In
most of the synods' resolutions concerning violence, the courts were
called upon to take a firm stand. In the late sixteenth century it was still
common for the judicial authorities to allow private reconciliations in
cases of homicide. They did not interfere when a killer had reached a

settlement with the victim's family; they might just impose a financial compensation on the former. Fugitive killers were convicted by default to a banishment from the jurisdiction, often consisting of a handful of villages. With a big smile the condemned paraded along the borderline, the synods complained. Clearly, the Church wanted the state to exercise its monopoly of violence through punishment. The churchmen admonished the secular authorities never to pardon those guilty of manslaughter and forbade their flock to hinder any criminal prosecution. Significantly, the ministers' definition of a duel stressed the fact that it involved two persons subject to the same authority. The duel was wrong because it meant an encroachment on the state's monopoly of violence.[48] The influence of these ecclesiastical admonitions is difficult to ascertain. It is unlikely that it was just pressure by the churchmen that caused the magistrates to stop recognizing private settlements in homicide cases.

The timing of the shift toward an ex officio prosecution of homicide probably varied with the jurisdiction. Undoubtedly, the Amsterdam magistrates were bent on repressing the knife culture from at least 1650 onward. In my series there is no trace of a positive view nor even a neutral view of the popular duel by the court. The "honorable" combat was unlawful without any question. The only lawful excuse for stabbing someone was self-defense. This claim was bound to strict rules, such as an unmistakable duty to retreat. The duty to retreat is plain in Claas Abrams's case, cited at the beginning of this article: even though the eventual victim had been the first to draw a knife, the Amsterdam *schepenen* found that the killer deserved the death penalty. When his adversary's knife broke, they argued, Claas should have taken the opportunity to flee. The court told other defendants who claimed self-defense that they could easily have retreated into someone's house. Needless to say, such acts of withdrawal would be a shame on an honorable fighter.

Changes in the knife culture's infrastructure were crucial, too. The court struck at it from time to time, but the magistrates do not seem to have been engaged in a systematic policy of suppression. The infrastructure's existence is revealed in trials against individual killers around 1700. The larger community to which knife fighters belonged, maybe even some respectable people, thought lightly about the popular duel. If a fight resulted in the death of one combatant, many people considered this an accident. They found capital punishment too severe a sanction. Consequently, they refused to turn in an "honest" killer, and some were prepared to help him escape. Of course, help came from family and friends in the first place, but even strangers might be indirectly involved. A few private persons caught a shoplifter in the act, then let him go when he confessed to having once committed manslaughter. They would have turned him in for theft, but they found it unreasonable that the poor wretch might get the death penalty for his earlier "accident." Some landlords, upon noticing a reputed killer in their bar, would ask, "Why are you still in town?" Once, we hear that money was collected in several bars in the street in which a knife fight had taken place, to support a killer in his flight from the city.[49] After 1720 the court records no longer contain references to this infrastructure. It may have faded away with the knife culture itself.

A case in 1795 suggests a changed attitude on the part of the tavern public: two men quarreled in a winehouse over a loan of money; they went outside; one of them returned to the winehouse a little later, carrying a bloodstained knife that he had used to peel a lemon when the quarrel started; he exclaimed, "Where shall I go to?" No one reacted.[50] Further research is needed to discover whether cooperation with the law became increasingly acceptable during the eighteenth century.

Conclusion

The knife culture that flourished in Amsterdam until about 1720 was rooted in "traditional" notions of masculinity and honor. The theme of honor has been studied by anthropologists as well as by some historians, but hardly so with reference to tavern violence in the towns of early modern Europe.[51] Therefore, the ritual character of one-on-one combats in Amsterdam forms a crucial finding. This evidence broadens our knowledge of duels, which up until now was based almost solely on the official aristocratic and military duel. The popular duel was first discovered by Beattie, studying eighteenth-century England. In England it was even more formal, often being arranged in advance. The preceding quarrel, for example, might be in a tavern in the afternoon and the combat would take place in the tavern's courtyard that night with the landlord acting as a witness.[52] In a similar vein, lower-class Parisians in the eighteenth century sometimes participated in prearranged fights.[53] Further research is needed to determine whether such customs existed in other countries and to discover the chronology of their rise and fall throughout Europe.

In Amsterdam the disappearance of the knife culture had consequences for the incidence and character of violence. After the first quarter of the eighteenth century, the homicide rate sharply declined. Ritual elements came to occupy a less prominent place in Amsterdam violence. The proportion of killings of strangers decreased, and the proportion of homicides of intimate persons rose.

Notes

Earlier versions of this article were presented as lectures for the Program for British Studies, University of Michigan, Ann Arbor, and the history departments at Georgetown University and the University of Stony Brook, and as a paper at the 1994 meeting of the Social Science History Association in Atlanta. I am grateful to the audiences for their comments, especially to the discussant in Atlanta, Daniel Cohen. I also have to thank Martin Wiener for pointing out an inconsistency in an earlier version.

   1. This had happened on 29 July 1685, also eventually leading to a homicide because of Jets. See Gemeente-Archief (Municipal Archive), Amsterdam: Archive no. 5061, Oud-Rechterlijk Archief (henceforth R.A.), no. 329, fols. 197–99.
   2. R.A. 336, fols. 129vs, 132vs, 138, 140vs; R.A. 596, fol. 177vs.
   3. Blok 1991.
   4. See Gurr 1981 and Stone 1983.
   5. For more details, see Spierenburg 1994 and 1996.
   6. R.A. 326, fols. 162, 165, 195, 201, 219, 221vs.
   7. R.A. 345, fols. 226, 227, 229vs, 257vs, 261vs; R.A. 346, fols. 24vs, 31vs, 36vs, 41vs, 119.
   8. R.A. 387, fols. 143vs, 146, 147, 151vs, 158, 159vs, 164, 174vs, 177vs.
   9. R.A. 368, fols. 241vs e.v.; R.A. 369, fols. 54vs, 75vs, 77, 107, 107vs.
   10. R.A. 356, fols. 82vs, 102vs, 104vs, 129.
   11. R.A. 378, fols. 29vs, 32, 34, 50.
   12. R.A. 336, fols. 145, 148, 151vs, 153, 155vs, 192; R.A. 596, fol. 216.
   13. R.A. 389, fols. 183, 192.
   14. R.A. 356, fols. 100, 102, 129vs.
   15. R.A. 364, fols. 161vs, 187, 236vs.
   16. R.A. 318, fols. 31vs–32vs, 33.
   17. R.A. 353, fols. 161vs, 163, 164, 165vs, 166vs, 170vs, 184, 189, 194, 195vs, 197vs, 220.
   18. R.A. 378, fols. 44, 47, 86.
   19. R.A. 378, fols. 51, 52, 53vs, 100.
   20. R.A. 345, fols. 226, 227, 229vs, 257vs, 261vs; R.A. 346, fols. 24vs, 31vs, 36vs, 41vs, 119.
   21. R.A. 378, fols. 91vs, 94, 96, 100.

22. R.A. 365, fols. 53, 61vs, 64, 78.
23. R.A. 349, fols. 246, 250, 262vs, 264vs, 265vs, 273, 277vs, 278.
24. Muchembled 1989, 167–83.
25. Cohen and Cohen 1993, 25.
26. R.A. 343, fols. 183vs, 204, 208, 210vs, 257.
27. R.A. 363, fols. 92vs, 98, 131, 139vs, 151, 156, 171.
28. R.A. 327, fols. 56 ff.
29. R.A. 338, fols. 149, 154vs, 202.
30. R.A. 366, fols. 23vs, 36vs, 38, 95.
31. R.A. 327, fols. 6, 10, 20, 22vs, 28vs, 43vs, 51, 54vs.
32. Frevert 1991; Nye 1993.
33. R.A. 309, fol. 1vs.
34. R.A. 355, fols. 2, 6vs.
35. R.A. 368, fols. 88, 93vs.
36. R.A. 345, fol. 118vs.
37. R.A. 362, fols. 207vs, 219vs.
38. R.A. 405, fols. 149vs, 154, 159vs.
39. Roodenburg 1990, 347–61.
40. R.A. 429, pp. 79, 111, 156, 233.
41. Sleebe 1994, 264–74. See also Rooijakkers 1994, 401–3.
42. Cf. Spierenburg 1994 and 1996. A few statements made there, based on the quantification of contextual aspects, should be qualified in view of the present analysis:

a. The distinction between strangers and acquaintances among homicide victims appears less relevant. Violence flared up among mixed groups in taverns and streets. The composition of these groups fluctuated; often they included a few friends of the eventual killer as well as a few others with whom he was previously unacquainted.

b. The proportion of strangers killed partly depends on the share of robbery-related cases. Trials against members of organized bands, however, were excluded from my series, and nonorganized robberies in which the victim was killed formed a fairly constant minority in it. (For violence by robber bands in the Dutch Republic, see Egmond 1993.)

c. My earlier distinction between killers who were professional criminals and those who were not seems less pertinent. The interrogation protocols reveal a much closer association with the world of petty crime than the listings of previous convictions or additional offenses in the sentences.

d. Whether or not one was born in Amsterdam hardly appeared to make a difference in the half-respectable community to which the knife fighters belonged.

These four corrections, however, do not diminish the reliability of the principal trend posited in the above-mentioned publications toward an increasing proportion of intimate victims of homicide.

43. Cf. Spierenburg 1994.
44. See, for example, Teellinck 1622; Udemans 1658; Koelman 1690.
45. Reitsma and van Veen 1892–99, 6:62, 133, 303; 8:69, 138–39.
46. Knuttel 1908–16, 1:477, 503; 2:69; 3:182.
47. Cf. Roodenburg 1981.
48. Cf., for example, Udemans 1658, 245.
49. R.A. 368, fols. 61vs, 69, 218vs, 220vs.
50. R.A. 477, pp. 189, 211, 317, 398, 492.
51. See my introduction to this book. There and earlier in this article I have referred to several studies based on court records, in which honor is a major theme. Others are Carrasco 1990; Dinges 1991; Egmond 1994; Gauvard 1991; Kuehn 1991; Keunen and Roodenburg 1992.
52. Cf. Beattie 1986.
53. Brennan 1988, 48–51.

5

Homicide and Knife Fighting in Rome, 1845–1914

DANIELE BOSCHI

Our plebeian Romans have no more contempt for a murderer than Parisians have for a man who has loyally killed his adversary in a duel. And indeed, murder, as it is practiced here, is a veritable duel. If, in the heat of their discussion, two men have exchanged certain words, they know that blood has to flow among them; the war is implicitly declared; the whole city is the chosen terrain: the crowd is the witness accepted by each party and the two combatants know they have to be on their guard every hour of the day and the night. Thus, the people believe — and this is a prejudice not easily eradicated — that the murderer is a just person.[1]

This is how Edmond About described popular attitudes toward homicide, on the basis of what he had learned during his stay in Rome in the late 1850s. Many other observers of social and cultural life regarded impulsiveness and an inclination toward violence as distinctive features of the common people of Rome during the nineteenth century. Writers and poets who were well acquainted with popular customs and culture considered the use of knives natural in the course of quarrels and brawls among the lower classes. They also frequently implied that ability and courage in knife fighting were essential to a man's honor. A woman, it was said, would not have been very happy to marry a man who had never shown his bravery in a knife fight.[2]

The aggressive nature of the Romans and their predilection for knife fighting were sometimes regarded as psychological traits related to the peculiar environment and traditions of the city.[3] By the end of the nineteenth century, however, criminologists and other experts had become aware that the abuse of weapons, especially of knives, was widespread in many provinces of central, southern, and insular Italy. They also suggested that the frequent abuse of weapons explained why the homicide rate in Italy was much higher than in the more "civilized" countries of central and northern Europe. Indeed, it was for this reason that in 1908 the Italian government requested and obtained from Parliament the approval of a bill hardening penalties for the unlawful carrying of weapons and for wounds inflicted with knives.[4] The introductory report to Parliament on this bill pointed out that, especially in some regions of Italy, the "savage" misuse of deadly weapons provided subject matter for newspaper reports almost daily, "making our country appear among the least civilized in Europe."[5]

As a matter of fact, official statistics provided enough data to show that the homicide rate in Italy was very high. In the 1880s and 1890s, criminologists and statisticians such as Luigi Bodio, Enrico Ferri, and Augusto Bosco had carefully analyzed homicide rates throughout Europe. Enrico Ferri's *Atlante antropologico-statistico dell' omicidio* had shown that around 1880 Italy had the highest rate of offenders condemned for homicide in Europe: 9 per 100,000 inhabitants every year. In the same period, France and Germany had rates lower than 2 per 100,000 inhabitants, and England and Scotland had rates lower than 1.[6] The situation had somewhat improved by the end of the nineteenth century, but the gap between Italy and the more "civilized" countries of central and northern Europe persisted.[7] Criminal statistics also showed that homicide rates throughout Italy were far from uniform. In the years 1880–84, the rate of prosecuted homicides varied from a minimum of 3.6 per 100,000 inhabitants in the district of Milan to a maximum of 45.1 in the district of Palermo. All eight districts of northern Italy had rates lower than 11, the

districts of central Italy had rates between 9 and 26, and almost all districts of the southern and insular regions had rates between 16 and 35.[8]

These data stimulate comparisons with the results of recent historical
research on homicide. A growing number of studies show that several European countries experienced a gradual decline of the homicide rate between the late Middle Ages and the eighteenth century.[9] In England and
Wales, a further decline took place in the nineteenth century and in the
first half of the twentieth.[10] Most scholars have connected this decline to
the modernization of western societies. There is no agreement, however,
on which aspects of the modernization processes were — or might have
been — crucial in this respect. The transition from feudal to bourgeois society, the growth of the modern state, the "civilizing" effects of religion
and education — all have been referred to as possible "causes" of the decline of the homicide rate.[11] The Italian case may add a new dimension to
this picture. The evidence collected so far on homicide in Italy in the late
Middle Ages and in the early modern period, combined with the data provided by official statistics for more recent times, strongly suggests that in
Italy the decline of the homicide rate took place much later or much more
slowly than in the countries of central and northern Europe.[12] Studies by
Ferri and others indicate that toward the end of the nineteenth century
the provinces of northern Italy, which were the most developed in the
country, also had the lowest homicide rates, whereas the highest rates
were registered in the more backward and traditional provinces of the
south and of the two main islands. Furthermore, between the 1880s and
the 1960s, the homicide rate in Italy underwent an almost steady decline,
seemingly parallel to the modernization of the country.[13]

Although a general pattern linking homicide rates to different levels of
modernization is apparent, a thorough sociological study of homicidal violence in Italy between the nineteenth and twentieth centuries has not yet
been attempted.[14] In order to accomplish this, we need more accurate statistical studies as well as in-depth and piecemeal analyses of the typology
of homicide in different areas of the country. This essay presents some of
the findings of a case study on homicide in Rome from the middle of the
nineteenth century to the beginning of the twentieth. I have chosen Rome
as the focus of my research not only for its long-standing tradition of violence but also because, after 1870, the city underwent major social and political changes.

At the middle of the nineteenth century, Rome was the capital of the

Papal States. It was the most populous city in the pope's dominions and the fourth largest city in Italy after Naples, Palermo, and Milan. Its growth in the past three centuries had been linked to its role as capital of a theocratic state and as center of the Catholic world. In the first half of the nineteenth century, the rulers of the Papal States had proved unable to keep up with the changes that were transforming the western world. The economic and political structures of the pope's dominions had rapidly become obsolete, and Rome had been no exception to the general decay. The city's traditional economy, for instance, had been severely disrupted by the importation of cheaper goods from abroad. The standards of living of the popular classes had considerably worsened. Nonetheless, the population of Rome continued to grow, because the city still catalyzed immigrants from rural areas, where the situation was even worse than in the capital. In 1870, Rome — and the other provinces of the Papal States that had remained independent after 1861 — were annexed to the recently founded Kingdom of Italy. As capital of the young national state, the city became the center of novel political, administrative, and economic activities, and it attracted a flood of immigrants from central and southern Italy. The city's population grew more than twofold between 1870 and 1914. Its inhabitants increased from 244,484 in 1871 to 542,123 in 1911. One of the aims of my research is to establish whether these developments, and other related changes, had any impact on the patterns of homicidal violence.[15]

This essay is divided into four parts: the first part deals with the homicide rate and its variations over time; the second illustrates the most recurrent features of homicidal violence; the third analyzes popular attitudes toward homicide; and, finally, the fourth briefly examines some of the possible causes of the "modernization" of homicide in Rome.

Homicide Rates

The first problem one confronts when studying homicide in Rome during the nineteenth century is to establish how high the homicide rate actually was and whether it varied significantly over time. Despite all their talk about lower-class violence, contemporary observers usually did not bother to provide reliable data to back up their assertions. Before 1870, under papal rule, neither the central government nor the local authorities published regular statistics on crime. After 1870, official statistics on crime and criminal justice, published by the central government of the recently founded Italian state, provide ample and relatively accurate data on all sorts of crimes perpetrated in the country; unfortunately, these data are usually disaggregated on a regional basis, so that no figures are available on crimes reported and prosecuted at a local level.[16]

Nonetheless, it is possible to get an approximate idea about the homicide rate in Rome during the nineteenth century from unpublished statistics for the period before 1870 and from statistics on the causes of death for the subsequent period. More accurate data can be collected by taking samples from the archival records of the main city courts, but these records become less and less complete as one nears the end of the period under examination.

In 1864 an investigation was made of all violent deaths reported to the judicial authorities in the southern provinces of the Papal States in the preceding decade. The data collected remained unpublished in the archives.[17] As shown in table 5.1, these data indicate that an average of 20 homicides a year (10.6 per 100,000 inhabitants) were perpetrated in Rome between 1854 and 1863. There is good reason, however, to believe that the homicide rate was unusually low in the mid-1850s and that the figures in the 1864 statistics, on the whole, underestimate the number of killings known to the judicial authorities. Research carried out directly on archival records for the years 1845–46 and 1865–66 shows, in fact, that

TABLE 5.1.
Homicides Perpetrated in Rome, 1854–1863

	Average Homicides per Year		
	N	N/100,000 pop.	Population
1854	15	8.2	182,232
1855	18	9.9	181,661
1856	7	3.8	182,998
1857	21	11.4	184,252
1858	27	14.6	184,659
1859	25	13.4	186,895
1860	20	10.6	188,517
1861	26	13.8	188,841
1862	16	8.3	192,185
1863	24	12.2	195,986
Yearly average	20	10.6	186,833

Source: See n. 17.

no less than 62 homicides were perpetrated in the first two years and no less than 73 in the second two years, resulting in rates of about 18 homicides per 100,000 inhabitants.[18] It is therefore unquestionable that the homicide rate in Rome was much higher than that recorded for other European cities and urban areas in the same period.

In the years 1851–70, the London homicide rate never exceeded 0.5 per 100,000 inhabitants, while the Liverpool rate was on average just under 2.[19] In the mainly urban department of the Seine, which included Paris, 2.6 persons per 100,000 inhabitants were tried for homicide in the period 1837–41, and this rate dropped to 1.3 in the years 1865–69. In the Bouches-du-Rhône department, which included Marseilles, a city with a long-standing reputation for violence, the offenders tried for homicide were 2.4 and 3.5 per 100,000 inhabitants in the periods 1837–41 and 1865–69, respectively.[20]

For the period 1871–1914, statistics on the causes of death, based on death certificates issued by the sanitary authorities, show that the homicides committed in Rome averaged about 33 each year in the period 1872–79, rose to about 40 in the first decade of the twentieth century, and then dropped to 27 in the period 1910–14 (see table 5.2). The homicide rate declined from about 12 homicides per 100,000 inhabitants in the 1870s to about 8 in the decade 1900–1909, and dropped further in the years 1910–14. Again, it is quite possible that these data underestimate

TABLE 5.2.
Homicides Perpetrated in Rome, 1872–1914

	Average Homicides per Year		Population
	N	N/100,000 pop.	
1872–79	33	12.3	270,242
1880–86	38	11.9	323,331
1895–99	35	7.8	439,542
1900–1904	41	8.5	480,771
1904–9	40	7.7	525,470
1910–14	27	4.8	576,368

Sources: Comune di Roma, Direzione Comunale di Statistica, *Annuario statistico di Roma, Anno II. 1886*, vol. 1 (Rome and Florence, 1890), 438; Ministero di Agricoltura, Industria e Commercio, *Cause di morte. Statistica dell' anno . . .* , years 1895–96 (Rome, 1897); idem, *Statistica delle cause di morte nell' anno . . .* , years 1897–1913 (Rome, 1899–1915); Ministero per l'Industria, il Commercio e il Lavoro, *Statistica delle cause di morte nell' anno 1914* (Rome, 1917).

the number of homicides known to the judicial authorities. As a matter of fact, the authors of the statistics themselves pointed out that homicides known to the sanitary authorities could not comprise *all* of the homicides known to the magistrates, because in some cases the physician writing the death certificate was only able to state the immediate cause of death — for example, an injury or asphyxia — whereas the magistrate might later establish that such a "cause" was actually the result of homicidal violence.[21]

Unfortunately, even archival records do not enable us to calculate the precise number of homicides known to the judicial authorities for the period 1871–1914, because some of the relevant criminal registers are missing. A number of parallel indicators do confirm, however, that there was a marked decline in the homicide rate. Official statistics on crimes known to the public prosecutor show a marked drop in the rate of homicides prosecuted in the district of Rome — a regional area centered around the capital — over the period 1881–1914.[22] Moreover, samples taken from the sentences passed by the assizes and by the correctional court also point to a consistent decline (see table 4, below). It seems, therefore, very likely that homicidal violence actually did decline in Rome between 1871 and 1914. Yet, even after this decrease, the homicide rate registered in the capital of Italy was much higher than those of other European cities such as London, Paris, or Berlin; it was also considerably higher than those of northern Italian towns, such as Turin or Milan.[23] As we will see, the decline between 1871 and 1914 was only the beginning of a longer decline that continued until the end of the 1930s.

A Typology of Homicidal Violence

The study of homicide rates must be supplemented with an analysis of the typology and of the social and cultural meanings of homicidal violence. Archival records are the first and most obvious source to use for a more detailed analysis of homicide in the context under examination. The only alternative source would be newspaper reports, but these are not equally reliable. Moreover, they are only available from 1871 onwards, because no free press was allowed under papal rule. Given the bulk of documents extant in the archives, I have chosen four sets of sample years: 1845–46, 1865–66, 1884 and 1888, and 1905–6.

Although I have been looking through all the available trial documents concerning homicides, the gaps found in the sources for the period

1870–1914 have made it impossible to collect complete data on homicides known to the judicial authorities. Thus, the data presented here refer only to the homicides that were judged by a criminal court. These data cannot, therefore, wholly reflect the patterns of the homicides known to the judicial authorities, because the probability that a homicide case could have resulted in an indictment before a court was not the same for all types of homicides and for all categories of offenders. Infanticides, for instance, were much less likely than adult homicides to reach the courtroom, and judges might find it harder to indict somebody for homicide if the victim had been killed by an unusual method or under rather peculiar circumstances. Nonetheless, when one considers that homicides judged by the courts generally comprised the majority of the cases known to the judicial authorities, and that some of the more unusual cases would be left out anyway—it being impossible to establish whether a homicide had occurred or not—one may be relatively confident that the data shown here are representative of at least the most typical cases of homicidal violence.[24]

Two major changes occurred in penal legislation in the period covered by my research. The first took place in 1870, when Rome was annexed to the recently founded Kingdom of Italy: the criminal laws of the Papal States, dating back to the early 1830s, were then abolished and the penal code of the Kingdom was extended to the newly acquired provinces. The second important change occurred in 1889, when a new penal code was introduced.[25] In order to avoid any serious distortion caused by varying legal definitions of homicide, I decided to include in my data all acts of willful violence that resulted in the death of the victim, no matter how they were defined in strictly legal terms. In tables 5.3 and 5.4, all cases of homicide, for which at least one defendant was indicted before a court, are classified according to the legal categories used by the magistrates of the time.[26]

The statistical distribution of homicides among different legal categories is partially a reflection of varying legal theories and criminal procedures, but it is also, to some extent, a reflection of the social reality of homicide in the context under examination. As shown in table 5.3, before 1870 most culprits would be indicted and sentenced under a charge of "voluntary homicide" (*omicidio volontario*): this meant that, in the eyes of the magistrates, the offender had acted with the precise intention of killing the victim. In some cases, the legal definition of the crime would be changed by the court to "malicious wounding" (*ferite, percosse*) on the

TABLE 5.3.

Homicides Perpetrated in Rome, 1845–1846, 1865–1866, by Type

	1845–46		1865–66	
	A	B	A	B
Premeditated homicide	4	1	3	1
Homicide in the course of robbery	1	1	0	0
Uxoricide	1	0	2	2
Infanticide	0	0	0	0
Voluntary homicide	46	35	39	35
Involuntary homicide	0	0	0	2
Malicious wounding followed by death	0	10	0	3
Total	52	47	44	43
Rate per 100,000 inhabitants	15.1	13.6	10.8	10.5

Sources: See n. 26.

Figures are based on the sentences passed by the Tribunale criminale del Governo di Roma, which was the main criminal court of the city under papal rule.

Note: A = homicides for which at least one culprit was indicted; B = homicides defined as such in a court sentence. The differences in the totals of columns A and B are due to the cases in which the sentence established that there was no proof that a homicide had been perpetrated.

grounds that some accidental factor, besides the perpetrated violence, had contributed to the fatal outcome of the aggression. In an even smaller number of cases, a charge of "voluntary homicide" (*omicidio colposo*) would be changed by the court to "involuntary homicide," indicating that the defendant had intended not to kill the victim but only to inflict bodily harm.[27]

After 1871, when the criminal codes of the Kingdom of Italy were extended to Rome, it was no longer possible to change an accusation of homicide into one of malicious wounding, even if it were proved that some other cause, besides the offender's behavior, had contributed to the victim's death. As shown in table 5.4, a great number of culprits would still be indicted under a charge of "voluntary homicide," but the courts would often lessen that charge to one of homicide committed "without intent to kill" (*ferimento seguito da morte; omicidio oltre l'intenzione*) meaning that the offender had acted with the aim of inflicting an injury rather than with the intention of killing.

Both before and after 1870, charges of aggravated homicide were rare, and it was even less common that a court actually condemned the

TABLE 5.4.

Homicides Perpetrated in Rome, 1884, 1888, 1905–1906, by Type

	1884, 1888		1905–6	
	A	B	A	B
Premeditated homicide	9	4	7	5
Homicide in the furtherance of another crime				
(robbery or rape)	2	1	0	0
Uxoricide	2	2	2	1
Infanticide	2	1	1	0
Voluntary homicide	40	27	54	27
Homicide without intent to kill	28	35	8	26
Excusable homicide	0	2	0	9
Unspecified	0	4	1	1
Total	79	73	71	68
Rate per 100,000 inhabitants	10.9	10.1	6.9	6.6

Sources: See n. 26.

The figures for the years 1884 and 1888 refer to the homicides judged by the correctional court and by the assizes, whereas the figures for the years 1905–6 refer only to the cases judged by the assizes (the records for the correctional court are missing). The data for 1905–6 are nonetheless comparable to those for 1884 and 1888, because in the first decade of the twentieth century homicides were rarely judged by the correctional court.

Note: See table 5.3.

"Homicides in the furtherance of another crime" and "uxoricides" must be subtracted from the totals because they overlap with other categories. "Excusable" homicides include those committed in self-defense or under the compulsion of mental illness. (There were no such cases for the years 1845–46 and 1865–66, which are shown in table 5.3).

culprit under such a charge, which in most cases entailed the death penalty (until it was abolished in 1889). In particular, in all four sets of sample years, only a few homicides were classified in indictments as "premeditated," and even fewer were so defined in the sentences passed by the courts (see columns A and B in tables 5.3 and 5.4). This was to a great extent a reflection of the social reality of homicide in this context. As will be shown with more detail, most homicides perpetrated in Rome throughout this period were the result of brawls or fights, which took place shortly after verbal exchange between the parties involved. Only in extremely rare cases were homicides the outcome of cold-blooded, treacherous attacks, which could more easily be classified as "premeditated" homicides.

Killings perpetrated in the furtherance of another crime were also very uncommon. Homicides connected with robbery or rape never made up more than 3 percent of the killings in each of the four samples (see tables 5.3 and 5.4). If it were possible to include *all* cases of homicidal violence known to the judicial authorities — which we can only do for the first two samples — the percentage of homicides committed in the furtherance of another crime would probably be slightly higher. In 1845–46, for instance, homicides occurring during robberies represented 4.8 percent of the killings reported to the authorities (3 cases out of 62, whereas there was only 1 case among the 52 homicides that were judged).

Turning to another category of aggravated homicide, the crimes defined as "uxoricides" in a court sentence never made up more than 5 percent of the total (see tables 5.3 and 5.4, column B). Given the ongoing debate about "family" or "domestic" homicide, it is convenient here to provide some data referring to these broader categories as well, although they do not correspond to any of the legal categories used in the period under scrutiny.[28] Homicides among spouses and lovers were totally absent from the cases judged in 1845–46 and amounted to 6.9, 2.7, and 5.8 percent in the subsequent three samples. Should we consider the even larger category of "homicides among intimates," as defined by Pieter Spierenburg, we would find that killings falling into this category are again totally absent in the first sample and make up 9.3, 5.4, and 10.2 percent of the other three samples.[29] Thus, throughout the period under examination, the vast majority of homicides were perpetrated by people who were not tied to their victim by love affairs, marriage, or close bonds of kinship. The most typical victim-perpetrator relationship was that of two people who knew one another *before* the occasion that gave rise to the homicide but were not closely connected.

In an overwhelming majority of cases, both offenders and victims of homicide were males.[30] Males represented between 94 and 100 percent of the offenders in each of the four sets of sample years, and the percentage of male victims of homicide oscillated between 89 and 96 percent. Males therefore stood a much higher chance than women both of killing and of being killed. This hardly applied, however, to males belonging to the upper and medium layers of the urban population. With few scarcely relevant exceptions, the men who were involved in these deadly disputes belonged to the lower strata of the population. This is shown not only by the distribution of offenders by trade (see table 5.5) but also by several recurrent features, such as the use of knives and the fact that the disputes

TABLE 5.5.

Homicides Perpetrated in Rome, 1845-1846, 1905-1906, by Trade of Offender

| | 1845–46 | | 1905–6 | |
	N	%	N	%
Artisans	22	43.1	28	38.9
Bricklayers	5	9.8	6	8.3
Carters, porters	4	7.8	14	19.5
Servants	2	3.9	1	1.4
Agricultural workers, shepherds	9	17.7	8	11.1
Hunters	3	5.9	0	0
Other manual workers	0	0	1	1.4
Shopkeepers, shop assistants	3	5.9	7	9.7
Others	3	5.9	7	9.7
Total	51	100	72	100

Sources: See n. 26.

Notes: The data include offenders who were acquitted because they were mentally ill or had acted in self-defense.

often broke out in taverns, where one could hardly expect to find people belonging to the upper or middle classes.

Data on the weapons used by the offenders show that between 67 and 79 percent of the homicides in each of the four samples were perpetrated by means of sharp instruments (almost invariably a knife). By contrast, killings committed with firearms never exceeded 12 percent of the total, and homicides perpetrated with blunt instruments decreased from 17 percent in 1845–46 to 6 percent in 1905–6, an indication, perhaps, that progress in surgery made it increasingly difficult to kill people with sticks, stones, and the like (see table 5.6).

The majority of homicides took place either in taverns or in the streets. In 1845–46, 25.5 percent of the killings were perpetrated shortly after a dispute had broken out in a tavern; the same dynamics appear in 30.1 percent of the homicides committed in 1905–6. In many cases, the homicide did not actually occur in the tavern, because the quarrellers would often challenge one another to go out into the street, or the barkeeper would try to push them out in order to avoid troubles with the police. Streets were also the theater of many homicides that had no apparent relationship with tavern quarrels. These latter episodes represented 42.5 percent of the killings in the years 1845–46 and 30.8 percent in 1905–6. Other homicides

TABLE 5.6.

Homicides Perpetrated in Rome, 1845–1846, 1865–1866, 1884, 1888, and 1905–1906, by Apparent Method

	1845–46		1865–66		1884, 1888		1905–6	
	N	%	N	%	N	%	N	%
Fire weapon	3	6.4	2	4.7	5	6.9	8	11.8
Sharp instrument	35	74.5	29	67.4	50	68.5	54	79.4
Blunt instrument	8	17.0	12	27.9	12	16.4	4	5.9
Hitting or kicking	0	0	0	0	1	1.4	0	0
Other	1	2.1	0	0	2	2.7	2	2.9
Not known	0	0	0	0	3	4.1	0	0
Total	47	100.0	43	100.0	73	100.0	68	100.0

Sources: See n. 26.

Note: "Homicides" include all deaths defined as such in a court sentence.

took place in workshops, private dwellings, public prisons, farmhouses, or the open countryside. On the whole, throughout the period under scrutiny, homicides committed in public spaces were much more frequent than homicides perpetrated in private dwellings. The latter represent only 6.3 percent of the total in 1845–46, whereas their share of homicidal violence amounts to 19.1 percent in 1905–6. This increase is not necessarily a meaningful one, given the unusual absence of homicides "among intimates" in the first sample.

A variety of disputes could lead to violence and homicide. What was at stake is not always easy to detect. The event that gave rise to the clash was often rather trivial, but even in such cases there may have been underlying sources of tension that were totally, or partially, ignored by the magistrates. An attempted classification of the apparent motives of homicide is shown in table 5.7. Statistical data alone cannot, however, fully describe the nature of the tensions and disputes leading to homicidal violence. I shall, therefore, illustrate them with a number of examples, highlighting some of the most recurrent features of these deadly disputes.

A great number of them apparently began over a joke, an arrogant reply, or other forms of sudden, gratuitous provocation. Disputes of this kind usually took place either in the streets or in drinking places, were related to the abuse of alcohol, and involved young men in their twenties or early thirties. A good example is provided by the brawl in which Sante Donati, a 22-year-old pasta maker, killed Enrico Toteri, a 45-year-old

TABLE 5.7.

Homicides Perpetrated in Rome, 1845–1846, 1905–1906, by Apparent Method

	1845–46		1905–6	
	N	%	N	%
Disputes over:				
Trivial matters	10	21.3	14	20.6
Game	8	17.0	9	13.2
Money or property	13	27.7	10	14.7
Relationships between men and women	5	10.6	8	11.8
Rules of conduct among family members,				
neighbors, or workmates	3	6.4	12	17.6
Other matters	3	6.4	8	11.8
Robbery	1	2.1	0	0
Rape	0	0	1	1.5
Not known	4	8.5	6	8.8
Total	47	100.0	68	100.0

Sources: See n. 26.

Note: "Homicides" include all deaths defined as such in a court sentence.

seller of aqua vitae. The two had probably never met, nor spoken to one another, before finding themselves in the same tavern on a Sunday evening at the end of September 1845. Donati had already spent several hours there, drinking with two acquaintances, when Toteri and his friends arrived and sat at another table. Donati approached them when he saw that Rosa Stocchi, his former lover, had joined their company. He spoke to Rosa and offered her a glass of wine, but she did not answer and retreated without even looking at him. Shortly afterwards, Toteri started making fun of Donati because he had been rebuffed by the girl; this caused a row, which a comrade of Toteri's unsuccessfully tried to stop; in the ensuing fight Donati managed to stab Toteri with his knife. Toteri died almost immediately.[31]

The disputes that arose in the course of games played either in taverns or in the streets were of a similar nature. Among the many cases of homicides stemming from quarrels of this kind, I will cite the one that led to the killing of Sante De Rossi, a 28-year-old carpenter. On January 1, 1845, De Rossi played several games on the bank of the river with Giovanni Quattrini, Marco Pichi and other young men. At the end of a game, an argument arose over a small sum of money that had to be paid by the losers.

For the moment the players continued their games, but shortly thereafter the argument resumed and the row soon turned into a violent confrontation, in which Quattrini managed to stab both De Rossi and Pichi with his knife. Pichi was only slightly wounded, but De Rossi died in hospital thirteen days later.[32] In this case, the game over which the argument had broken out was *garaghé*, a game of chance which was quite popular in Rome during the nineteenth century. But all sorts of games could give rise to heated quarrels: games of cards (e.g., *tresette*), *morra*, and, most of all, the notorious *passatella*, a game which, by its very structure and rules, was almost bound to lead to disputes.[33]

Quarrels arising over trivial matters and games were thus among the most common apparent causes of homicides. In many other cases, however, homicidal violence was related to disputes of a more serious nature, mostly concerning money or property, relationships between men and women, and rules of conduct among family members, neighbors, and workmates. I will first give two examples of homicides stemming from quarrels concerning money or property.

In September 1846, Giuseppe Polidori, a 24-year-old bricklayer, was mortally wounded by his workmate, Francesco Zannini. The latter, who was only sixteen years old, owed a small sum of money to Polidori's friend Giovan Battista Amici, from whom he had bought some food. On a Saturday evening, a row broke out in the street between Zannini and Polidori, caused by Zannini's refusal to discharge his debt with Amici. After Polidori had beaten Zannini with his bare hands, Zannini hit him on the head with a stone and seriously injured him. Polidori died five weeks later.[34] In this case, the apparent motive of the dispute was not so trivial, but the dynamics of the event were similar to those of the previous examples: here, too, homicide appears to be the result of aggressiveness suddenly roused by a quarrel between men who had previously been on good terms with one another.

In other cases, however, the aggressive drive clearly stemmed from long pent-up tensions finally erupting into homicidal violence. A prolonged conflict over small objects of personal property lay, for instance, at the root of the killing of Tommaso Moretti by his brother-in-law, Stefano Cecchi. The latter, a 61-year-old shoemaker, had married the widowed Caterina Moretti and had lived for some time under her roof, together with her mother and her younger brother, Tommaso. Cecchi and his wife frequently quarrelled with Tommaso, because the latter was in the habit of embezzling his sister's personal belongings to make a living. The couple had eventually moved to another house, but the bad blood between the two men persisted. On August 24, 1845, a quarrel started among the three, and after Tommaso had wounded Caterina with a glass, Cecchi stabbed him to death with a kitchen knife.[35]

Relationships between men and women were also a fairly common cause of disputes leading to homicide. An example of this is the homicide perpetrated by Luigi Pala, a 19-year-old carpenter. Pala could not stand the illicit relationship that had developed, in the absence of his father, between his mother, Maria, and Nicola Palombelli, and he resented Palombelli's arrogant behavior toward him and his sister, Rosa. One evening a quarrel arose, and Luigi mortally wounded Palombelli with a kitchen knife.[36] An extramarital relationship was also apparently the source of tension between Giuseppe Proietti, a 32-year-old stonecutter, and Agostino Bellini, a 34-year-old carpenter. Although both were married, the two men had tried to win the favors of Chiara De Angelis, a woman who had a bad reputation. It is not clear whether either of the two had had any success, but it seems that Proietti could not stand the rivalry of Bellini. When, on a Sunday afternoon, he met Bellini in the street near Chiara De Angelis's home, he provoked him and then mortally wounded him with his knife.[37]

Finally, I will take the killing of Antonio Mariani as an example of a homicide caused by a dispute over the rules of conduct among workmates. In the afternoon of September 4, 1845, Gioacchino Grimaldi, a 42-year-old stevedore, was working under the supervision of Antonio Mariani. At some point, Grimaldi refused to comply with Mariani's orders concerning the procedure to follow in unloading a cargo of wood from a boat. The two men quarreled, and Grimaldi pushed Mariani off the river bank, causing him to hit his head on some rocks. Mariani died two days later. Grimaldi apparently had never quarreled with Mariani before, but one witness remarked that all stevedores resented Mariani for the strict surveillance he exercised over their work.[38]

The Social and Cultural Meaning of Homicide

A clear pattern seems to emerge from the archival records concerning homicides perpetrated in Rome during the nineteenth and early twentieth centuries. Homicide was a disproportionately male and lower-class phenomenon, and it was usually the outcome of impulsive (as opposed to planned or premeditated) violence. It was typically the outcome of sudden outbursts of anger and it occurred much more often in the public than in the private sphere of human relations. In many respects, this pattern is very similar to the one that seems prevalent in several European countries in the early modern period.[39] The fact that this traditional pattern of homicidal violence was still dominant in Rome (and probably in the rest of central and southern Italy) in the nineteenth and early twentieth centuries further supports the hypothesis of a late "modernization" of homicide in Italy.

But now that we have described the typology of homicidal violence, what can we say about its social and cultural meaning? Are we to trust those writers, such as Edmond About, who tell us that people in the lower classes usually considered killers were men who had rightly defended their honor? Was homicide the outcome of patterns of behavior common to most men in the lower ranks of the urban population, or was it linked to a code of honor mainly followed in the restricted milieu of the "tough" guys called *bulli*?[40]

In the first place, we must bear in mind that although the homicide rate in Rome appears very high in comparison with the rates calculated for other urban areas in the same period, most instances of interpersonal violence led neither to homicides nor to serious woundings. This is clearly shown by a series of statistical tables concerning crimes reported to the main city court in five years between 1851 and 1863.[41] In these tables, homicides and malicious woundings "endangering the victim's life" (*ferite con pericolo di vita, con qualche pericolo di vita*) represented only about one-tenth of all violent crimes reported to the court. In other words, people who were involved in fights and brawls did not, in most cases, hurt or wound one another so seriously as to put human life at risk. This indicates that men and women who resorted to violence did not usually act under a cultural or psychological imperative to kill their opponents, or at least such imperatives were not strong enough to prevent a peaceful settlement of the dispute. What did homicides then represent? Were they just the exceptional cases in which the situation unpredictably got out of hand? Or were they rather the result of crimes committed by individuals who had a special inclination toward violence? And, in any case, how was homicide looked upon by the lower strata of the population?

To answer these questions I will first examine the previous criminal records of the people who committed homicide in four sample years (1845–46, 1905–6). Second, I will consider how killers and their victims are described in trial documents. Third, I will question whether homicide may have been positively or negatively valued depending on the observance of rules of fairness in knife fighting.

Out of fifty-one individuals who committed homicide in the years 1845–46, seventeen (or 33.3%) had been previously convicted at least once. Ten had been convicted for other crimes against the person, four for crimes against property and three for both types of crime. The situation seems to have changed considerably in the following sixty years. Out of seventy-two persons who committed homicide in the years 1905–6, as many as forty-three (or 59.7%) had been previously jailed at least once. Twelve had been sentenced for offenses against the person, thirteen for property offenses, and seven for both types of offense. Apparently, therefore, there was not only an increase in the percentage of killers with previous criminal records but also a significant rise in the percentage of people who had been convicted of property crimes. It would be possible to argue from these data that at the end of the period under examination homicidal violence had become more closely connected with a milieu of poor and marginal people, who were inclined to thefts and even to more serious property crimes. However, I would be cautious in embracing such an explanation, especially because the criminal justice system was certainly much more efficient in the period 1871–1914 than it had been in the last decades of papal power (see the discussion below). This factor alone could explain the rise in the proportion of killers with previous criminal records. It could also perhaps explain the increase in the percentage of killers who had previously been convicted of crimes against property, for it is to be expected that a very lax penal system, such as that operating in Rome until 1870, was less successful in prosecuting property crimes than in pursuing those who committed crimes of violence.

Whatever changes may have occurred, it is clear that both before and after 1870 a significant percentage of killers had previous criminal records, and we may easily imagine that some of them were violent individuals who committed homicide after they had been involved in several episodes of violence. In this respect, descriptions found in trial documents are perhaps more eloquent than numbers. The men involved in these deadly disputes sometimes had a reputation as violent and dangerous individuals even before they killed or were killed. Their violent habits were in many cases connected with the abuse of alcohol. Lorenzo Loffredi, a 27-year-old painter, had already been condemned for homicide and for several other crimes against the person before he was again convicted for taking part in the murder of Benedetto Morelli on April 3, 1845. According to some witnesses, he habitually became "nasty" and lost control after getting drunk.[42] Similarly, Sante Quintavalli, a 25-year-old fisher, condemned for the homicide of Lorenzo Ciccoricco, was described as a man who was "addicted to wine and to brawls" and who became "nasty" whenever he drank.[43] Orazio D'Annunzio, a 51-year-old barber, who was found guilty of killing Natale De Angelis on July 18, 1905, was depicted by an acquaintance as follows: "I know D'Annunzio because he served with me in the papal army. He has always had a violent and overbearing character and he told me that in America he killed a mulatto. He also told me that many years ago he almost slaughtered a man with a piece of glass and the court condemned him to one month of jail for malicious wounding."[44]

Such testimonies do not always imply a clear-cut moral judgment on the part of the witness. Indeed, it is rare to find, in criminal sources, explicit and unambiguous moral evaluation of the human character of the perpetrators and victims of homicide. This indicates, perhaps, that most homicides were not perceived by the majority of people as something so bad as to require outright condemnation. It is interesting, however, to examine in greater detail those cases in which a clear moral judgment was made. I will take the killing of Olivo Compagnucci as an example. Compagnucci, a 22-year-old shoemaker, was mortally wounded on September 1, 1845, during a fight with his workmate, Giovanni Silla.[45] The two had been on bad terms for a long time. Giovanni Compagnucci, Olivo's brother and employer, owned a shoemaker's shop in the street of Tor de' Conti. When summoned before the magistrate, Giovanni gave a vivid portrait of his dead brother.[46] The latter, he testified, was a totally unreliable character, who loved to spend much of his time drinking in taverns, where he got involved in brawls with whoever had the misfortune of meeting him. Owing to his loose conduct, Olivo had proved incapable, or unwilling, to run the shop with him. Giovanni thought that he was "dishonored" by Olivo's behavior and had thus resolved to send him away from his home. In 1841, Olivo had killed a man and had been sentenced to three years of hard labor.[47] After being released in 1843, he had a row with another shoemaker, who stabbed him in the throat with his knife. He survived only to be killed by his workmate, Giovanni Silla.

To some extent, this portrait may be a reflection of the mentality of a rather well-off artisan, showing little sympathy for the habits and lifestyle of the lowest ranks of the popular classes, to whose level his younger brother, Olivo, had debased himself. But Giovanni was not alone in judging Olivo so sternly. Several of Olivo's workmates did not hesitate to utter their resentment toward him: "Olivo's death is not mourned by anybody," one of them said, "not even by his own brother, because he was a young rascal guilty of homicide, and he went about beating and threatening everyone, picking quarrels with whoever he came across." "Everybody feared him," said another witness, "and almost nobody chose him as his companion." Yet, we know from his brother's testimony that Olivo had "bad companies," so we may easily imagine that, at least within a restricted circle of comrades, Olivo's rowdy and violent behavior was valued in a positive manner. It is also worth noticing that Olivo's workmates, in condemning the young "rascal," were all, at least implicitly, justifying his killer's behavior: having being provoked and assailed by Olivo, Giovanni Silla had been forced to kill him in self-defense.[48] In fact, the judges themselves were lenient with Silla, because they only sentenced him to three years of hard labor.

What we learn from this and other similar cases is that the use of violence, especially when going beyond certain limits, did not necessarily enhance one's reputation; it might do so in a restricted milieu of restless and unruly young men, but their opinion might be in contrast with that of other members of the community, and especially with that of the elder and/or better-off individuals. On the other hand, when somebody was provoked to violence and subsequently killed his opponent — as had been the case with Giovanni Silla — people belonging to his community might be prepared to justify and pardon him, being all too conscious that they themselves might have done the same, had they been in his position.

The human character of the people involved in interpersonal violence and the circumstances of each episode were thus important factors in determining the level of violence that would be reached and the attitudes of third parties toward the perpetrators and the victims of violent crimes. But did moral judgment also depend on the observance of rules of fairness in fighting? Literary sources and direct testimonies of Roman "toughs" (*bulli*) tend to emphasize that in knife fights men had to be fair. A knife should not be used against someone who was not armed with a similar weapon; when somebody was challenged, he might refuse to fight, although by doing so he would lose his "honor." Indeed, many episodes of violence are described in these sources as popular duels (*duelli rusticani*) rather than as brawls.[49] On the contrary, popular duels appear very rarely in trial documents. This is partially due to the peculiar nature of these sources. In homicide trials, and more generally in trials for crimes against the person, each of the two parties involved had a strong interest in minimizing his own contribution to the criminal act and in exaggerating the other party's responsibility. No matter how the confrontation had actually occurred, the victim, if still alive, often claimed that he had done no harm to the offender, whereas the latter usually endeavored to show that he had acted in self-defense or under strong provocation. If we add that witnesses were not always impartial, it is no wonder that in criminal trials the dynamics of violent confrontations are often described in a blurred and contradictory manner.

The tendency to understate the intentional character of violent acts makes it inevitable that popular duels are to some extent underrepresented in trial documents. One of the few homicides that clearly appears to have stemmed from a duel with knives was the killing of Pietro Del Proposto by Enrico Federici, an 18-year-old carpenter. It is worth noticing that we only know with certainty that a duel had taken place, thanks to the testimony of a single witness. This was a barber named Pasqualini, an acquaintance of Federici, to whom the latter had incidentally spoken a few hours before killing Del Proposto on December 8, 1888. Though Federici admitted he had killed his rival, he skillfully made this event seem the immediate result of a quarrel: while arguing with him, Del Proposto had suddenly attacked him with a knife, and he had wounded Del Proposto in self-defense. In fact, the authorities were able to establish that the row had occurred not a few minutes but several hours before the fight and that the two men had agreed to meet in the square of San Pietro in Montorio to fight a duel with knives. Before going there, Federici had told Pasqualini that, by the end of the day, he would be either in hospital or in jail, but everybody in Rome would know what a man from Ascoli—his native town—was worth. The duel was instantaneous: Federici stabbed Del Proposto in the heart but was himself badly wounded—in fact, almost killed—by his opponent.[50]

It is very likely that more homicides were the outcome of popular duels than is apparent from trial evidence. Yet, there is reason to think that popular duels were by no means the most typical pattern of male violence in the lower classes. In many cases, trial documents clearly show that no formal and explicit rules were followed in violent confrontations. Verbal insults and challenges often provoked immediate physical retaliation, and in many cases the first physical contact was followed by a rapid escalation of violence, with no guarantees that the parties involved would be equally armed. This does not necessarily mean, however, that there was no fairness in fighting. In most cases, a clear pattern of behavior was almost automatically followed. When the verbal confrontation between two men had gone beyond certain limits, each of them knew that he could be assailed by the other and thus tried to anticipate his moves. If one of the men was unarmed, he would often rush to the nearest place where he could find a knife, or any other instrument that could be used as a weapon, and then quickly return to the place where the quarrel had broken out. Because insults so easily led to violence, acquaintances, friends, and even passers-by frequently intervened to calm down the angered men, so as to avoid at least the worst possible consequences of a fight.

This pattern is clearly visible in the brawl between Francesco Avvisati, a 42-year-old shoemaker, and Benedetto Melucci, a 32-year-old barber. Their shops faced the same street, the via del Teatro Marcello, in the very heart of the city. Melucci was angry because Avvisati was in the habit of taking Melucci's workers' attention off their job. One evening, after Avvisati had taken one of the barber's workmen away with him for the whole day, the two men had a row in the street, in front of their shops. Melucci insulted Avvisati and threatened him with his razor. They then entered their shops, where Melucci armed himself with a shovel and Avvisati picked up a shoemaker's knife. The two men were about to engage in a fight, but Melucci was checked by the people who were in his shop and could not go out into the street again. Two acquaintances of his, Giuseppe Vitali and Luigi Ermini, apparently succeeded in calming him down. A few minutes later, Ermini took Melucci out of the shop for a drink. But when Melucci saw Avvisati near the door of his shop, the verbal confrontation started anew. Melucci rid himself of Ermini, ran toward Avvisati, and wounded him in the head with his razor. Avvisati was quick to respond, hitting Melucci in the belly with his knife. Melucci died in hospital the following day.[51]

Though it is not possible to quantify the incidence of the various types of physical confrontation, it is reasonable to maintain that brawls were much more frequent than popular duels. It is also possible that precise rules were more regularly followed in the restricted circles of *bulli,* whereas people who were less addicted to violence were also, perhaps, less able to control their aggressive drive and/or less sensitive to the blow that their public image might suffer from an unfair use of violence.[52]

My inquiry into the social and cultural meanings of homicide in Rome leads me to conclude that in the lower classes the degree of involvement in interpersonal violence varied considerably from one individual to another, and so did the attitudes toward homicidal violence. Some people were involved in episodes of violence much more often than others and therefore stood a much greater chance both of killing and of being killed. For these individuals, violence was often associated with a lifestyle in which the world of taverns and popular games played a prominent part. Some of these violent folks were also probably linked to an underworld of small thieves, a connection that set them apart from the wider working-class community. More peaceful men probably refrained from violence as a rule, but they might nonetheless be driven to violence, and even to homicide, by the force of circumstances: indeed, the widespread use of knives as weapons entailed that even men who were not particularly prone to violence could unpredictably commit homicide or seriously injure other people. Views and perceptions of physical violence were also far from uniform. Most violent offenders probably regarded their own violence as a rightful means of preserving their honor, but their violent acts were not necessarily approved by other people. For most people in the popular classes, moral judgment of violence, whether leading to homicide or not, depended on the circumstances that had given rise to the events and on the evaluation of the human character of the perpetrators and victims of violent acts. Gratuitous violence was generally criticized, but a violent reaction to a serious provocation was considered legitimate; if this resulted in homicide, most people would probably consider the killing either an accident — a fatal event for which the killer was not entirely responsible — or a well-deserved punishment for the victim's unjust behavior.

Possible Explanations of the Long-Term Trend

The inclination toward violence and the knife-fighting culture that were so typical of the popular classes in Rome in the middle of the nineteenth century were gradually uprooted in the period that followed the annexation of the city to the Kingdom of Italy. As I have already shown, the homicide rate declined steadily between 1870 and 1914.[53] Official statistics on crimes prosecuted in the district of Rome indicate that the decline of the homicide rate continued from 1915 until 1939.[54] More qualitative evidence suggests that by the middle of the twentieth century the knife-fighting culture and the gangs of *bulli* that were associated with it had almost disappeared.[55]

Such changes are no doubt connected to the "modernization" of Rome and its surrounding rural areas. Although the new capital of the Kingdom of Italy did not industrialize, it did undergo profound social, cultural, and institutional changes. At present, it is not possible to indicate which of these developments was crucial in determining the decline of the homicide rate. Only a comparative study of the patterns of homicide in different cities and areas of Italy toward the end of the nineteenth century could produce something more solid than a number of plausible hypotheses. Case studies, however, are equally important, because they enable us to select a limited number of hypotheses which may be tested later in more wide-ranging analyses. I will thus indicate two factors that seem prominent among those that may have had a "modernizing" influence on homicidal violence in Rome: the development of a working-class movement and the modernization of the criminal justice system.

Under papal rule, guilds and confraternities had been the only legitimate forms of association among artisans and other working-class people.[56] The scene changed radically after 1870, when freedom of speech and association was introduced in Rome and the city became one of the main centers of political life under the constitutional regime of the recently founded Italian state. Initially, working-class associations took the form of societies for mutual aid, but these paved the way for more advanced forms of social and political action.[57] Strikes for better pay and better working conditions became more frequent, and a growing number of working-class associations began to operate as modern trade unions.[58] Anarchist and socialist ideals slowly spread among the working people, and by the beginning of the twentieth century the Socialist Party had established its roots in the lower classes of Rome.[59] These developments may have helped to reduce the incidence of homicidal violence insofar as working-class solidarity restrained intraclass violence and diverted aggressiveness toward social and political targets. Yet, it is likely that between 1871 and 1914 the development of the working-class movement had a marked and profound effect only on a minority of the popular classes of the capital, while its impact probably became stronger as the twentieth century progressed.

Thus, in the first decades after 1870, the second factor I have pointed to, the modernization of the criminal justice system, was probably more important. There had been, in the Papal States, a long-standing tradition of indulgence toward interpersonal violence. Throughout the early modern period, people accused of violent crimes, other than homicide, easily managed to avoid at least the most severe forms of punishment, thanks to a complex system of judicial pardons and private reconciliations. Even people who committed homicide were treated with leniency when they had killed in the heat of a quarrel.[60] Although by the early 1830s a series of reforms had swept away from criminal laws the remnants of the ancien régime, the reformed system of criminal justice failed to operate with efficiency. A recent study of the administration of criminal justice in Rome in the period 1849–59 has shown that the main criminal court of the city (the Tribunale criminale di Roma) received several thousand reports each year, concerning a wide variety of crimes allegedly committed in the capital, but effectively dealt with a very small portion of these offenses. This was also true of offenses against the person. Out of 1,133 malicious woundings reported to the court in 1849, only 52 (or 4.5%) were punished. Nor was this low percentage due to the particular situation of that year, which saw the rise and fall of the Roman Republic. In 1859, the cases of malicious wounding reported to the court were 630: only for 75 (or 12%) the court convicted and sentenced the offenders. To be sure, the percentage of offenders condemned was considerably higher for homicides. However, since assaults with knives only exceptionally resulted in the death of the victim, it is unlikely that frequent punishment of homicide may have had a strong deterrent effect, as long as potential offenders knew that less serious crimes would only occasionally be punished. It is, therefore, reasonable to conclude that before 1870 the judicial system only exerted a moderate deterrent power over potential killers.[61]

This situation changed considerably after 1870, as official statistics on criminal justice clearly indicate. The available data refer to the district of Rome rather than to the city itself, but it is very likely that the pattern of punishment in the capital was similar. To take just one sample, in the period 1896–1900, the cases of malicious wounding for which prosecution was undertaken were on average 4,824 every year; in the same period, an

average of 3,836 offenders were indicted each year for malicious wounding, out of which 1,903 (or 49.6%) were condemned. Moreover, the percentage of offenders condemned was much higher among those who were
tried on more serious charges: out of 549 defendants indicted on average
every year for aggravated crimes of violence (other than homicide), as
many as 467 (or 85%) were condemned.[62]

Thus, a process of modernization of both society and institutions apparently lay at the root of the decline of the homicide rate in Rome in the
late nineteenth and early twentieth centuries. A parallel decline of the
homicide rate took place, over the same period, in many other districts of
central, southern, and insular Italy.[63] It is plausible that a connection between modernization and decreasing homicide rates could be established
for some of these areas as well. However, little work has been done so far
on the nature and incidence of violent crimes in these regions.[64] We must,
therefore, conduct further research before a more precise assessment can
be made about the nature and timing of the modernization of homicidal
violence in Italy.

Notes

This essay is based on my doctoral thesis, "L'omicidio a Roma fra la metà dell' Ottocento e
la prima guerra mondiale, 1841–1914" (University of Rome, 1996).

1. About 1861, 132 (editor's translation).

2. See Bresciani 1862, 61–62, 64–65, 97–99, and passim; Gabelli 1881, xxx-xlii; Picca
1907; Zanazzo 1908, 201–3, 212–15. Many rhymes by poets writing in dialect, such as
Gioacchino Belli, Cesare Pascarella, and Giggi Zanazzo, touching on the violent habits of
the lower classes of Rome, are quoted in Rossetti 1978. Among more recent publications on
the topic of violence in Rome in the nineteenth and early twentieth centuries, see esp. Mariani 1983. For a broader interpretation of lower-class violence in the past centuries, especially of knife fighting, see Baronti 1986.

3. See Picca 1907, 260; Rossetti 1978, 115–24.

4. The text of the law can be found in the *Raccolta ufficiale delle leggi e dei decreti del Regno
d'Italia, Parte principale* (Rome, 1908), 4:2779–81.

5. See the *Raccolta degli atti stampati per ordine della Camera, Legislatura XXII, Sessione
1904–1909*, vol. 6 (Rome, 1909), n. 106A, p. 1.

6. E. Ferri, *Atlante antropologico-statistico dell' omicidio*, published as an appendix to Ferri
1895 (246–49, 281). Ferri's statistics referred to seventeen European countries. The figures
for Italy include individuals convicted for attempted homicides. It seems that the same

criterion was used for all other countries except Spain, England, Ireland, and Scotland; for the latter four countries, offenders guilty of shooting and similar crimes, which were roughly the equivalent of the Italian category of attempted homicide, were not included. Comparisons among crime rates recorded in different countries are a very complex matter, and Ferri's attempt was not without flaws; in the case of homicide, however, it seems unlikely that differences so sharp as those discovered by Ferri and other criminologists of his time could be explained simply as the result of differences in legislation and penal policies. This argument is all the more cogent for the differences in homicide rates throughout Italy, where a uniform legislation and judicial system were in force after 1870 (only the region of Tuscany was allowed to preserve its own criminal code, until 1889).

   7. See Negri 1908, 555–57.

   8. Rates are calculated on the basis of the data provided by Ferri in his *Atlante,* 1895, 252–53. Again, Ferri's figures comprise both completed and attempted homicides. They cannot, therefore, be directly compared with the figures on homicides in Rome, which will be given below, because the latter always refer to completed homicides only. See also Bodio 1885; Bosco 1898.

   9. For a general overview see Rousseaux 1994. A review of historical studies of homicide in medieval and early modern England is found in Gurr 1981. For the early modern period, more recent studies dealing with homicide in particular towns or areas include Beattie 1986; Cockburn 1991; Spierenburg 1994.

   10. See Cockburn 1991, 78; Gatrell 1980, 286–87.

   11. See esp. Gatrell 1980, 300; Gurr 1981, 341–44; Spierenburg 1994, 702–3; Stone 1983, 29–30.

   12. On homicide in Italy from the late Middle Ages to the eighteenth century, see Becker 1976; Fiume 1990; Folin 1990–91; Fosi 1992; Padovan 1988; Ruggiero 1980.

   13. The national homicide rate declined from an average of 13.9 per 100,000 inhabitants in the 1880s to 4.2 in the 1930s and further dropped to 2.6 in the 1960s. Thereafter, the rate has tended to increase but has stayed well below the level of the late nineteenth century. In the years 1990–94, it oscillated between 5 and 7 homicides per 100,000 inhabitants. All these figures include attempted homicides. See Istituto Centrale di Statistica (hereafter ISTAT), *Sommario di statistiche storiche dell' Italia, 1861–1975* (Rome, 1976), 68–69; ISTAT, *Statistiche giudiziarie penali, Anno 1994* (Rome, 1995), 437.

   14. Studies by criminologists and statisticians of the nineteenth and early twentieth centuries contain detailed analyses of the serial data published in official statistics, but they hardly make any serious attempt at explaining the incidence and evolution of homicide in sociological terms. Beside the works already quoted, see Spallanzani 1917.

   15. On the general history of Rome in the nineteenth century, see Bartoccini 1985; Caracciolo 1984; Friz 1974 and 1980; Seronde-Babonaux 1983.

   16. On the Italian statistics on crime and criminal justice see Saraceno 1984.

   17. See State Archive of Rome (hereafter ASR), *Miscellanea statistica,* 42, *Morti violente verificatesi nel decennio 1854 a 1863, Tavola IV. Numero degli Omicidj avvenuti, denunciati e giudicati dai Tribunali di Civitavecchia, Frosinone, Roma, Velletri, Viterbo nel decennio 1854 a 1863.*

   18. Details may be found in my doctoral thesis: Boschi 1996, 100–104, 287–88. The figures on population I have used are the following: 1845, 170,988 inhabitants; 1846, 174,058; 1865, 202,457; 1866, 205,435. Since the average population was 172,523 in the

first couple of years and 203,946 in the second, the exact rates per 100,000 inhabitants were 17.96 in 1845–46 and 17.89 in 1865–66.

19. Monkkonen 1989, 86.

20. Zehr 1976, 118.

21. See Ministero di Agricoltura, Industria e Commercio, *Statistica delle cause di morte: Morti avvenute nei comuni capoluoghi di provincia e di circondario. Anno 1882* (Rome, 1883), xxvi n. 1.

22. The rate of successful homicides known to the public prosecutor in this area declined from 13 per 100,000 inhabitants in the period 1881–86 to 7.0 per 100,000 in 1912–14. For the absolute figures on homicides, see Ministero di Agricoltura, Industria e Commercio, *Statistica giudiziaria penale* for the years 1881–86 (Rome, 1884–88); Ministero di Grazia e Giustizia e dei Culti, *Statistica giudiziaria penale* for the years 1912–14 (Rome, 1916–18). Data on population were drawn from the national censuses of 1881, 1901, 1911, and 1921 and interpolated.

23. On homicide rates in Italian cities in the years 1907–11, see Spallanzani 1917, 614; on London, see Monkkonen 1989, 86; on Berlin and Paris, see Zehr 1976, 118; see also, however, on Berlin, McHale and Bergner 1981, showing that the homicide rate in the capital of the German Reich, which was fairly low in the last two decades of the nineteenth century, underwent a dramatic upswing in the years 1905–12. More generally, on homicide rates in Europe in the nineteenth and twentieth centuries, see Gurr 1981, 310–12, 334–40.

24. In the years 1845–46 and 1865–66, the homicides on which sentence was passed made up 83.9 and 60.2 percent of the total number of homicides known to the judicial authorities: Boschi 1996, 288–89. For the period 1870–1914, archival records do not enable us to calculate the percentage of prosecuted homicides over the total number of killings perpetrated in the city of Rome. In the district of Rome, however, prosecuted homicides (excluding attempted homicides) amounted to 81.8 percent of the total number of killings known to the examining magistrates for the period 1880–86. This percentage dropped slightly to 77.6 percent in the years 1890–95. These calculations are based on the data provided in Ministero di Agricoltura, Industria e Commercio, *Statistica giudiziaria degli affari penali per l' anno 1880* (Rome, 1883); ibid., *Statistica giudiziaria penale* for the years 1881–86, 1890–95 (Rome, 1884–88, 1892–97).

25. On the history of criminal legislation in the Papal States after the Restoration of 1814, see La Mantia 1884, 608–18; Castracane Mombelli 1979. On the criminal codes of the Kingdom of Italy, see Pessina 1906, 638–70, 685–708, 733–64.

26. For the sake of clarity and consistency, not all subspecies of homicide have been considered in disaggregating the data but only those that appeared to be the most relevant and the least affected by changes in penal legislation. Data in tables 5.3, 5.4, 5.5, 5.6, and 5.7 are drawn from the following sources: ASR, *Tribunale criminale del Governo di Roma, 1814–1871* (from 1847 onwards *Tribunale criminale di Roma*); *Registri delle sentenze*, 20–21, 36–38; ASR, *Tribunale penale di Roma*, 5585–88, 5890–91, 5634; ASR, *Corte di appello di Roma (1871–99)*, 651–56, 668–73; ASR, *Corte di appello di Roma (1894–1921)*, 371–76; ASR, *Corte di assise di Roma, Sentenze penali (1871–1920)*, 305–7, 309–11, 326–28. When the information provided by the sentence was not satisfactory, the data were taken from other trial documents.

27. After 1870 the expression "involuntary homicide" was only used, in legal language,

to indicate homicides caused by a reckless or negligent, rather than malicious, action. In the Papal States, however, the expression could also refer to homicides that would have been classified as "homicides without intent to kill" (*ferimenti volontari seguiti da morte, omicidi oltre l'intenzione*) after 1870. On the latter category of homicides, see below in the text.

28. On family homicides, see esp. Cockburn 1991, 93–98; Spierenburg 1994, 705–6, 709–12.

29. Both in Spierenburg's data and in my own, "intimates" include spouses, lovers, and immediate family. See Spierenburg 1994, 710, 716n. 41.

30. All the data on "offenders" presented in this essay refer not only to the culprits who were convicted but also to those who were acquitted for having killed in self-defense or under the compulsion of mental illness.

31. ASR, *Tribunale criminale del Governo di Roma (1814–71), Processi,* vol. 227 (old numeration), file 29154.

32. Ibid., vol. 206, file 27599.

33. On popular games in Rome during the past centuries, see Rossetti 1978, 200–210, 228–30. The rules of passatella are explained in Zanazzo 1908, 375–83; see also J. Davis 1964.

34. ASR, *Tribunale criminale del Governo di Roma (1814–71), Processi,* vol. 278, file 31183.

35. Ibid., vol. 216, file 28550.

36. Ibid., vol. 200, file 27105. The homicide was committed on September 19, 1845.

37. Ibid., vol. 218, file 28670. The homicide occurred on August 3, 1845.

38. Ibid., vol. 243, file 29631.

39. Contextual evidence on homicidal violence in Italy in the early modern period can be found in Baronti 1986. On France, see esp. Muchembled 1989. On the Netherlands, and for more general considerations, see Spierenburg 1994.

40. The word *bulli* began to be used only after 1870. It indicated men who were known for their bold and sometimes overbearing manners. *Bulli* regarded themselves as "men of honor" and usually had a reputation for knife fighting. See Mariani 1983.

41. See the *Quadri numerici delle cause introdotte e decise dal Tribunale Criminale di Roma* for the years 1850–51, 1852, 1854, 1856, and 1863. ASR, Ministero di Grazia e Giustizia, 407; ASR, *Miscellanea statistica,* 40, 43.

42. ASR, *Tribunale criminale del Governo di Roma (1814–71), Processi,* vol. 221, file 28869.

43. Ibid., vol. 289, file 31515.

44. ASR, *Corte di assise di Roma, Processi (1897–1931),* vol. 137, file 34.

45. ASR, *Tribunale criminale del Governo di Roma (1814–71), Processi,* vol. 222, file 28915.

46. Ibid., fols. 18–22.

47. According to Giovanni Compagnucci, the punishment inflicted on his brother had been so mild because the homicide charge had been changed at court stage into one of malicious wounding followed by death (ibid., fol. 21). It was not uncommon, however, that people guilty of homicide were sentenced by the papal courts to what appear to us nowadays very mild penalties.

48. Ibid., fols. 49–50, 35.

49. See Rossetti 1978, 190, 221–23, 231, 249; Mariani 1983, 42–44, 50–51, 65–67, 123–25.

50. ASR, *Corte d'appello di Roma (1871–1899),* vol. 673, sentence no. 475.

51. ASR, *Corte di assise di Roma, Processi (1897–1931)*, vol. 125, file 61.

52. See Mariani 1983, 42–44, 50–51.

53. It is not possible to explain this decline as a consequence of progress in medicine and surgery. The period under examination is indeed the one that saw the birth and the development of modern surgery (see Maconi 1991). However, while it seems beyond doubt that over the very long run progress in medicine and surgery has helped to push — or at least to keep — the homicide rates down, it is not at all certain that the improvements made in the second half of the nineteenth century had any significant effects on homicide rates. As a matter of fact, in the case of Rome, the available data show that the mortality rate for serious injuries did not decline but increased, in contrast with our expectations. In the years 1871–76, out of 468 patients who received treatment for serious injuries caused by sharp instruments in the hospital of Santa Maria della Consolazione, 12 percent (56) died. The mortality rate for the same kind of injuries rose to 14.4 percent in the period 1892–97 and to 19.3 percent in the years 1902–4 and 1909. The figures cited are calculated on the basis of the data provided in *Saggio di statistica illustrata eseguito nell' Ospedale di S. Maria della Consolazione di Roma* (Rome, 1878), and in Regio Commissariato degli Ospedali Riuniti di Roma, *Statistica sanitaria degli ospedali per gli anni 1892, 1893, 1894 e 1895 compilata a cura del Dott. Achille Ballori medico direttore dell' arcispedale di S. Spirito* (Rome, 1896) (and similar volumes for the following years).

54. In the 1920s and 1930s the district of Rome no longer coincided with any of the areas whose population is known thanks to census data. Therefore, it is no longer possible to calculate the homicide rate for this district on the basis of aggregate census data. It is known, however, that the homicides known to the public prosecutors of the district (excluding attempted homicides) decreased from an annual average of 94 in the period 1920–24 to an annual average of 61 in the years 1936–39. Over the same period, the inhabitants of Rome — who were the core of the population of the district — increased from 691,661 inhabitants in 1921 to 1,179,037 in 1936. We may thus deduce that a consistent decline of the homicide rate took place in the period 1920–39. For the data on homicides, see Ministero di Grazia e Giustizia, *Statistica giudiziaria penale* for the years 1920–35 (Rome, 1925–39); ISTAT, *Statistica giudiziaria penale* for the years 1936–39 (Rome, 1939–41). For the data on the population of Rome, see Comune di Roma, Ufficio di Statistica e Censimento, *Annuario statistico della città di Roma: Anno 1864 con dati retrospettivi per il decennio 1955–1964 e serie storiche secolari* (Rome, 1969), 27.

55. See Rossetti 1978, 258–75; Mariani 1983, 4–6 and passim.

56. Guilds had been abolished in 1801 by Pope Pius VII. Pope Pius IX tried to reintroduce them in 1852, but only a few were reestablished. See Scacchi 1981, 63.

57. Ibid., 63–78, 113–25; Basevi 1954, 10–11. Societies for mutual aid grew rapidly from 50, numbering about 8,500 members in 1873, to 274, numbering more than 40,000 members in 1894, when their expansion reached its peak.

58. Scacchi 1981, 85–87, 95–100, 115–17.

59. Basevi 1954, 12–15; Cafagna 1952; Della Peruta 1952.

60. See Cajani 1991, 526–27.

61. Cerroni 1995, 56–182; see also n. 24 above.

62. The data on malicious woundings known to the public prosecutor are drawn from Ministero di Agricoltura, Industria e Commercio, *Statistica giudiziaria penale* for the years

1896–1900 (Rome, 1897–1901). The data on offenders indicted and condemned are taken from Ministero di Agricoltura, *Notizie complementari alle statistiche giudiziarie penali degli anni 1896–1900* (Rome, 1909), 107, 235, 377, 515, 653.

63. See Spallanzani 1917, 623–76.

64. See, however, Baronti 1986, esp. 76–89; Da Passano 1984; Pompejano, Fazio, and Raffaele 1985; Rosoni 1988.

6

Fights/Fires: Violent Firemen
in the Nineteenth-Century American City

AMY SOPHIA GREENBERG

Harry: Come, Mose, let's be off.
Mose: [Astonished] What! Widout a fight? No, sir-ree—
I'm goin' to have a speech from the landlord—den for a
knock-down and a drag-out—den I retires like a gentleman.
—*A Glance at New York*

Benjamin Baker's 1848 melodrama,
A Glance at New York, launched the career of the character Mose
Humphreys, also known as "Mose the Bowery B'hoy," "Fighting Mose,"
and "Mose, Hero of a Hundred Muses."[1] Mose was a seegar-smoking,
rowdy volunteer fire laddie who emerged from an otherwise ordinary production to magnetize the country in over one thousand performances in
the 1850s.[2]

Mose was a fireman who liked to fight. In his first appearance on the
stage he professes, "I've made up my mind not to run wid der machine any
more," because the chief engineer had hit him "over the goard wid a trumpet" for insubordination. Of course, he cannot resist the lure of fire fighting for long. "I did think yesterday I'd leave de machine, but I can't do it;
I love that ingine better than my dinner."[3]

In *A Glance at New York* Mose fights, or threatens to fight, in every
scene in which he appears. He does not fight indiscriminately, however.
He fights thieves and politicians, loafers and landlords, but is gentle with

159

the naive country boy, George. "I wouldn't hurt him for the world," Mose promises. His fighting also never interferes with his duty as a fireman.[4] He is an honorable, fearless, and notably masculine figure. When his educated and refined friends decide to infiltrate a women's bowling league in drag and persuade him to come along, Mose betrays them and his own masculinity by kissing a matron, who quickly forgives him his transgression.

Despite Mose's own claim, it is not his fire engine but the fighting that really binds him to his volunteer company. Within his fire company, Mose reigns supreme, respected for his ability in a "knock-down and a drag-out," as well as for his ability with a fire hose. The volunteer fire company provides Mose with the perfect forum for his pugilistic prowess, and it is the respect of his fellow firemen that allows him to retire "like a gentleman" after a fight. Within this fictional and very popular world of volunteer firefighters, honor and violence, justice and masculinity are joined together and personified by Mose.

Mose's impact on the nonfictional world of the real urban volunteer firefighter was intense and lasting. As urban citizens first began to consider paying firemen to fight fires, rather than relying on volunteers, the image of the rowdy, violent volunteer was put to use to justify the expense of municipal forces. As the Mose character grew in popularity, so too did the belief that volunteer firemen were inveterate fighters. Many audiences wondered if Mose, "one of the fire b'hoys, full of fun, frolic and fighting," was an appropriate stage presence in cities troubled by actual firemen's battles.[5] Indeed, a national increase in violence among urban firemen was noted, discussed, and condemned by more law-abiding citizens in the 1840s and 1850s. While Mose was celebrated for his fighting, real volunteer firefighters in Baltimore, St. Louis, and San Francisco, the three cities examined here, saw their institutions dismantled as a result of their own perceived violence. In the late 1850s, as Mose's fame reached its peak, reformers agreed that urban volunteer firefighters posed a serious threat to public order and that firemen stood outside the law, answerable to no power greater than their own. While Mose could have a "knock-down and a drag-out" and then retire "like a gentleman," the firemen of St. Louis, San Francisco, and Baltimore found it impossible to fight and then retire with dignity and reputation intact, in part because of the fictional fireman.

This essay will explore the context and extent of violence among volunteer firemen in nineteenth-century urban America by closely examining when and why firemen in Baltimore, St. Louis, and San Francisco chose to fight. Although firemen in all three cities were reputed to be "violent," these firemen did not share a uniform honor code, nor did they engage in identical modes of behavior. The paradigmatic form of fireman violence was the fire "riot," in David Grimsted's definition, an incident "where a number of people group together to enforce their will immediately, by threatening or perpetrating injury to people or property outside legal procedures but without intending to challenge the general structure of society."[6] Such a riot occurred at a fire or alarm of fire only once in San Francisco, twice in a short period in St. Louis, and countless times throughout the tainted history of Baltimore's volunteer fire department. This article will consider why firemen fought one another in the mid-nineteenth century and why the public reacted to fighting firemen as it did. Did firemen in different cities really exhibit similar behavioral patterns? Did urban volunteer firemen share a masculine culture in which regular acts of violence were sanctioned and necessary? If not, why did urban citizens in the late antebellum period believe this to be true?

The Firemen of Mob-Town

Historians have identified the middle decades of the nineteenth century as a time of disorientation for urban men. Industrialization and the decline of the apprentice system increasingly forced working-class men to acknowledge the limits of their economic opportunity, whereas middle-class men were forced to balance home and work environments that were sharply at variance. Masculinity itself had reached a point of transition for both groups, and specific class-related social activities emerged. Middle-class men joined literary clubs and temperance and other reform organizations. Or, as Mark Carnes has shown, they joined fraternal orders with rituals that promoted "emotional transition from an identification from feminine domesticity to the relentlessly aggressive and competitive demands of the masculine work place."[7]

Working-class male culture, in contrast, was increasingly organized around drinking, gambling, theaters, whoring, and, above all, physical violence. Urban workers repaired from their anonymous workplaces to saloons, where they found the camaraderie and respect that was missing from their jobs. They also found fistfights, dogfights, and rat-bating contests organized by saloon keepers as entertainment. One way working-class men earned the respect of their peers was through their physical strength and ability to dominate others. Indeed, physical violence was central to urban working-class masculinity, which celebrated bare-knuckle boxing as well as less orchestrated exhibitions of virility. Personal acts of physical violence were common within saloon culture and also among working-class street gangs. By midcentury, both working- and middle-class men had developed masculine cultures that offered approval and respect distinct from any performance in the workplace. These two visions of masculinity were increasingly opposed to one another.[8]

The volunteer fire department offered men a third option, a vigorous masculine culture that combined aspects of working and middle-class culture with cultural forms singular to the fire department. In a period when leisure activities were increasingly segregated by class, the three volunteer fire departments considered here all contained memberships that were heterogeneous with regard to class and ethnicity. In Baltimore and St. Louis, volunteer fire departments were primarily composed of men who practiced low white-collar occupations: clerks, shopkeepers, small businessmen, and those laborers who practiced skilled trades. In San Francisco, the volunteer fire department was substantially more elite in occupational profile, but welcomed many skilled and some unskilled laborers. In all three cities, a higher proportion of volunteer firemen practiced white-collar professions than did the population at large up until the decade before municipalization. The volunteer firefighter was just as likely to be a clerk or merchant as he was to be a butcher, like Mose.[9]

Volunteer fire companies offered a heterogeneous membership some of the trappings of the middle class — fine houses, libraries, even an occasional piano — along with the physicality and excitement of working-class culture. The volunteer fire departments of urban America developed a vision of masculinity that was accessible and appealing to men of different social strata. Firefighter masculinity lacked the constraints and hierarchies of middle-class cultural forms and celebrated physicality within narrower parameters than working-class culture. Firemen held banquets, tea parties, and balls like middle-class men, but they had no elaborate rituals like those of middle-class fraternal organizations during this period. The ideal of decorum prevailed even when its practice failed. What the fire department offered men was an opportunity to race, parade, wear a uniform, and match strength with other like-minded men, regardless of occupation.

In Baltimore, this masculine subculture produced and supported extensive violence, but not because it became a working-class institution. Historians of the fire departments of Philadelphia and New York have attributed the violence among firemen in those cities to transformations in the class and ethnic compositions of fire-fighting forces. In both cities, "perfectly respectable" departments were altered by the coming of industrialism and population growth. The departments came under the control of working-class rowdies, who engaged in increasingly violent expressions of their competitiveness until an exasperated public saw no choice but to replace them. In Philadelphia, in the 1830s, "intercompany rivalries were still relatively benign." A decade later they had developed into "brutal clashes between warring white traditionalists." By the 1850s arsonists were burning down rival firehouses, and firemen preferred to shoot at each other rather than fight with more primitive and traditional weapons, such as brickbats or fists.[10]

Although this decline narrative may accurately represent the history of the volunteer fire departments of Philadelphia and New York, none of the fire departments considered here experienced this trajectory. Not only did the heterogeneous composition of these departments differ from that of Philadelphia, where, we are told, the white-collar workers fled in terror from their companies, but the actions of the volunteers differed as well. Baltimore's volunteer fire department certainly did not conform to the precedent of New York and Philadelphia. Baltimore's department maintained a heterogeneous membership with regard to ethnicity as well as class. As late as 1858, the year the volunteer department was disbanded, 42 percent of active Baltimore firemen locatable in the city directory were listed as either owning shops or practicing white-collar occupations. Eight percent of the firemen were identified as high white collar, such as merchants, doctors, lawyers, and manufacturers. These figures do not include honorary members of the companies, those members who supported the department financially but were not required to fight fires themselves. Nor do these figures include veteran members, who had served seven years of active duty and now held emeritus status. Honorary and veteran members of Baltimore's department in many cases identified themselves with volunteer fire fighting as vigorously as any young volunteer fireman, and they were even more likely to practice white-collar occupations than were the active members.[11]

Baltimore's department differed from the Philadelphia department in another way: it supported a culture of violence almost from its origins.

Unlike Philadelphia, Baltimore had no Benjamin Franklin to set the tone for their eighteenth-century department, and troubles in Baltimore started early. Between 1763, when the Mechanical Fire Company was formed, and 1782, when a group of firemen split off and formed the Union Company, there was peace in Baltimore. The motto of the second company, "In union there is strength," was quickly belied, however. According to an early source, "rivalry sprung up between the two companies," and the disaffected met in 1785 to form a third company, which "with a view of reconciling all the then difficulty" took the name Friendship.[12]

The first surviving fire company records in Baltimore document disputes. A meeting of the Mechanical Company in 1813 condemned the lack of orderliness at fires and "great neglect of duty" by the company. One of the earliest entries in the Union Company's ledger is a resignation letter from a member who complained of being "badly insulted" by another member.[13] By the 1830s Baltimore had gained the sobriquet "Mob-town" because of its frequent riots, some of which originated within the fire department. Both newspapers and company ledgers document serious volunteer troubles, including a battle between two companies at the scene of a fire, shootings, and arson.[14]

Despite attempts in the early 1830s by both the firemen and the city to bring the firemen's behavior under control, violence worsened. Although fights seemed always to center around the firehouse, or fire itself, firemen pointed to outsiders as the cause of the violence. In the 1830s three firehouses were torched by unidentified arsonists. Riots were nearly weekly occurrences. Yet the press failed to identify firemen as the perpetrators. "When shall we be able to pass a Sabbath day without being called upon to record some act of disgraceful violation of the peace, some daring outrage amounting almost to bloodshed?" asked the Baltimore *Sun* on January 16, 1838, after one of these riots. "Not, we fear, until the originators of these riots, the master spirits who excite the evil passions of gangs of thoughtless, unruly boys, and lead them on step by step from simple brawls to riot, arson, and murder, receive their just dues." The *Sun* did not suggest that the master spirits might be firemen.[15]

Firemen maintained that they were blameless in these doings, but fire companies began internal reforms. Company members signed pledges that they would discontinue the use of "ardent spirits at fires" and that they would "refrain from giving any cause of offense to the members of any other company." Rather, they would take care to remember "the honour of the company" of which they were members and the "character of the Firemen of Baltimore."[16]

Much of the problem, however, lay in this question of honor. It was unclear whether a volunteer fireman's code of honor would be better served by fighting or not fighting. The ledger of the Mechanical Company in 1839 commends the Independent Fire Company for attacking the Patapsco Company (the Mechanical Company's particular enemies) because of the latter company's "continued disorderly conduct, and the low character of the man of fellows of which it is composed — a disgrace to the Fire Department of Baltimore."[17] In the eyes of the Mechanical Company it was perfectly all right for an honorable company to attack a company made dishonorable by its own fighting.

The Volunteer Fire Department Standing Committee also considered honor a legitimate reason to start a fight. "It will not be maintained," the committee declared, "that any company should remain quiet and permit itself to be taunted, insulted, or mistreated."[18] In fact, members of the committee were not above such concerns themselves. According to fire company notes, in 1840 a fracas was instigated by one of the members of the committee whose "taunts and vociferous noises" were sufficient to start a riot on a "most beautiful and moonlit night!"[19]

This tacit recognition of an honor code that condoned violence under certain circumstances helps explain the great number of disputes brought before the standing committee. In the highly charged and competitive world of antebellum fire fighting, insults lurked everywhere. The first years of the committee, between 1834 and 1840, saw an astounding array of cases, from relatively minor infractions involving racing, or one company throwing water upon another, to serious threats, bludgeonings, theft, and "general outrages by firemen." The United Fire Company ran their hose carriage into the Washington Company's engine. Was it deliberate? Unclear. Was it reason for a fight? Yes. Was the threat "to split your head open" made by a member of the Columbian Company simply high spirits, or was it an insult to the member of the Deptford Company against whom it was made?[20]

Committee members clearly felt ambivalent about firefighter violence. They recognized that sometimes fighting was justified, and they were firemen themselves. They rarely reached any conclusions. Subcommittees were often appointed to look into disputes, but they do not seem to have reported back. Even when evidence was forthcoming, the committee was loath to lay blame within the department or to pronounce any serious punishment, perhaps out of concern for the department's public image. After all, a volunteer fire company survived on the goodwill and financial contributions of its neighbors. It was not in the interest of the standing committee to make violent conflicts more visible than they already were. The same parties reappear with similar complaints. The New Market Company, generally considered to be a "bad lot," was accused of "using implements and carrying clubs and weapons not required by their duties, and frequently applied to purposes subversive of the public peace." In one particular 1838 battle against the Union Fire Company, New Market members or their "runners" killed two men. Yet no one was punished, and the firemen continued fighting. It is unclear whether the committee was astounded or resigned that two deaths did nothing to tame the disorder in the fire department. Indeed, the committee noted, "Riots, turbulence, disgraceful conduct and personal violence have since repeatedly occurred. The name of the fireman has almost become a badge of obloquy, and an emblem of disorder."[21] Fire company records show that the deaths made little impact on the firemen and that even firemen who condemned "disgraceful" companies could still take a lurid pleasure in the violence of others. "The Patapsco and Friendship came in collision and ended in a *glorious* fight," the secretary of the Mechanical Fire Company wrote in his ledger on August 22, 1840.

The standing committee must have done an excellent job of keeping volunteer difficulties private. Although the name of the fireman might be on the way to becoming a "badge of obloquy" far into the 1840s, the press refused to locate the source of rioting among the firemen. Perhaps this was due to the firemen's capable performance at a series of large fires or the role the firemen played in controlling an 1835 bank riot.[22] In any case, although firemen engaged in frequent and extensive episodes of violence, they were not publicly identified as violent during the 1830s. In 1838 the Baltimore *Sun* clearly attempted to exonerate the firemen of any charges of misbehavior. Although the paper acknowledged that some people once suspected that the firemen themselves were starting riots, "this opinion . . . is nearly exploded." The *Sun* offered an alternative explanation, elaborating and expanding on the favorite excuse of the firemen: "We say the cause is this: Baltimore City, like all other large places, contains some five or six dozen flash fellows — fancy rattlers — men who are a sort of half and half — who dress with more ease than grace, and now and then with more grace than ease: a species of nondescript, being neither professional men, mechanics, or laborers — a something, nothing, a kind of wandering beings." After elaborating upon the details of these "confidence men," who wander from eating house to tavern bar, flashing showy jewelry and drinking late into the evening, the paper revealed their fiendish designs. Intent upon fighting, "according to their own conception, a sort of civil drubbing, which some particular man, or set of men, has in some way earned," their intention is conveyed "to the various engine houses (at most of these in the evening are collected large gangs of half-grown boys); they hear of the coming battle with the greatest joy, and off they scamper to the battle ground." The paper concluded that it was the responsibility of parents and masters to keep children and apprentices at home late at night and that no one under the age of twenty should be allowed to collect in gangs or at engine houses.[23]

Outside agitators did help incite firemen's riots. According to fire company minutes, rabble-rousers might shout inflammatory remarks at the firemen or throw bricks and stones at them during or after fires. Often these fights originated in political disputes between Whig and Democratic political clubs, which associated at the privately owned firehouses or at taverns near the firehouses. On August 18, 1844, the secretary of the Mechanical Fire Company reported that the engine of the Vigilant Company was "seized by a party of rowdies, who threw their hose in the Falls. The Columbia Carriage was likewise seized and partially destroyed. Beautiful Conduct!! Brick bats flew like hail, pistols were fired in every direction." This company believed that rowdies, and not firemen, were the source of their troubles. The secretary of this company was clearly concerned that "there is now no safety for those that are well disposed," and he predicted that "something must be done or the department will be in the hands of these rowdies completely!"

But firemen were not the innocent victims of rowdyism and political difference. The firemen also contributed to these scenes, and "disgraceful fights" in which "axes, torches, knives and pistols were freely used" were attributed by firemen to their brethren as well as to "rowdies" who might or might not be connected to the department.[24] Yet in reports of riots at fires and false alarms in the 1830s and 1840s, firemen were rarely identified. On the rare occasions that combatants were arrested, they were reported to be "youths not believed to be firemen" and unidentified belligerents.[25] Clearly, many of these individuals, arrested or not, were firemen. A particularly disgraceful fight occurred on Easter 1844 after a false alarm. The ledger of the Mechanical Fire Company commented that on this occasion, "Easter morning trial of apparatus turns into a fight in which members of all companies participated." The *Baltimore American* stated conservatively on April 9 that they "observed a general melee going on, but as to who was at fault, or who were the belligerents, we could not ascertain." In 1838 legislation was passed making the intentional injury of a fireman a crime punishable by a month's imprisonment.

A combination of internal reforms and a new municipal "minor law" banning minors from companies in 1844 worked to dispel both the boys and riots. The secretary of the Mechanical Fire Company commented with some amazement in April 1845 that the recent legislation "is found fully to effect the object for which it is designed—scarcely a boy is seen with any of the Reel Suctions. . . . A most admirable regulation and calculated to do away with the broils and riots which have disgraced the Fire Department for so long past." But the minor law was soon ignored, and by the summer of 1847, rioting had again become "so bad that it is dangerous for peaceable persons to go to fires, for fear of being shot, or knocked down by a brick."[26]

After the two-year hiatus on disorder, the press became far less sympathetic to the firemen. In an article on September 11, 1847, entitled "Firemen's Riots—What Can the Matter Be?" the Baltimore *Sun* scorned the excuses they had once believed. "We find bonfires built in some remote section of the city, merely to cause an alarm and draw the firemen together for the purpose of a fight, and have seen the apparatus of certain companies taken out when there was no alarm and run into a section of the city where a collision was most likely to take place." Although adult men, in the uniform of firemen, always appeared to be in charge, "when a collision occurs," the reporter sneered, "we have every assurance given that those who participated in them are half-grown boys, and not members of the companies" Or, as another *Sun* article stated skeptically on October 28, "It certainly seems strange that these rioters, if not members of the companies they run with, should be allowed to take out their apparatus."

Apparently the public was losing interest as well. For the first time, the Mechanical Company Collecting Committee decided in December not to request funds from the neighborhood, due to "the impression which may have been made on the public, by the rioting of several Companies in the city." Instead, they decided that they "had better defer it until peace and harmony was restored." That time never came. By late 1848, another person had died, and at least five observers had been injured by the flying bricks, missiles, and bullets that marked the firemen's battles.[27]

During the period of calm in the mid-1840s, "arrests of minors were made, all rioting among firemen ceased, and there were not near so many fires as now," as one fireman later put it. It appears that large numbers of Baltimoreans took advantage of the peace following the passage of the minor law and reexamined their assumptions about rioting in Baltimore.[28]

In the 1830s and early 1840s, riots frequently did not involve firemen. Many were perpetrated by unhappy segments of the population to protest social ills. Riots in Baltimore were both expressive and recreational, to borrow Michael Feldberg's terms. The Bank Riot of 1835 was one of three riots in Baltimore in a two-year period clearly expressive of protesters' sense of economic or political injustice. An 1840 attack by "a large party of rowdies with the New Market and United companies . . . on a crowd of Whigs assembled at the Patriot office" offers another example of expressive rioting. "Several pistols were discharged by the Whigs but no one was killed . . . great political excitement between the Whigs and Democrats, threatening riot and bloodshed."[29]

Other riots, involving rowdies and firemen, appear to have been purely recreational in nature. These riots may have reinforced the solidarity of the group or upheld a group's honor code, but such riots did not express any larger dissatisfaction with the status quo.[30] Those riots in which the firemen took part (according to their own records) were therefore easy for the public to blame on other troublemakers, and the confidence man served this purpose well. Firemen could not be expected to be in control in an environment where no one else was, either. If boys ran with their machines and bashed one another with bricks, well, they might have done as much elsewhere just as easily. The firemen blamed the police for not keeping order, and in fact they had to act as police to protect public order during the Bank Riot. It was also difficult for the public to decide whom to blame when the police consistently failed to arrest rioters.

But by 1846, there is evidence of a dramatic decline in expressive rioting and a decline in the number of riots *not* related to fire fighting. Virtually no reports of riots without firemen can be found in the newspapers of the late 1840s.[31] The link between firemen and riots probably became clear in the 1845–46 period of calm in the fire department. As a result, all later riots could be blamed on the firemen, who clearly were rioting for recreational purposes. Thus a solution to all riots was sought in relation to the fire department.

In fact, rioting among firemen had only marginally worsened. Individual riots of the late 1840s in Baltimore were particularly violent, and for a period in 1847 firemen battled each other weekly, but there were also particularly violent battles in 1835 and 1840 and an extended series of battles throughout the period. Rioting appeared worse in the late 1840s, not simply because it was, but because there was no longer a background of lawlessness to soften its edges. "Mob-town" may have been an appropriate description of Baltimore in the 1830s, but by the late 1840s, Baltimoreans were looking for a more dignified title.

Firemen were perceived to be rioting more often because they were more likely to be identified as such in Baltimore *Sun* reports in the late 1840s, a fact possibly related to the rise of "Fighting Mose" in 1848. Fights involving firemen were also more likely to be labeled "riots" than in earlier years. "A Riot and Brutal Murder," in February 1849, is actually the story of a barroom brawl involving perhaps four people, all of whom unfortunately belonged to fire companies and one of whom was stabbed to death. A postfire disturbance a week later was saved from becoming "a riot of considerable extent" by the "efficient and extraordinary efforts" of the police. An engine collision on Baltimore Street led to insults, followed by two injuries. A brick thrown by a member of the Watchman Company hit a member of the United Company on the head, and a United member retaliated by smacking a Watchman fireman with a pipe. The police, the *Sun* reader is told, saved the day. "The very moment that manifestations of disorder appeared, [the police] were on the spot amidst the uproarious crowds that filled the street, and regardless of danger or injury promptly arrested the offending parties."[32] This event would hardly have merited a paragraph in the 1830s, but in the 1830s the police would not have taken preemptive action. The melee would have taken its own course, either dissipating, as such events often did according to fire company records, or developing into a full-fledged riot.

What is clear from this passage is the new interest and demand for order in Baltimore, focused on preventing disorder, not simply controlling it. As in other cities, order was enforced in Baltimore by growing numbers of professional police. Police expenditures in Baltimore more than tripled between 1845 and 1855, and by 1856 an expanded and centralized Baltimore police was uniformed, reflecting and legitimating their growing semimilitary status in the city. In 1849 the mayor of Baltimore divided the city into fire wards to which the companies were then assigned and allowed to leave only upon permission of the mayor.[33]

These two preemptive strikes against the firemen in 1849, one by the police at a disturbance and one by the mayor, could only help convince the public that a nonviolent fire department was nonviolent because it was externally controlled, not because of any internal restraints. In fact, the police were utterly unable to control a truly riotous crowd, as was made clear in Baltimore's election riots of 1856–59, the most violent election riots in U.S. history. The perception that the police alone could provide control helped them to widen their own sphere of influence. Starting in the mid-nineteenth century, it also helped the police to justify ever-increasing force sizes and expenditures when they failed to provide that illusive control.[34]

There is no evidence of any firemen's riots, or other major public disturbances by the firemen from 1850 to 1855, although there were a great number of false alarms and fires, averaging almost one of each per day in 1851. Two or three minor attacks by one company upon another are documented in the company ledgers, but these events do not seem to have resulted in major injuries or to have been publicized.[35]

The decline in violence does not seem to have improved the public standing of the fire department. Perhaps this was because their behavior was now viewed within the paradigm of police control, their orderliness viewed as the result of effective policing. The press portrayed it as such, commenting, when a serious riot broke out in August 1855, that for some time, "there has been every indication of a serious struggle between them [the New Market and Mount Vernon Companies], though they have been kept in check by the police, who were always on the watch, in consequence of the anticipated rupture. Notwithstanding their vigilance, however, they have, at last, succeeded in their disgraceful designs." The results were indeed disgraceful. One fireman was killed by a member of his own company (who was aiming at a policeman). Also killed were a young bystander and a former fireman, killed by a shot to the breast. Three other men were injured, and the crowd at large was "armed, and for the most part, incessantly firing." After two more election-day riots, in 1856 and 1858, the volunteer department was dismantled, although the firemen's role in each riot was exaggerated.[36]

Given the strange trajectory of the Baltimore volunteer fire depart-ment—a membership which clearly did not reflect the ruffian reputation it acquired in the 1850s, a long and involved history of recreational rioting which had no impact on the reputation of the department until the late 1840s, and increasing public condemnation of behavior which did not substantially worsen—it becomes difficult to accept traditional explana-tions for firefighter violence. Baltimore's volunteer fire department did not decline from a bastion of middle-class respectability to a mob of working-class and immigrant rowdies. Volunteer firemen in Baltimore rather found their traditional concepts of honor, and means of expressing that honor, increasingly under fire amidst changing demands for order and respect-ability in the larger society. Baltimore's behavioral norms had changed more than had the behavior of the firemen.

St. Louis Rowdyism

The violence of the St. Louis volunteers seems playful in comparison, more rowdy than riotous. Firemen did not begin to fight in St. Louis until 1849, and they employed primitive weapons in primarily minor skir-mishes. Only one fatality can be directly attributed to the Volunteer Fire Company's record of rowdyism, and up until they were disbanded, fire-men in St. Louis showed a willingness to reconcile with their sparring partners, which highlights the casual nature of most of this fighting. Fire-men in St. Louis shared a code of honor, but the behavior it sanctioned was far more limited than that of the Baltimore volunteers. Here, as in Baltimore, the department contained a larger percentage of white-collar members than did the city at large, as well as a membership of diverse eth-nicity. As in Baltimore, the record of firefighter violence does not fit a simple decline narrative.

The first five permanent fire companies in the frontier city of St. Louis were established between 1832 and 1835, with the first recorded fighting occurring in 1849. Their first fight was really a riot, although it was not re-ferred to as such at the time. This may have been because the firemen did not attack each other but the Irish inhabitants of the appropriately named "Battle Roe." The fight resulted in worse press than injuries, although not as bad, of course, as if the firemen's victims had been "Americans." The Irish deckhands of this area were renowned brawlers. Native-born residents of St. Louis were not sympathetic to these violent immigrants. One contemporary account of this thumping only stated: "A fight occurred between the firemen and a gang of Irish. The firemen came off the victors. Loss $130,000." In the report of a fireman, the Irish had "got what they deserves," after the firemen finished "run[ing] the Irish all over the upper part of town."[37]

Fire companies in St. Louis maintained their honor in the 1840s by racing to fires, raising false alarms, and stealing the engines out of other companies' firehouses. Engine racing was treated as a major problem by many of the companies, who passed legislation to expel any member who engaged in such an activity, and warned of the "many evil consequences ensu[ing] from persisting in such practices such as unnecessarily injuring the apparatus and endangering the lives and limbs of members." The lives and limbs of nonmembers were also endangered by this practice. The Missouri Fire Company admitted to running over four people with their engine in two years, none of whom, amazingly, were seriously hurt.[38]

The 1843–49 records of the Phoenix Fire Company, the "most turbulent" company in the department, and the one containing "more of the Eastern rowdies than the rest combined," according to one historian of the department, reveal that the company in this decade had more interest in entertaining other companies, parading, and attractively dressing both its engine and members than in fighting (men or fires). The most disturbing event of the 1840s at the Phoenix firehouse was a threat made by a member to shoot the watchman if he rang the bell. This transgression occupies an entire month of debate in the record book. Fines were also instituted for members caught racing or ringing the bell in a false alarm of fire.[39]

The Franklin Company also expelled a member for "misbehavior and stating a gross falsehood to the company." St. Louis fire companies favored the threat of expulsion, and expulsion itself, as a way to control behavior, and to accept a previously expelled fireman into your company was a mark of great dishonor.[40] Four offenses merited expulsion from the Laclede Company in 1850: "giving false alarm of a fire," "disobedience of the order of a Superior," "loud, vulgar, or obscene language either at the engine house or when on duty," and quarreling. These transgressions appear quaint in comparison with the arson, battery, fighting at a fire, and shooting another fireman that resulted in expulsions in Baltimore.[41] In

March 1852, the Missouri Company threatened to expel any member who appeared drunk at a fire twice or made any noise "deemed injurious to the character and reputation of the company."[42]

Even flagrant provocations of another company appear to have diffused themselves fairly well in the 1840s. The Missouri Fire Company stole the Union Company's engine out of their house "without authority" in 1846, in a clear violation of that company's honor, and felt no repercussions for four years. "Union Fire Co. awfull keen for a muss, they had better keep cool," the Missouri secretary remarked in March 1848.[43] Only with the onset of the tumultuous 1850s could the fight they had "been expecting for some time" begin. The description of this fight reveals a joy in pure physical violence lacking in any of the surviving materials from Baltimore. The fight began as the Missouri Company returned home with their engine from a fire. As they passed the Liberty hose truck, the captain of the Liberty Company, known to the writer as "Big Six," ominously approached Mr. Dickey, assistant foreman of the Missouri Company.

> Big Six struck at Mr. Dickey but missed him. In turn, Dickey knocked him down, and so the fight began. Both companies fought like h —— l. At last the Liberty Hose Co. run, and I thought the fight was ended, but not so, for just as we started home again, the Union and Liberty Companies came at us with stones, clubs, spanners, and wrenches. Our boys tried to stand their ground, but it was no use, they were too much for us. . . . There was as many as 20 of the Liberty and Union members at Mr. Dickey at once, and if ever a man fought hard, Dickey did, and I believe he would have undid them all, but one of the Liberty's members jumped on the fence and struck Dickey in the back of the head, which knocked him down.

The fight ended with Mr. Dickey's fall. Three Missouri members were injured, but only Dickey had to be carried home. The writer proudly announced that more Liberty members were injured than their own members, but he closed with a sobering evaluation of the afternoon's activities. "All I wish is that there will never be such another fight again. . . . This scrape will be the means of breaking down the Missouri. P.S., we will have a slap at them again some day."[44]

Intradepartmental fighting began in St. Louis in 1850, but firemen continued to exhibit restraint. As the Missouri secretary indicated, firemen in St. Louis felt ambivalence about physical combat. They may have enjoyed the excitement of the battle and felt the desire to avenge previous wrongs with more fighting, but they could also hope that "there will never be such another fight again." This regret is entirely absent from the surviving records of the Baltimore fire companies.

The Union Company and Missouri Company seemed to drop their differences after this fight, although the Union Company went on to fight with the Liberty and Phoenix Companies in 1852. The Missouri had the chance at another "slap" at the Liberty in 1854 when the latter company "accidentally" ran their engine into the path of the Missouri engine. The Missouri men practiced restraint, although the Missouri secretary did not mince words about the "dirty low blow hards" that made up the Liberty company. "The D — n Rowdies are a perfect nuisance, and the company from its commencement was a quaralous, low, rowdy company, and instead of getting better, they got worse. A bigger set of Cowards never pulled on a drag rope of an Engine." The secretary's comments upon this occasion reveal a firefighter code being broken by the Liberty Company, and a real fear of the ramifications fighting would bring on the department. "It is this company of our once Respectable Department [that] from their first organization . . . would take in members expelled from other companies. . . . They now talk of breaking up, and the sooner the better for the city and department."[45]

It was probably this fear for the reputation of the department, in the light of developments in eastern departments, which kept fights from escalating into riots in St. Louis. A "muss" broke out in 1851 after the Washington Fire Company threw water on the St. Louis Fire Company, with "plenty of Brick Bats thrown by the St. Louis," but the Washington Company did not retaliate.[46]

Fire companies in St. Louis fought throughout the 1850s, but also repeatedly attempted to work out their differences with apologies or meetings with other companies, indicating that the firemen hoped to limit the extent and ramifications of their rowdyism. In 1856, the Missouri and Franklin Companies, who had fought on and off for several years, held a "friendly visit" as they both pledged to "stand by each other as friends, and to do all in our power to cement the bonds of friendship more closely than ever."[47] Problems between the Franklin and Liberty Companies proved difficult to solve. Differences between the two originated when the

Franklin was "attacked by members of the Liberty . . . on their way to take up some Hose" in 1851. After three years of occasional fights after fires and false alarms, the Franklin Company held a meeting with members of the Liberty Company to attempt to finally resolve their difficulties.[48] Fighting continued, and in May 1855 the Liberty Company was suspended for six months for damaging the Franklin Company's engine, the same month that the Washington Company was suspended for breaking the windows of the Liberty Fire Company.[49] The injury to engine led to the only verified violence-related fatality in St. Louis. Before these two companies were finally reconciled, a Liberty Company member was shot and killed, the only documented case of a fireman in St. Louis using a pistol against another fireman.[50]

Within its own context, the fact that only one St. Louis fireman was shot is somewhat remarkable. Firefighters in St. Louis deserve credit for not resorting to firearms again. By the mid-1850s, nearly all firemen carried them for protection against mobs at fires, according to one volunteer who claimed he "would not have gone to that fire without his revolver under any consideration." Yet if guns were carried, they do not appear to have been drawn, or if drawn, they certainly were not fired at other firemen.[51]

On the eve of the Civil War, St. Louis was a town seething with sectional violence, where "Bibles and Sharp's rifles were associated as correlating agencies of civilization."[52] Advertisements for rifles appeared on the front pages of St. Louis newspapers. Yet firemen in this city did not use firearms regularly. Fights in St. Louis emerged out of races to fires, competitions over fire hydrants, and turf disputes, as they did in Baltimore and other cities. Some St. Louis firemen clearly enjoyed fighting. But the firemen of this city exhibited clear restraint considering the weapons on hand and the precedent set by departments on the East Coast. The volunteer firefighter culture in St. Louis sanctioned only limited forms of violence.

Although there may have been an internal control and possibly even order to the St. Louis fighting, by the mid-1850s the firemen had alienated their public as thoroughly as had the Baltimore volunteers. In another ethnically based disturbance in July 1854, the firemen attempted to impose their values outside their organization. They demanded beer from a German beer-house keeper, and when that beer failed to materialize, they "began to break the bottles in the house, and in other ways damaging the furniture in the room." The angry brewer shot one of the firemen in the face, and shot at several people in the crowd outside as well.[53]

As in the earlier Irish-bating episode, the sympathy of the public was fully with the firemen. Perhaps if the St. Louis volunteers had limited their attentions and demands to immigrants and one another they could have continued in this manner for some time, harassing ethnic groups and throwing bricks at rival engines. But by the 1850s, the values of the firemen and the larger society were clearly diverging. The *Missouri Democrat* complemented the firemen on their "effective work in subduing the flames" at the fire near the beer house, but complaints about the firemen's behavior elsewhere began to increase.

The firehouse became a central site of contention in St. Louis in the battle over behavioral norms. Men drank in the firehouse and sometimes fought. Occasionally the fights were of a formal nature. Robert Dunn was expelled from the Laclede Fire Company when he did "to the great scandal of the company and disturbance of the neighborhood bring hither into our engine room two men as Principals to fight a prize fight—they, the said Robert Dunn and Wm Boyd, aiding and abetting them in the capacity of seconds." Generally the fights were of a more banal sort. The Laclede records also report that "Peter Holden did while in an intoxicated state come into our engine room and then and there violently assaulted a member of the company," for which he was not expelled.[54]

Firehouse neighbors complained of the constant noise and disorder emanating from almost all of the houses throughout the 1850s, a situation firemen were either unable or unwilling to rectify.[55] The mayor of St. Louis focused on the disorderly firehouse in his report to the city council in 1855. In his opinion, the volunteer system was "demoralizing" because of its impact on the young and on families. Firemen, "particularly the more youthful, will and do congregate, as they feel free to do, in and about their engine house, day and night, and on the Sabbath, in great numbers, and indulge in conversation and conduct, not only unbecoming, but highly indecorous and obscene." The mayor continued, warming to his subject. "No one who has a decent regard for what is polite, refined or virtuous, has lived in the vicinity of, or passed near one of the houses in the evening or on Sunday, and not been disgusted with the exhibitions there witnessed."[56] The polite, refined, and virtuous were more actively assaulted when missiles thrown in one 1856 battle between the Liberty and Franklin Companies damaged several houses, not firehouses, in the neighborhood.[57]

Members of the middle class of St. Louis were actively working toward the gentility of Boston and New York in the 1840s and 1850s, and they were insecure about how well they were progressing toward this goal. Boosters and middle-class transplants from those cities valiantly strove to bring refinement to St. Louis at the exact time that the behavior of the firemen was degenerating. The morality of the firemen became the object of public outrage, and their behavior in the streets was almost as loudly bemoaned as their behavior in the firehouse. This was because the street, like the home, was an especially contested battleground in the struggle for refinement in America, as Richard Bushman and others have illustrated. In the streets of St. Louis, the refined were forced to interact with everyone else. And the firemen were not only actively visible in the streets but actively crude in their behavior.[58]

It was appropriate that the final confrontation between the norms of the firemen and those of the polite, refined, and virtuous would transpire in the streets. Only two months after Mayor King's report on the indecorous firemen, he and a number of "ladies and gentlemen" were interrupted on a promenade down a "crowded thoroughfare" by the Phoenix Hose Carriage. The carriage, drawn by "a set of Wildmen and half-grown boys on the sidewalk," threatened the "lives" of the decent citizens as well as their control of the streets. When the mayor heard "the yell as of so many savages," he stepped in and attempted to use his authority to stop the "disgraceful act" of firemen running their engine on the sidewalk. Perhaps the greatest crime that afternoon was not the misuse of the sidewalk but the fact that Mayor King, in his own words, "was not only disregarded, but insulted by a louder yell when they learned who I was."[59]

The savages had squared off against the protector of ladies and gentlemen and won a Pyrrhic victory. In April 1857 the city of St. Louis passed an ordinance to provide for a paid steam fire department.[60] Legislated out of existence, the final year of the volunteer department was marked by arson and active resistance to the new paid organization. Nonetheless, as the department apologist pointed out correctly, "The record of dangerous injuries due to the spirit of 'sport' during its whole existence, is not comparable with that often resulting during a single season from the rivalry in sport among 'teams' of leading universities, between 1898 and 1905."[61]

St. Louis's fire department was never an unruly mob. Although they may not have shown sufficient respect for elected politicians, violence within the department was almost always internally controlled. But history has not been kind to the St. Louis volunteers; their record of violence continued to expand long after their institution was dismantled. The most famous nineteenth-century historian of St. Louis, John Thomas Scharf, spared no venom in his portrayal of the firemen as nearly Baltimorean in character (which, considering he had written *The Chronicles of Baltimore* nine years earlier, is perhaps not surprising). The volunteer system, he wrote, "had become a standing outrage" and was responsible for all manner of urban crimes. "The spirit of rowdyism which had grown up under it, not satisfied with an occasional demonstration at fires, turned to the highways and assailed the inoffensive citizen as he walked to his home."[62]

Strangely enough, firemen also contributed to the mythologizing of fireman violence. Thomas Lynch, a veteran firefighter, apparently manufactures a dramatic riot in his 1880 history of the St. Louis Volunteer Fire Department. The supposed riot is undocumented in any previous work, including the leading newspapers of the period. The "Dog-Fight Riot" of 1853, according to Lynch, occurred when a fireman interfered in a fight between a large bulldog and its small victim in his "desire to see fair play." The owners of the bulldog resented the interference, and soon a riot between the firemen at large and the bulldog's supporters interrupted the peace of a St. Louis Sunday.[63]

Could Mose be responsible for these developments? Both Scharf and Lynch attribute the rise of rowdyism in the St. Louis Fire Department to the "acquisition of members . . . of a lot of refugees from justice and chronic roughs from the departments of the Eastern Cities." Although the names of these rough characters are not given, both authors provide clues to their exact identities. According to Lynch it was the "typical 'B'hoy' or 'Syksey'" (another character in the fictional Mose drama). According to Scharf, "This class were those who styled the apparatus 'de masheen!' who said 'nah!' and 'yaas!'" Both authors indicate that Mose, in his most threatening and dangerous form, came to St. Louis at just the time when his character would have graced the stages of St. Louis.[64]

Not only did Mose, in the form of East Coast rowdies, enter St. Louis, but Lynch reports that St. Louis began to produce its own Moses as well. "The character of 'Mose' brought out about this time at the theaters contributed largely to give 'éclat' to the sayings and doings of these parties, and especially in molding the future character of the younger members."[65]

The influence of Mose was far greater than either of these commentators realized, however. Mose was not only able to change the character of the department after his arrival, as they suggest, but to re-create its entire history in his image. Who but Mose would stand up for the rights of the literal "underdog" with his fists, as the firemen of the imaginary "Dog-Fight Riot" did? The victims of the real St. Louis firemen, the Irish in 1849, and the German tavernkeeper in 1854, would have been beneath the notice of Mose, or at least would not have figured in his adventures. The persecutors of small dogs are precisely the sort that Mose would revel in fighting. It appears that Mose not only enabled those outside the fire department to understand rowdyism within it but also enabled members of this masculine subculture to construct their own behavior and history.

The "Model Fire Department of the World"

Almost from their organization in 1849, the firemen of San Francisco considered themselves the "Model Fire Department of the World." In part this was due to the "strict observance of its laws, and . . . brotherly feeling which has always distinguished them."[66] In part it was because the San Francisco volunteer fire department was among the most elite departments in the country. In 1860, after the Baltimore and St. Louis volunteers had been forcibly disbanded, San Francisco's volunteer fire department contained far more white-collar members than members who were laborers. Nearly 60 percent of volunteer firemen in this city practiced white-collar occupations, and fully 18 percent practiced high white-collar occupations. The department was ethnically diverse but less so than the gold-rush city to which it belonged. In a city where only half of all residents were native born, one-third of all firemen were foreign born in 1860. San Francisco's department was a model of wealth, decorum, and middle-class trappings.[67]

Because they organized so much later than did East Coast or Midwest departments, the San Francisco firemen understood the wages of violence. They correctly observed that "one blow struck in anger in the public street, while in the Fireman's garb, will be like a cancer, eating gradually into the vitals of the Department."[68] As a result, violence in San

Francisco had a different character than it did in Baltimore or St. Louis. Each violent episode in San Francisco can be traced to a concrete source of "ill feeling" among the participants, and in each case, the resulting violence was read by the participants as a legitimate reaction to perceived wrongs. The San Francisco firemen were not riotous, as the Baltimore firemen were, or rowdy, as were their St. Louis brethren. They shared a code of honor, but it sanctioned very few expressions of violence. Like the other departments, however, the San Francisco volunteers alienated their public with scenes of public disorder at odds with an increasingly orderly urban context.

Volunteer fire fighting in San Francisco was not free from the rivalry and competition that marked other departments. Starting in 1849, when the department was organized, firemen raced each other to fires, allowed boys to run with their engines, and even "saved" hydrants at fires. Yet those activities, which provided the impetus for so many of the fights in other departments, had little effect on the good feeling among firemen in San Francisco. As volunteer Robert S. Lammot wrote, "After it [a fire] is over, instead of stopping a while to have a fight, as they file past one another on their way home, you hear such cries as Hurrah for the 'Howard'! She's always the first in service — Three cheers for the 'California' — she is *some* at a fire — There comes the 'Monumental'! good for the Baltimoreans."[69]

Antagonism and rivalry could and did appear. After a trial of apparatus in front of five thousand spectators, and a $500 wager, the Monumental and Vigilant Companies nearly came to blows. They published insulting letters to one another in San Francisco's newspapers, but were reconciled during the visit of a Stockton fire company to the city, before a self-described "war of water" could become a "war of blood."[70]

Similar tensions arose for the same reasons between the Howard and Knickerbocker Companies (who wagered $6,000 on a contest of machinery) and were heard to growl "instead of giving three cheers for each other as they ought to have done" when returning from a fire.[71] In the letters exchanged between these companies, also published, each company attempted to negotiate terms of the contest most favorable to them, while accusing the other company of demanding unfair advantage. These correspondences finally degenerated into accusations of dishonesty on both sides, and the refusal of the Howard Company to compete at all was based on the assertion that "judging from several previous transactions with [the Knickerbockers], there is no honor or probity among them as a company."[72] Although honor was at stake, no blows were exchanged between these companies.

San Francisco also suffered from many of the same external stresses that troubled other departments. Fights between boys running with engines occasionally began, but were generally controlled by "the promptitude and decision of MEN in the department." Unruly crowds interfered with firemen in their discharge of duty. Firemen in San Francisco, like those in Baltimore and St. Louis, complained that there were often no police at the scenes of fires to aid firemen in crowd control.[73]

As in East Coast departments, youth gangs found firemen a tempting target. In 1855 rowdies attacked the firemen on at least three occasions, yet the firemen refrained from battling with rowdies. Truly, they were tested. Although "bullied and attacked on the streets, and followed by their assailants to the very portals of their engine houses" and "the hot blood of a rightful indignation at the insults heaped upon them has mounted to their cheeks," the firemen never forgot who they were. As the press reported, "the thought of their own unsullied reputation" prevented them from retaliating, as they wished to do. Overall, the San Francisco firemen "displayed a forbearance which their best friends did not give them credit for," and they did so out of a sense of honor. Until 1856, in fact, the editor of the *Fireman's Journal* could with some truth report that "blows in anger" had never been exchanged among the firemen (although the editor himself had a year earlier been attacked by the chief engineer).[74] Neither competition, wagers, boys, nor rowdies could compel the "model fire department of the world" to fight, but politics could.

A highly contested 1857 election for chief engineer would provide the impetus for the "one blow struck in anger" that would, as warned, eat away at the department. A five-vote victory of one candidate over another in 1857 left the San Francisco department badly divided. Until January 1860, when the California Supreme Court finally decided the contested election, the department lacked any consensus as to who was in charge as well as a strong leader to discipline disgruntled firemen. False alarms and other difficulties resulted. In December 1857 the *San Francisco Bulletin* began to report on the "Rowdyism in the Fire Department." After nearly every fire, firemen became "a little ugly." Generally this involved members of different companies squaring off, exchanging dirty looks and threatening remarks. In one example, an engine blocked the path of another company on its way home, "whether by design or not, we can not say," the *Fireman's Journal* reported. After an "unreasonable" delay, "sharp words passed." At that point, matters heated up quickly, at least by the standards of this department. "The foreman of Manhattan company, was observed to have his coat off, and to talk more than the occasion required. . . . Some one halloed out 'Three cheers for Jim Nuttman!' [one of the candidates] and there was a response, which was not calculated to calm the feelings of the companies towards each other. . . . There was considerable noise made, but all ended in smoke." On at least one occasion, blows were exchanged as well as insulting remarks, although examples of "smoke" were far more common.[75]

Sarcastic cheering, passive-aggressive engine placement, a foreman removing his coat: this was not rowdyism as practiced elsewhere in the country. The public recognized this fact, but panicked none the less. "Heretofore, the Department of this city, with a few exceptions, has been a model for similar institutions in the Union. . . . They [the firemen] are of our quiet, orderly, law-abiding citizens, who have discountenanced all attempts at rowdyism or open violations of the peace."

The firemen's restraint can be attributed to the deeply held belief in law and order among San Franciscans in the wake of the 1856 Vigilance Committee. The open antagonism in the fire department appeared to some to be the first step in the fall of the department and a return to the disorder which San Franciscans believed had plagued the city in the early 1850s. "If such a spirit is allowed to gain a foothold, all decent men will leave the Department in disgust, and it will fall into the hands and control of rowdies," wrote the *Bulletin*.[76]

Six months later, with no improvement apparent, the *Bulletin* was nearly hysterical with the possibility of disorder. "When it became evident that if the insurrection was not nipped in the bud, our streets might run in gore, our city be disgraced with such riots as have from time to time occurred in eastern cities . . . it was necessary to take decisive action." The city supervisors "have the benefit of the record of similar difficulties in eastern cities," they pointed out, "and should prevent the difficulties from occurring." The paper also suggested that "it is time for all good citizens, who wish bloody riots prevented, to interfere." Others agreed. One letter writer to the *Bulletin* advised, "In times of insurrection and rebellion, the first step is everything." He suggested that the entire department be abolished, while admitting that "riots, quarrels and disgraceful scenes are unknown" among the firemen. In light of the developments in cities like Baltimore, where many of the members of the San Francisco Fire Department had served, it was perhaps not unreasonable to assume that unchecked riot was just around the corner. But as of yet, that riot had failed to appear.[77]

The first "disgraceful fight" took place in August 1860. "Fists, and even harder weapons were freely used, and numbers of bruised faces and bloody noses attested to the prowess of the rival combatants." Apparently that harder weapon was a fireman's trumpet, and the firemen's paper warned against using "the most dangerous of weapons . . . as sharp as an ax and three times as heavy." Three months later, the foreman of the Volunteer Engine Company was knocked down and beaten with a hose pipe and iron wrench during a fire, by unidentified "members of other companies."[78]

The same tensions motivating these acts of violence appear to be at the heart of the dramatic 1865 firemen's riot in San Francisco, although there are no recorded episodes of fighting in between. Short-term hostilities had been building over several days, as firemen collided at various false alarms and fires. The department picked an extremely bad time to finally riot: Sunday afternoon, December 18, on a street filled with citizens returning from church. The peace of the Sabbath was "suddenly broken by shouts, curses, pistol shots, blows from spanners, billets of wood and paving stones, to the great terror of men, women and children, who fled from the disgraceful scene in the utmost consternation and confusion."

Between five and fifteen shots were fired as the Knickerbocker Fire Company, with assorted members of other companies, battled the combined forces of the Howard and Monumental Companies. The participants were careful not to damage the fire engines, but they did much damage to one another. An assistant foreman was shot through the arm and clubbed on the head. Another fireman was shot in the foot. Several firemen were hit with stones, clubs, and spanners. Chief Engineer Scannell immediately suspended the three companies involved in the brawl. This riot not only justified the warnings of the department's earlier naysayers but furnished "the enemies of the Volunteer system with an unanswerable argument in favor of its early and entire abolition."[79]

After nine years of condemnation for minor acts of violence, one riot was enough to finish off the fragile department. In 1866 the department was disbanded. The San Francisco Volunteer Fire Department, a group which neither sanctioned violence nor regularly engaged in it, was disbanded in the same manner and amidst the same accusations as was the Baltimore Volunteer Fire Department seven years earlier.

Some Conclusions about Fire Department Violence

The decline of the volunteer fire department in the opinion of the public was paralleled by the decline of Mose, who was reduced from a "robust drama-cycle" to "vestigial skit." Mose's principal actor identified the "era of steam fire-engines" as marking the demise of Mose the Bowery B'hoy, but in doing so he mistook cause and effect. For a time in the 1850s, volunteer fire departments could, and sometimes did, support rowdy behavior. A visitor in 1855 observed that Baltimore's fire companies, perhaps the most violent in the nation, were "jealous as Kilkenny cats of one another, and when they come together, they scarcely ever lose an opportunity of getting up a bloody fight. They are even accused of doing occasionally a little bit of arson, so as to get the chance of a row."

Yet this same observer could also write that "when extinguishing fires, they exhibit a courage and reckless daring that cannot be surpassed and they are never so happy as when the excitement of danger is at its highest."[80] This was the era of Mose, the symbol of the fireman who was both a great fighter and a great firefighter. This was also an era when the masculine code of honor that bound firemen in Baltimore had not yet come in conflict with the norms of the larger society.

The separation of fighting and fire fighting, which reduced Mose to an anachronism, was fully accomplished by the "era of the steam-engine," or paid fire department. The strengthening of the police and the decline of other rioting in Baltimore in the 1840s produced the impression that firemen had suddenly become violent in that city. In St. Louis, efforts at refining the city cast that department's behavior in an increasingly negative light. In San Francisco, violence was rooted out and condemned, even where it did not exist.

While it is undeniable that firemen in each of these cities fought in the 1850s, there is no uniform explanation for violence among American volunteer firefighters. Firemen within cities seemed to share a code of behavior that sanctioned some forms of violence, while keeping that violence within certain bounds. Firemen did not share a uniform behavioral code

nationwide, although in all three of these cities the public believed that
their firemen had devolved into an uncontrollable mob by the 1850s.

What this perception reflected was not the reality of violence among
firemen, or uniform changes in class and ethnic composition across departments, but a widespread desire for order in the city. It also reflected a
decreasing tolerance, on the national level, for the masculine culture represented by the character Mose. In Baltimore, firemen were certainly uncontrollable, but this was no new development of the late 1840s. San
Francisco's fire department was far from an unruly mob: the department
remained primarily low white collar through 1860, with a stable ethnic
composition of one-third foreign born. In St. Louis, the most extensive riots expressed nativist hostility on the part of the firemen, yet these incidents had less of an impact on the reputation of the firemen than did lesser
events that threatened the comfort of the polite and refined segments of
the population.

In none of these cities was the behavior of the firemen what it appeared to the public, and in all three departments, Mose was the figure
who came to represent the volunteer firemen. The American volunteer
fireman was celebrated for his violent masculine subculture on the stage,
but he was ultimately destroyed by that same celebrated image. This was
true even when, as in San Francisco, actual volunteer firemen were not
notably violent. Municipal firefighters were not permitted to fight one another, to get drunk at fires, or to otherwise indulge in the excesses for
which the volunteers had gained their infamy. The public order of the late
nineteenth century had no room for masculine pugilists like Mose or for
any version of the masculine honor code that supported the brotherhood
of volunteer firefighters.

Notes

1. B. Baker 1857.
2. Dorson 1943, 288–89.
3. Ibid., 9, 24.
4. B. Baker 1857, 19.
5. Dorson 1943, 295.
6. Grimsted 1972, 365.
7. Doyle 1977, 347; Carnes and Griffen 1990, 48.
8. On the development of urban working-class culture see Gorn 1986 and 1987;

Stansell 1987, chap. 5; Hirsch 1987, chaps. 1, 2, and 5; Rock 1979; Kingsdale 1973. On the crisis in masculinity in general during this period see Johnson and Wilentz 1994.

    9. Statistics on the class and ethnic composition of the volunteer firemen are drawn from research into the census returns and city directories in San Francisco, Baltimore, and St. Louis. See Amy Greenberg 1995, introduction and chap. 3, for more on the failings of a class-based analysis of the volunteer fire department.

    10. Laurie 1980, 58–61, 151–56; Neilly 1959, chap. 9; Wilentz 1984, 258–63.

    11. Statistics based on four fire company rosters. Of the 491 active firemen taken from these lists, 222 individuals were locatable and identifiable in Boyd 1858. The 1858 Mechanical Company roster in McCreary 1901. The 1859 Pioneer Hook and Ladder Company roster, 1857 New Market Company roster, and 1858 Deptford Company roster, all from the special collections at the Peale Museum, Baltimore. Occupational scale drawn from Thernstorm 1975, 289–302. Even given the white-collar bias of city directories in this period, the occupational profile of these Baltimore firemen, the year before municipalization, presents a dramatically different vision of who belonged to a volunteer fire company than that previously presented by historians like Bruce Laurie and Sean Wilentz.

    12. Forrest 1898, 13; Holloway 1860, 3.

    13. Mechanical Fire Company volume of quarterly meetings, 7 December 1813, in the Maryland Historical Society manuscripts division (hereafter MdHS); Union Fire Company records, 3 August 1824, vol. 3, MdHS.

    14. Dukehart 1877; Union Fire Company records, 10 February 1832.

    15. Forrest 1898, 67.

    16. Mechanical Fire Company records, 11 December 1834; Union Fire Company records, 9 January 1835.

    17. Mechanical Fire Company records, 15 September 1839.

    18. Records of the Volunteer Fire Department Standing Committee, 1837, MdHS documents collection.

    19. Mechanical Company records, 15 August 1840.

    20. Ibid., 1834–1840.

    21. Ibid., 1837.

    22. Grimsted 1972, 374; Feldberg 1980, 71–72; Cassedy 1891, 30–31.

    23. Baltimore *Sun*, 20 January 1838. On the potent image of the confidence man in middle-class culture, see Halttunen 1982.

    24. Mechanical Fire Company ledgers, 9 August 1841; J. Baker 1977, 121–22.

    25. Baltimore *Sun*, 21 July 1843, 19 March, 1 April 1844.

    26. Mechanical Fire Company ledgers, 13 April, 2 and 20 September 1847.

    27. Mechanical Fire Company ledgers, 2 December 1847, 22 October 1848; Independent Fire Company ledger, 27 September, 10 December 1847; Forrest 1898, 77.

    28. Baltimore *Sun*, 23 September 1847.

    29. Mechanical Fire Company ledgers, 3 November 1840.

    30. Feldberg 1980, 55–83. Other major "expressive" riots in Baltimore included an earlier Bank of Maryland riot in March 1834 and a Whig-Democratic political riot in April 1834. Neither involved the fire department. See Prince 1985.

    31. Scharf (1874, 528) mentions one, between rowdies and the *Baltimore Clipper* in 1848, after the result of the election for sheriff had been ascertained.

    32. Baltimore *Sun*, 6 and 12 February 1849.

33. Forrest 1898, 67. In 1845 the police cost the city $70,238, in 1850, $110,102, and in 1855 they cost $232,629 (Browne 1980, 156, 203, 210). On uniforms see "The Re-Organization of the Police and Night Watch," Baltimore *Sun,* 29 November 1856; The nineteenth-century expansion of police and their duties has been well documented by historians. See Lane 1975; Monkkonen 1982.

34. J. Baker (1977, 133) points out that the Know-Nothing police stood by passively at election riots.

35. Independent Fire Company ledger, 1850–1855.

36. Baltimore *Sun,* 20 August 1855, 9 September 1856; Cassedy 1891, 43–45; Scharf 1874, 570–71; J. Baker 1977, 129; Forrest 1898, 78–79. That, as Forrest claims, "the elections year after year became less and less free from intimidation and terror" cannot be attributed to the firemen.

37. Dana 1858, 179; Adler 1991, 101–2; Missouri Fire Company records, 29 July 1849, vol. 10, Volunteer Firemen Collection, Missouri Historical Society (hereafter MoHS). A large number of volunteer firemen in St. Louis had Irish surnames, although it is impossible to say whether these members participated in the riot.

38. Union Fire Company records, 30 May 1845, vol. 14, MoHS; Missouri Fire Company records, 5 March 1848.

39. Phoenix Fire Company records, 10 February, 10 March 1845, 9 March 1846, 1 March 1848, vol. 11, MoHS; Lynch 1880, 40.

40. Phoenix Fire Company records, 13 January 1845; Franklin Fire Company minutes, 5 September 1850, vol. 2, MoHS.

41. Laclede Fire Company records, 11 March 1850, MoHS.

42. Missouri Fire Company records, 4 March 1852.

43. Ibid., 16 November 1846, 5 March 1848.

44. Ibid., 18 November 1850.

45. Ibid., 23 July 1854.

46. Union Fire Company minutes, 26 June 1850.

47. Missouri Fire Company records, 11 October 1856; Franklin Company records, 11 October 1856.

48. Franklin Fire Company records, 17 July 1851, 26 September 1854.

49. St. Louis Firemen's Association minutes, 8, 21, and 23 May 1855.

50. E. Edwards 1906, 73.

51. Lynch 1880, 78.

52. E. Edwards 1906, 73.

53. *Missouri Democrat,* 19 July 1854.

54. Laclede Fire Company records, 3 September 1857. On the appeal of fighting among the working class see Gorn 1986.

55. Laclede Fire Company, 12 May 1851; Missouri Fire Company, 25 June 1855, 3 and 18 January 1856.

56. *Mayor's Message,* 14 May 1855.

57. Dykstra 1974, 58.

58. Bushman 1992, 353–401; Adler 1991, 103–9. On the battle over street behavior, see also Ryan 1990, chap. 2; S. Davis 1986.

59. Firemen's Association minutes, 3 July 1855, MoHS.

60. St. Louis Firemen's Fund, *History of the St. Louis Fire Department* (St. Louis, 1914), 168.

61. *Missouri Democrat,* 21 February 1858; E. Edwards 1906, 73, 277–79.

62. Scharf 1883, 796.

63. Lynch 1880, 91. I was unable to find any account of a riot in 1853 in either the *Missouri Democrat* or the *Missouri Republican.* Edward Edwards (1906, 70–71) believes this riot to be a conflation of the riot of 1849 and some other minor dog-related event, resulting from the general disturbances of the period.

64. Scharf 1883, 797; Lynch 1880, 11–13; see also Dorson 1943, 289n. 5.

65. Lynch 1880, 12.

66. *Fireman's Journal,* 4 August 1855.

67. Statistics on the San Francisco volunteer fire department drawn from a voting roster for the 1860 department election. Of the 859 members of the department entitled to vote, 427 were locatable in either the 1860 census or 1860 city directory.

68. *Fireman's Journal,* 4 August 1855.

69. *California Spirit of the Times and Fireman's Journal,* 21 July 1860; Robert S. Lammot, 2 March 1851, in Lammot Family Correspondence, Bancroft Library.

70. *Fireman's Journal,* 9 January, 16 February, 12 July 1856.

71. Ibid., 30 August, 27 September 1856.

72. *San Francisco Bulletin,* 22 and 23 September, 2 October 1856; *Fireman's Journal,* 18 October 1856.

73. *Fireman's Journal,* 4 August 1855 (emphasis in the original); 11 August 1855; 19 April 1856.

74. Ibid., 9 June 1855.

75. *Evening Bulletin,* 9 December 1857, 8 December 1857, 11 May 1858.

76. *Evening Bulletin,* 8, 10, and 12 December 1857.

77. *Evening Bulletin,* 18 May 1858; Dolores Waldorf, "Baltimore Fire Laddie — George Hossefross," *California Historical Society Quarterly* 23 (1944): 69.

78. *Alta California,* 29 August 1860; *California Spirit of the Times and Fireman's Journal,* 1 September 1860; *Alta California,* 23 November 1860.

79. *Alta California,* 18 December 1865.

80. Dorson 1943, 297; Murray 1855, 354–55.

THREE

VIOLENCE AND THE STATE

THE STATE is a major factor in violence per definition. The final three essays discuss the state's role in curbing male aggression and the partial tolerance of aggression by persons in authority. Whether curbing or condoning prevails in a particular society is largely determined by the extent to which the state is able to maintain a monopoly on violence. In a society where such a monopoly has developed only weakly, ruling elites themselves partake of a culture of violence, being likely to appreciate certain forms of private aggression. On this point, the contrast between the centralized United Kingdom and most of the southern United States is obvious: a contrast exacerbated by the issue of race. Acting in an increasingly pacified society, British courts were able to lead the way toward a change in concepts of masculinity; from a position of strength, they consciously strove to curb male violence, criminalizing it to a greater degree than ever before. In the American South, on the other hand, more traditional notions of private violence in defense of one's honor persisted, related to white racial hegemony. The result was a tension between upholding the law (i.e., state power) and condoning at least some forms of lynching. This tension was not fully resolved until after the First World War, which, incidentally, put an end to dueling on the other side of the Atlantic.

These two contrasting situations are studied according to different methods. Whereas the chapter on Britain is analytical and quantitative, the chapters on South Carolina are narrative, making use of case studies. Wiener analyzes the records of various institutions of social control in nineteenth-century Britain and attempts to trace changes in the way these institutions dealt with men and violence. He is able to document a process of change indeed. Typically male forms of behavior, in particular those involving violence, were increasingly proscribed by law. Consequently, a growing proportion of serious criminal prosecutions and punishments were aimed at men. The net result was an increasing criminalization of men. In other words, a new masculinity was created, at the expense of a masculinization of crime.

In the southern United States, old masculinity continued to prevail. The narrative approach of chapters 8 and 9 suits their particular subject. Although they both deal with South Carolina, the themes they discuss have ramifications for the postbellum South as a whole. Moreover, they introduce a new element not discussed so far, that of race. The factor of race not only influenced concepts of honor and masculinity but it also colored the relationships between the state and local communities. This is especially apparent in Kantrowitz's contribution. He pays ample attention to one lynching, a notorious case in the town of Denmark in 1893. The major issues of race, honor, and state control all came together in the Denmark lynching. The chain of events leading to it demonstrated the practical impossibility of Governor Tillman's attempt to reconcile white supremacist justice with the rule of law. Like many other white southern politicians, Tillman identified with the spokesmen for racial hegemony, but he wanted to remain in control of its implementation. In the end he had to cede some measure of control. The Denmark lynching was a clear-cut example of popular (or, rather, nonstate) justice (without the official requirements of due process). Tillman's own views on white supremacy and honor eventually led him to condone this act of nonstate justice.

Masculinity, rather than honor, is the principal issue in Finnegan's case study, dealing with a lynching in Abbeville County in 1916. The men who murdered Anthony Crawford felt that his behavior constituted a challenge to their own male pride. When African Americans aspired to an equality with whites, the existing patriarchal social order was perceived to be at stake. But of course white men's perceptions of their male pride and patriarchal authority were bound up with traditional notions of honor. So, the themes covered by Kantrowitz and Finnegan actually converge. More important, for the overall subject of violence and the state, they both show that lynching meant an encroachment by members of a local community upon state prerogatives, which did not prevent politicians from taking the community's side. The attorney Sam Adams, for example, who ran for the South Carolina legislature in 1916, took a leading role in Crawford's lynching. State control vs. private violence in local communities, then, is a prominent theme in both contributions on the South.

In a way, private justice by white supremacists in the American South resembled the drama of Mafia clan conflict in Sicily at about the same time. In both cases, local communities afterwards pleaded ignorance. When a Mafia hitman had tracked down his opponent, say, in a small-town square on a Sunday afternoon, the square would suddenly become empty. The townspeople knew what was going to happen, but they preferred not to see it. When a southern mob killed an African American, many people did watch, but the case was closed with the classic statement that the victim had met his death at the hands of parties unknown. Willful ignorance prevailed in both situations: in the first for fear of retaliation, and in the second because the witnesses approved of the act. The state's role also was slightly different. Sicilians preferred not knowing, because the Italian state at least had the power to start an investigation and interrogate witnesses. In America, federal institutions had no authority to interfere in individual states' judicial affairs. Southerners could afford to be witnesses, because they knew no one would come to ask them questions.

Based on the essays in part 3, we can formulate a general hypothesis: where state control is weak, older notions of masculinity and a forceful defense of one's honor tend to remain dominant; state strength facilitates the development of a new masculinity and spiritualized notions of honor.

7

The Victorian Criminalization of Men

MARTIN J. WIENER

In recent years much attention has been given to the ways in which "Victorianism" bore down upon women throughout the western world in the nineteenth century. The ideologies of true womanhood and separate spheres have been shown to have enclosed, restricted, and disciplined women through a multitude of practices. Their nature redefined as peculiarly moral and nurturing, Victorian women tended to be more confined to domestic duties than hitherto.[1] Explorations of this gender shift have certainly deepened our understanding of nineteenth-century society. It is time, however, to broaden and deepen our vision yet further. Despite the new appreciation of gender inspired by feminism, comparatively little attention has been paid to the growing pressure of nineteenth-century institutions of social control upon *men*. Feminist historians themselves are beginning to recognize and indeed argue that a gender perspective requires attention to the construction and expression of masculinity as well as femininity.[2] However, such arguments have usually been accompanied by a flattening assumption that gender relations have always and everywhere been structured similarly, with men as the collective exercisers and beneficiaries of power, and women as its collective objects and victims. Such a "power essentialism" does not always encourage the fullest exploration of changing gender constructions in the past. By no means was every mode of "gendering" necessarily to the advantage of men or the disadvantage of women.

A close look at the relations between the criminal law and men in nineteenth-century Britain shows a more complicated picture. If women were being culturally reconstructed and subjected to new gender-based disciplines in the nineteenth century, the same can be said of men. The early Victorian reconstruction of womanhood was paralleled and complemented by a much less well known reconstruction of manhood, and a full understanding of the relations between gender and culture requires that *both* processes (intertwined, of course) receive their due. This essay is therefore not meant to be a complete or balanced account of these relations but, rather, a complement to existing accounts focused on the treatment of women.

Gender and Violence

The most direct institution of social control in nineteenth-century Britain was its rapidly expanding criminal justice system. If this system was in many ways "classed," as many historians have usefully argued, it was also gendered. When historians of the criminal law *have* taken notice of gender, however, it has usually been for one purpose only: to target the stigmatization and control of women, as in the treatment of prostitutes or of unmarried mothers.[3] Yet there is more to be done in bringing gender and justice into fruitful historical interplay. In particular, it is time to examine a little-noted but pervasive pattern emerging in the course of the nineteenth century, in which the law increasingly stigmatized and proscribed long accepted modes of *male* behavior.

Central to "traditional" patterns of male behavior in eighteenth-century Britain was the acceptance of a high degree of physical aggressiveness, both against other men and against women. Men were far more likely than women to exhibit general physical aggressiveness and also to commit outright violence. This was true of early modern Europe in general. As Robert Muchembled has observed of France in the fifteenth through seventeenth centuries, not only were homicide rates far higher than in modern times, but even more, "violence is at the very heart of life" and "especially attached to male roles." He described it as playing a fundamental role in young male life, as cementing group bonds and providing rites of passage into adulthood. The Belgian historian Marie-Sylvie Dupont-Bouchat has recently gone even further. Noting that something like half of all homicides took place in or about taverns, she has found violence to be almost "exclusively a male thing." Similarly, Pieter Spierenburg has recently described a pervasive lower-class male "knife-fighting culture," centered around taverns, in seventeenth-century Amsterdam, which produced remarkably high homicide rates. Eighteenth-century Britain was no exception. In Surrey between 1660 and 1800, about 85 percent of grand jury "true bills" for assault were against men; the proportion actually prosecuted was even higher. Indeed, in eighteenth- and early nineteenth-century Essex, 92 percent of those prosecuted for assault were male.[4]

These figures, of course, are of prosecutions only; yet, as far as we can tell, the bulk of the almost surely much larger domain of unprosecuted interpersonal violence, including behavior (like settling disputes by "fair fights") that was not even clearly disapproved of was *also* male. And if men dominated the ranks of those prosecuted for assault, the same is true of homicide (except for the killing of infants, which required, significantly, much less physical aggressiveness, often being accomplished simply by abandonment). This eighteenth-century pattern was no historical anomaly but, it would seem, deeply rooted. Almost every historical, sociological, and anthropological study of violence has found it to be highly gendered.[5] Indeed, in virtually all times and places, males have accounted for a very disproportionate share of physically aggressive behavior. Of the 241 women officially recorded as murdered in the United Kingdom in 1991, to cite a particularly striking statistic (as well as one close to home), every single known killer was male.[6] We do not need to resolve the long-standing causal debate as to how much of the pronounced gendering of aggression and violence is "natural" and how much "social" or "cultural" to accept the fact that violent behavior has been in the past and is today very disproportionately male.[7] Given that circumstance, any change in the social valuation of physical aggressiveness carries clear gender implications. To increasingly stigmatize and criminalize the personal use of physical force is to very disproportionately stigmatize and criminalize *men*.[8] Such stigmatization and criminalization is precisely what took place, in Britain and elsewhere, in the course of the nineteenth century.

This stigmatization and criminalization of violence would appear to be part of a long drawn-out process of character reshaping in which, throughout "western" societies, internal psychic controls on the expression and immediate gratification of impulses were heightened. This "civilizing process," as Norbert Elias termed it, was probably related to the growth of states, cities, and a market economy — in short, to the structural processes of "modernization," reinforced by the deliberate efforts of increasingly powerful states. Much has been written about the "civilizing process" since Elias coined the term, particularly about its class implications. The "civilizing offensive" that warred on much of the traditional culture of the populace has been identified with the rising bourgeoisie, whose way of life was so much more in harmony with its values and whose interests it could be said to have served.[9] Yet if the process was "classed," it also had specific gender implications that have generally been overlooked. Indeed, more than merely "implications": it is not too much to say that the "civilizing process" was fundamentally and deeply gendered. Just as the universal prescriptions of "civilized" behavior bore down with different force and consequences on the poor and on the rich, they affected men and women differently. The nature of new restrictions on impulsiveness varied: while the "civilizing" of women proceeded particularly around their sexuality (a well-known story), that of men, by contrast, focused primarily around their aggression.[10]

This process, elements of which can be detected from the sixteenth century, accelerated with the breakthrough in the pace of social change in the later eighteenth century. The readiness to resort to violence that lay at the heart of "traditional" manhood was then challenged by several new and rapidly advancing cultural movements. The "culture of sensibility" and the Evangelical religious revival shared a commitment to a "reformation of male manners," an ideological and affective "domestication" of men that complemented their better-known domestication of women. Throughout the new sentimental fiction of the eighteenth century, which drew an unprecedented number of female readers, G. J. Barker-Benfield has shown, "men are depicted as savage hunters, trappers, and fishermen, with women as their prey." Much of this fiction did not merely register anxiety about male predatoriness, but yearned to change men, to make them less frighteningly aggressive: to turn the macho "man of honor" into the domestic "man of feeling."[11] The Evangelical revival, from rather different origins, worked in the same direction. Evangelicals regularly denounced the worship of "honor," and sought to replace it by the conjoined ideals of "sympathy" and "prudence."[12] Accordingly, in the rapidly growing and increasingly influential religious middle classes male selfhood came to depend less on physical virility and more on occupation, on "rational" public activity, and on one's role as husband and father—a shift which was to spread both to the aristocracy and to the working classes during Victoria's reign.[13]

Similarly, the "civilization of the crowd" that both secular and religious reformers of manners opposed was predominantly a male culture, and its most authentic emblem was Punch beating his wife (and child). The Victorian era gradually softened Punch's fierce brutality and aggressive sexuality, turning him from a figure of adult entertainment to one confined to juvenile audiences, as was happening with the wider male culture he symbolized.[14] Domestication was also overtaking the violent and quasi-pornographic popular literatures of "true crime" and criminal fiction that had exploded with the coming together of a mass rudimentary readership and cheap printing early in the century. After describing with outrage the prominent illustrations of brutal and gory crimes displayed in store windows to sell broadsheets and "penny dreadfuls," Charles Dickens's periodical *All the Year Round* asked, "Is it good for the audience of men and boys" that was "never wanting" for such exhibitions "to be familiarised with these things? . . . when the time of temptation comes his nature will be all the less ready to resist, because of the habitual familiarity with violence."[15] Under a combination of overt moralist pressures and a "civilizing" audience, such literature was gradually transmuted into several tamer genres, among them "boys' adventures" and detective fiction.

In such ways, the reaction against the expression and display of violence that steadily advanced in nineteenth-century Britain became closely associated with the specific desire to change men, to redefine the "ideal" or "natural" attributes of masculinity. Indeed, the one exception to the trend to stigmatize, criminally prosecute, and punish more severely more instances of violence underscores its gender affiliations: the only form of violence in which women predominated—the killing of newborn infants—was the one that in certain ways defied this trend, being in fact increasingly likely to be punished less severely than before.[16] It is not that the violence of infanticide became any less shocking; indeed, prosecutions for the noncapital offense of "concealment of birth" (which stood to infanticide roughly as manslaughter stood to murder) *rose* from 1803 (when its penalty was reduced) until about 1865.[17] However, the blame for such violence was progressively shifted to male seducers—men "of dissolute principles," working on "the tender minds of our various females," as one broadside put it, or even to overly punitive fathers.[18] "Let the frailties of human nature be what they may," another broadside writer observed, "and in an unguarded moment a female be led astray and wander in the paths of illicit intercourse; it is much to be regretted that the laws operate so severely against them, and that the finger of scorn is for ever to be pointed at the despised victim of man, and drive them to commit acts at which human nature shudders, rather let us follow the example of him who said on a similar occasion, 'Let him that is without fault cast the first stone at her.'"[19]

As such sentiments were ever more widely accepted, penalties for both concealment of birth and the capital charge of willful child murder became ever milder. After midcentury, almost every convicted "murdering mother" was respited from hanging; as a local petition, supported by the judge, observed in one such case—that of an eighteen-year-old who had killed her three-month-old child—they "deeply pity her, both on account of her youth and in consideration of the gross wrongs she has suffered at the hands of her seducer."[20] During the nineteenth century, capital sentences upon women were ever more widely regarded with horror. As Vic Gatrell has recently noted, "Women whose sufferings ensued from misguided sexual passion or loyalty to powerful men became subjects of sympathy, and male villainy became the active principle in such stories."[21] A sea change in constructions of gender was thus taking place in tandem with a similarly fundamental alteration in constructions of violence, reshaping the cultural context within which criminal justice operated.

The Criminalization of Violence

What was happening, specifically, to legal constructions of "violence"? For eighteenth-century English criminal law, neither in principle nor in practice was personal injury a major concern. Whereas theft of property valued as low as a shilling was a felony, punishable at least in principle by hanging, assault was not—unless the victim died. Even manslaughter—culpable but nonintentional killing—carried a maximum penalty of only a year's imprisonment. Even the minimal sanctions against violence available in law, moreover, were only rarely applied; most cases of private violence in the eighteenth century seem not to have reached the courts, and even those that did were generally viewed as essentially private matters.[22] Sexual violence received even less attention: not only did the law make rape extremely difficult to prove, resulting in a very high acquittal rate, but most complaints of rape or attempted rape seem to have been dismissed by JPs or grand juries without ever reaching trial.[23]

This legal tolerance of interpersonal violence began to change during the second half of the century, with administration preceding the formal law.[24] The treatment of assault hardened in two ways: the size of fines tended to spiral, and courts became increasingly willing to order some time in jail in cases of serious violence. By the 1820s, the typical penalty for most assault convictions had altered from a nominal fine to the clearly harsher one of imprisonment. Similarly, in manslaughter cases by the turn of the century the jury's finding that the victim's death came by way of accident did not necessarily, as earlier, lead to a discharge; in such cases, if offenders had shown recklessness or imprudence, they were increasingly likely to be sentenced to some jail time.[25] Concern for personal security also seems a major motive behind the war on juvenile crime that began in the 1790s and accelerated after 1815. Just as the growing intolerance of violence was chiefly impacting upon men, this new effort against youthful delinquency was disproportionately directed against boys, whose prosecution rose faster than that of girls. Boys, who were far more likely than girls to combine theft with a degree of personal violence, were perceived as a threat in a way that girls were not.[26]

After 1800 judges and juries showed a new interest in prosecuting violence in jurisdictions traditionally outside their sphere, such as among the military and at sea; both these realms, of course, were traditional strongholds of aggressive male culture. Soldiers first appeared in Kent assizes as accused killers in 1806, although that county's dockyards and ports had long been home to an unruly military population. Similarly, it was only after the turn of the century that efforts were made in Kent courts to impose liability upon ships' masters who had killed men under their command.[27]

New legislation increased the potential penalties for violence. Lord Ellenborough's Act in 1803 made possible capital prosecution of attempted murder or even in certain cases of mere attempts to commit serious injury, if firearms or sharp instruments were employed. And Lord Landsdowne's Act in 1828, which replaced the 1803 act, dropped the requirement of use of such weapons. Also in 1828, magistrates in petty sessions were given wider jurisdiction over common assault and battery, including the power to imprison. In 1822 (the same year in which cruelty to animals was first criminalized) the maximum penalty for manslaughter was increased to three years imprisonment or transportation for life; in 1837, while a great many property offenses had their penalties reduced, those for various kinds of assault were raised.[28] All of these measures tended to augment the number and the proportion of men being prosecuted and more severely punished. Even as the number of assault cases prosecuted in London and Middlesex, for example, rose sharply between 1760 and 1830, the proportion of female offenders (always a minority) fell.[29] More prosecutions and convictions for assault thus meant a growing criminalization of men and a complementary "masculinization" of the social perception of "the criminal."

Even more obviously gendered was the new attitude toward killings in defense of honor or status, which began to lose their traditional excusable character. Spokesmen (and spokeswomen) for a broad spectrum of cultural and intellectual movements, from Evangelicalism to Utilitarianism, converged in condemning the masculine culture of honor. Dueling, long technically criminal, now began to be seriously proscribed. In August 1838 a successful prosecution for murder placed the institution in the dock of public opinion: four gentlemen were convicted at the Old Bailey (London's chief criminal court for serious offenses) of murder for a death resulting from a duel on Wimbledon Common; although the mandatory death sentence was of course commuted, they did suffer a rather severe twelve months' imprisonment, which marked a watershed in judicial treatment of dueling. Within a few years the military code was revised to provide severe penalties for the practice. This was paralleled for the lower classes by a hardening official attitude toward pugilism, whose practitioners were increasingly liable to criminal prosecution if serious harm or death resulted. Following his 1875 decision to award only a week's imprisonment to participants in a working-class "set fight" in which a man died, Mr. Justice Brett was roundly criticized for leniency by the *Times*. "It is one of the first conditions of civilised society," the newspaper announced, "not to mention Christianity or morality, that men should abstain from fighting out their quarrels, and that they should be content to seek from the law the redress of any real injury they may suffer. The mass of people are not of so mild a temper that a laxer doctrine can be safely encouraged among them."[30]

In line with this custom, the leading stimulant of violence, drunkenness, was becoming less likely to mitigate one's responsibility for disorderly behavior. In sentencing one wife slayer at the Old Bailey in 1839, Mr. Justice Parke observed that "the barbarity of the act admitted of no excuse, and only one circumstance could possibly be suggested as to the cause of the dreadful crime — namely, that he was intoxicated at the time. The law, however, could never admit intoxication as an excuse for such a heinous offense; for if it did, the most dreadful crimes, many of which were committed under the baneful excitement of drink, would go unpunished."[31] As another judge declared in an 1865 case of wife murder, "To have one law for drunken or angry and another for sober or quiet people would be subversive of all justice and order in this country."[32] Correspondingly, the Home Office was ever less likely to make allowances for drunkenness in deciding on reprieves from capital sentences. In the 1839 case, despite a deputation to the Home Office that included sheriffs and aldermen, the man was hanged. The Home Secretary told the deputation that "he regretted to say that murders committed under the excitement of drink had become of late so frequent, that it was necessary an example should be made."[33]

What was applied to drunkenness held also for other forms of loss of self-control. In 1852, Mr. Justice Cresswell, later to be placed in charge of the new divorce court (and there to become the single most influential arbiter of Victorian marriage behavior), rejected an accused wife-murderer's plea for reduction of the charge to manslaughter by reason of provocation by taunting language, emphasizing the traditional, but oft-ignored, points of law that words could form no justification for mortal violence and that death produced by a willful and unprovoked blow was murder, although the blow may have been given in a moment of passion or intoxication.[34] In the realm of violence against women, judges tended to be ahead of the broader (male) public (or just more generally punitive): here, for example, despite Cresswell's argument, the jury (probably focusing on the defendant's apparent drunkenness) found the lesser verdict of manslaughter. It was only gradually that the taunts of "bad" wives or tavern-fellows ceased to be readily allowed by juries as provocation in assault and homicide cases. Nonetheless, the trend throughout the century was clearly in the direction of more severe prosecution of such violence.[35]

Both Victorian antidrink campaigns and Victorian feminism drew much of their emotional force and moral authority from denunciation of male violence, particularly against women and children. Judges increasingly joined in such denunciations, not just on behalf of long-suffering domestic "angels," but even where the violence had been clearly provoked by bad wifely behavior. The highly publicized 1819 case of Henry Stent may have marked a watershed in this regard: Stent, a respectable middle-class man, attacked his wife, attempting but failing to kill her, after she had run away with a lover and then, remorseful, sought to return. Although judge and jury expressed sympathy with Stent, he was nonetheless convicted of attempted murder and imprisoned for two years.[36] In 1841 James Taylor, a Salisbury pig-dealer, shot his wife to death after she eloped with a man who had lodged in his house. He was promptly convicted of murder. The jury urged mercy, and many leading citizens of Salisbury, "taking into account the circumstances under which the crime was committed," petitioned for clemency; however, the judge withheld his support for their plea, and the man hanged.[37] At every level of the criminal justice system, men were increasingly expected to exercise a greater degree of control over themselves than ever before.

Judges, juries, and lawmakers also began to display a new attitude toward sexual violence. Prosecutions and convictions for sexual assault rose after 1800, and legislation in 1828 removed the need to prove seminal emission in rape, making any degree of penetration, if forced, sufficient. This change in the law had a double significance: practically, it made prosecution easier while, ideologically, it more clearly defined the offense as one of violence rather than of illegitimate taking, a crime against a woman as a person rather than as the property of her husband or father. Anna Clark has minimized the "progressive" aspect of this alteration, arguing that it was not a desire to convict rapists but "moral objections to women recounting explicit details in open court [which] seem to have provided the main impetus behind the 1828 legislation."[38] However, while one can readily grant that the rise of sexual prudery and an ideology of female purity was operating here, to see the change *only* as "silencing" women, as Clark does, and not also stigmatizing and criminalizing their assailants, seems much too one-sided. For the prosecution of sexual assault did eventually rise markedly—if not in the early Victorian years, then in the second half of the century (aided by the undoubtedly puritanical Criminal Law Amendment Act of 1885, which among other things made it easier to prosecute molesters of young girls).

At the same time, both judicial tolerance and popular acceptance of violence against wives were fading. The shaming sanction of "rough music" came to be deployed less against female scolds and male cuckolds and more against wife-beaters.[39] In the 1820s newspapers, seeking to boost their circulation, lowered their prices and turned to exposing crimes against women. Even the comparatively expensive *Sunday Times* followed innovating Sunday papers like *Lloyd's* and *Reynolds'* by expanding its coverage of "dreadful" and "horrible" crimes, particularly murders and rapes. By the 1840s, this journalistic turn had become a well-nigh universal preoccupation.[40] Although some of these sensationalizing news stories had female villains (a poisoner was always a good seller), among the "heavies" men clearly predominated.

At all levels the courts were paying growing attention to domestic violence. After summary jurisdiction was extended in 1828 to common assault and battery, providing a cheaper and quicker venue than jury trial for complaint and remedy, abused wives came to form a larger part of the growing business of magistrates' courts.[41] And in the higher courts, judges increasingly pressed reluctant juries to punish life-threatening violence against spouses, heaping some of their fiercest abuse on convicted wife-killers.

As much of the press, and most of the judges, took up the cause of reforming men, domestic violence for the first time entered national political debate, leading to the first legislative measure specifically addressing the problem. The 1853 Act for the Better Prevention of Aggravated Assault upon Women and Children set the first clear ceiling on the degree of "chastisement" permitted husbands and fathers. The act extended summary jurisdiction to aggravated assaults, and allowed magistrates, without juries, to punish attacks on all females and on males under fourteen that resulted in actual bodily harm by up to six months imprisonment with hard labor (raised in 1868 to one year).[42] Prodded by voluntary bodies like the Society for the Protection of Women and Children from Aggravated Assaults, founded in 1857, which sent observers into magistrate's courts, this trend to criminalize violence against women continued through the late nineteenth century, with prosecutions for assaults on females rising even as total prosecutions for assault (most of which were male-on-male) began to fall.[43] Every decade produced new legislation—in 1878, 1886, and 1895—providing increased legal recourse, both criminal and civil, for victims of marital violence. Such measures reflected two desires, interrelated but distinct: to better protect women and to reform men. As one MP observed in introducing a bill in 1856 to make such violence punishable by flogging, the issue was at root not a woman's but "a man's question. . . . It concerned the character of our own sex, that we should re-press these unmanly assaults; and he believed that upon the men who committed them they had a worse and more injurious effect than they had upon the women who endured them."[44]

Meanwhile, the draconian earlier penalties for property crime (in which women formed a higher proportion of offenders than in crimes against the person) were being reduced, in particular by the wholesale re-moval of capital offenses. After the passage of the Criminal Law Consoli-dating Acts in 1861, although by modern standards crimes of theft were still punished severely and crimes of violence lightly, the relative scale of penalties for these two types of offense had been significantly rearranged. This rearrangement continued, as the next few decades witnessed re-peated violence "crises" like the "garroting panic" of the sixties and the excited discussions in the seventies about a supposed wave of "brutal assaults" on women and children, both of which produced official in-quiries, new legislation, heightened penalties, and increased propensities to prosecute.

Even beyond criminal law the same gender tendencies were at work. Marriage law, which was in the nineteenth century quasi-criminal in its use of public stigmatization, was also moving to rein in male aggressive-ness. In that domain the concept of violence began to expand in 1790, in Lord Stowell's ruling in *Evans v. Evans* that "apprehension" of violence, though it had to be "reasonable," could take the place of actual violence as grounds for divorce. The impact of this concession was limited not only by judicial conservatism but by the very small amount of divorce litigation under the extremely restrictive procedures in effect before 1857. The cre-ation of the divorce court in that year, as James Hammerton has recently shown, widened the stream of litigation and accelerated the development of case law: within the next few years the threshold of "reasonableness" for such apprehensions was lowered by a series of rulings. At the same time, the threshold of provocation for marital violence was raised: a greater degree of wifely misbehavior came to be necessary to excuse hus-bandly violence.[45] Nor was divorce the only form of civil litigation fur-nishing increased opportunities for stigmatizing and "punishing" bad men. Growing numbers of actions for seduction and for breach of promise of marriage, at home and in the colonies, were providing the scandal-hungry press with new male targets.[46]

The Criminalization of Men

As more crimes against the person were defined and prosecuted, and as conviction and the severity of punishment, in crimes against property as well as against the person, came increasingly to depend upon the degree of violence or threat to personal security involved, the ranks of those criminally prosecuted and, even more, of those punished became ever more male. The total prosecutions of females at assizes and quarter sessions between 1805 and 1842 rose four times, from 1,338 to 5,569, which certainly seems large; but in the same period prosecutions of males rose eight times, from 3,267 to 25,740. Although this expansion of prosecution thereafter slowed markedly, and later in the century reversed, the gender trend continued. Just as the rise in prosecution, conviction, and incarceration in the first half of the century had been disproportionately concentrated on males, so the decline in the late nineteenth century was disproportionately female.[47] An emerging disenchantment with the use of imprisonment focused first on its use for women.[48] At the same time, while a growing number of deviant women were coming to be seen as mentally ill and were diverted to asylums and reformatory institutions, this psychiatrizing tendency was slower to affect deviant males.[49] As a consequence, the proportion of men prosecuted at the Old Bailey, which had risen from an eighteenth-century average of about two-thirds to about three-quarters in the 1820s, rose to almost 90 percent by the end of the century.[50] On a national level, men formed an increasing proportion of those proceeded against by indictment (the more serious form of criminal proceeding), rising from 73 percent of the total in 1857 to 81 percent by 1890.[51] Moreover, throughout the century male defendants remained somewhat more likely to be convicted and to receive longer sentences and thus formed an even higher proportion of those undergoing criminal punishment. By 1900, more than 85 percent of inmates of local prisons (for short sentences) and about 96 percent of convict (longer sentence) prisoners were male.[52]

This "masculinization" of crime and punishment was one of the most notable, but least noticed, facts of nineteenth-century British (and, indeed, western) criminal justice history.[53] It suggests not only an increasing "male" focus on the part of the criminal justice system but, even more, a long-term expansion and intensification of the legal disciplining of men relative to women. This was a development of the greatest importance for the shaping of modern society and culture, but it has been sadly neglected. The new attention to gender in history ought to help end that neglect.

Notes

1. At least as an ideal and goal: in practice, economic pressure ensured that many women — even married women — continued to be employed outside the home.

2. For examples, see Allen 1990, pt. 1, sec. 2; Dubinsky 1993, 168; more theoretically, Howe 1994, 158.

3. On prostitution, see Backhouse 1985; Levine 1993; Mahood 1990; Walkowitz 1980. On unmarried mothers, see Higginbotham 1989. A sociological counterpart of these historical works is Cain 1989.

4. Beattie 1986, 404; Dupont-Bouchat 1994; King 1996; Muchembled 1987; Spierenburg 1994.

5. See, for example, Counts, Brown, and Campbell 1992; Gottfredson and Hirschi 1990, 144–49; Muchembled 1987; Riches 1986.

6. *Independent on Sunday*, 12 January 1992.

7. However one wants to explain it, this well-nigh universal gender gap in regard to violence cannot be ignored. Some feminist criminologists have indeed begun to focus their attention on this apparently universal gender difference: for example, Maureen Cain (1990, 11) has recently declared that "the most consistent and dramatic finding from Lombroso to post-modern criminology is not that most criminals are working class — a fact which has received continuous theoretical attention from all perspectives — but that most criminals are and always have been *men*. Yet so great has been the gender-blindness of criminological discourse that men as males have never been the objects of the criminological gaze." Indeed, Judith Allen (1989, 19) has somewhat melodramatically observed that "the spectre of sex [now] haunts criminology," and she has gone on to suggest that "the capacity to explain the high sex ratio and sexed character of many criminal practices might be posed as a litmus text for the viability of the discipline."

8. And *young* men in particular, more prone to violence than their elders. As a diminishing tolerance of violence worked to "masculinize" crime, it also worked to "juvenilize" it (another important story, but one not to be dealt with here). As the female proportion of criminal offenders declined, the average offender's age also declined.

9. See Elias 1978; Lagrange 1993; Muchembled 1985; Rousseaux 1993; Wrightson 1982.

10. Indeed, this disciplining of males continued through the twentieth century, even as the sexual disciplining of females relaxed. See the comparative remark of an Australian feminist scholar that "the masculinisation of criminality rather than the sexualisation of female delinquency" is the more pressing question in contemporary criminal justice: Carrington 1990, 31.

11. Barker-Benfield 1992, 234. See also Armstrong 1987.

12. See Andrew 1980; McGowen 1986.

13. See Davidoff and Hall 1987; Trumbach 1978.

14. Leach 1985.

15. "Nothing like Example," *All the Year Round* 19 (30 May 1868), 585.

16. For important evidence, see Monholland 1989; Morgan 1993.

17. Emmerichs 1993, 108; see also Behlmer 1982, 18.

18. Quoted broadside in Gatrell 1994, 169.

19. "A full and particular account of the apprehension and taking of Anne and Mary Brinkworth, for the willful murder of the infant child of Anne Brinkworth, 15 September 1824."

20. Public Record Office, HO45/9358/31576 (case of Elizabeth Ellen Trevett, 1874). The judge recommended a mere three months imprisonment; the home secretary, concerned about such a precedent in a year of moral panic about violent crime, demurred and awarded six years.

21. Gatrell 1994, 336; Gatrell describes the growth of a trope of "the wronged woman" in early nineteenth-century reform discourse. See similar observations in Backhouse 1984 and 1986.

22. Beattie 1985, 42–43, 49–50; also Beattie 1986, 75–76, 457–61; Emsley 1987, 141.

23. Simpson 1986, 123 and passim. At the Old Bailey between 1770 and 1800, out of forty-three men tried for rapes of females over twelve, only three were found guilty (and two of them had raped fourteen-year-old girls). See Clark 1987, 58. Clark also found that in the northeast circuit in the later eighteenth century, only one out of three men accused of raping adult women was actually tried (ibid., 54).

24. Popular tolerance also seems to have entered a decline around this time: examples of execution-crowd execration of murderers cited by Gatrell (1994) all date from after 1820.

25. Beattie 1985, 48–49; Beattie 1986, 609; King 1996.

26. See King and Noel 1993. The inference concerning violence is mine. King and Noel suggest that, with the decline of the predominantly male institution of apprenticeship and the gradual feminization of domestic service, job opportunities in London for young males may have been declining in this period, rendering them more likely to fall into crime.

27. Cockburn 1991, 88–89.

28. Stephen 1884, 79, 116–17.

29. See G. Smith 1995. The gender proportion of the rising numbers indicted for assault in Essex remained about 92 percent male (King 1996, 55).

30. *Times*, 10 April 1875. The more severe attitude was evident in the appeal case of *R. v. Coney* (1881–82), in which, although the conviction of witnesses to a prizefight of aiding and abetting a felonious assault was narrowly quashed, all the judges agreed in denouncing the barbarity of the event (Cox Crim. Cases 46).

31. "Sorrowful lamentation of William Lees, now under sentence of death at Newgate" (1839).

32. Mr. Justice Mellor, *Times*, 6 March 1865.

33. *Times*, 17 December 1839. The Home Office also refused to intervene in the 1865

case noted above. For the official dismissal of drunkenness as a mitigating factor in Home Office reprieve decisions in the second half of the century, see Chadwick 1992, 383.

34. *R. v. Noon* (1852), 6 Cox Crim. Cases 137.

35. See Chadwick 1992, 383, and Conley 1991, chaps. 2 and 3. The same trend is evident in the United States: see Lane 1979, 68–76.

36. Morgan 1993, 146–47. He was sentenced to death with a strong recommendation to mercy, and the sentence then was commuted to two years imprisonment.

37. *Times*, 13 and 18 March 1841.

38. Clark 1987, 60, 63; Morgan 1993, chap. 5.

39. Thompson 1972. Thompson has more recently qualified this claim: Thompson 1991, 467–538. While similarly cautioning about the excessive Whiggism of this view of rough music, A. James Hammerton (1992) nonetheless provides additional evidence of rising early Victorian concern, popular as well as middle-class, about domestic violence.

40. Even the *Times* followed: in the decade 1810–19, it reported 48 cases of rape; in the following decade, it reported 147; its coverage of domestic violence also expanded sharply. Some examples from the 1840s are cited in Knelman 1993.

41. See J. Davis 1989, 418–19.

42. See May 1978.

43. Gatrell 1980, 291. A local study that bears out this national trend is Emmerichs 1991.

44. Lewis Dilwyn, M.P.: Hansard's Parliamentary Debates, 3d series, House of Commons, 7 May 1856, 142, col. 169.

45. Hammerton 1992, 120–29.

46. See Backhouse 1986; Coombe 1988; Frost 1991.

47. See Gatrell and Hadden 1972, 392–93 (table 3). Even as the total number of persons apprehended for indictable offenses (those more serious offenses which had not been turned over to summary jurisdiction) fell between 1857 and 1890 by almost half (from 32,031 to 17,678), the female proportion of this declining total fell from 26.9 percent to 19.3 percent. The female proportion of those committed for trial and those convicted and imprisoned fell even more. See Zedner 1991, 316–23.

48. See Wiener 1990, 309–10.

49. See R. Smith 1981; Zedner 1991.

50. Feeley and Little 1991, 722.

51. Zedner 1991, 36.

52. Annual reports of the prison commissioners; annual criminal statistics.

53. It also seems to have been true in western Europe and North America: as early as 1975 the study of criminal justice developments in France suggested to Michelle Perrot that a "fear of young men came to permeate" nineteenth-century French society; for women, on the other hand, "their weight on the scales of Justice became lighter." The percentage of French women arraigned declined from 19 percent in assize courts and 22 percent in lesser courts of correction in 1826–30 to 14 percent in both by 1902 (Perrot 1975; translated and republished in *Deviants and the Abandoned in French Society*, ed. Robert Forster and Orest Ranum [Baltimore: Johns Hopkins University Press, 1978]). Helen Boritch and John Hagan (1990), studying Toronto from 1859 to 1955, described a similar shift in the gender ratio of criminal involvement.

8

White Supremacist Justice and the Rule of Law: Lynching, Honor, and the State in Ben Tillman's South Carolina

STEPHEN KANTROWITZ

In June 1892, before an audience of white Democratic primary voters, South Carolina's incumbent governor took an aggressive stand on lynching. Demanding that the rule of law be respected, Ben Tillman promised to remove local sheriffs who allowed prisoners in their custody to be seized and lynched. Although this position deviated from the general rule of white men's local autonomy in matters of crime and punishment, Tillman's words would most likely not have surprised his audience. Barely a year and a half before, in his inaugural address, the governor had called the lynching of black South Carolinians "infamous" and "a blot on our civilization." Then and since, he had demanded that criminals be punished by legal means. "Every Carolinian worthy [of] the name," Tillman had insisted, "must long to see the time when law shall reassert its sway."

But in June 1892, this was not the whole of Tillman's position on lynch law. A mere moment after declaring his hostility to lynching—indeed, in almost the very same breath—Tillman offered a crucial caveat: he himself would "willingly lead a mob in lynching a negro who had committed an assault upon a white woman." Law and order were suddenly cast aside in favor of vigilante justice, with the governor himself not only cooperating but taking a leading role.[1]

Those familiar with Tillman's reputation as one of the period's foremost white supremacist spokesmen may be tempted to focus on his justification for lynching and to dismiss his condemnation as simple hypocrisy. This would be a serious mistake. Tillman's need to take both positions at once flowed directly from the nature of his white supremacist program. To explain why this was so, we must consider the historical context in which Tillman came to power and the conflicting political imperatives that confronted him. Seeking to ensure the political and economic primacy of white farmers through a strengthened state government, Tillman not only had to wrestle with the aspirations of African Americans and the white Conservative Democratic opposition; he had to find ways to respond to the vigilante acts of his own core constituency. The authority of the state to shape or limit the violent local enforcement of white supremacy was at stake in this mediation. So were the lives of black South Carolinians. In the pages that follow, we will then see how rival groups of South Carolinians joined the debate over lynching and how their contributions reflected their competing conceptions of race, justice, and honor.

Tillman's Rise to Power

Ben Tillman's 1892 pronouncement on lynching reflected the complex, sometimes contradictory lessons that white men had learned. Since emancipation in 1865, and especially during Reconstruction, southern white men had encountered substantial challenges to their local and regional dominance, often for the first time in their lives. The expansion of state government under Reconstruction Republican rule, ranging from labor laws to state-mandated public education, helped South Carolina's black majority attain a measure of political power and economic progress. In the mid-1870s, white Democrats (Ben Tillman among them) responded by seeking to overthrow the biracial Republican government. In 1876, their campaign of terrorist violence succeeded, and control of the state government returned to the all-white leadership of the Democratic Party.[2]

This successful insurrection was dubbed "Redemption," but the Redeemer regime had no plan for bringing prosperity to most white men. As a result, during the cotton depression of the 1880s many grew dissatisfied with the state's new leadership. White dissidents' options were limited, for those disgruntled enough to participate in political alliances with black Republicans were quickly brought to heel by the same white Democratic violence that had brought Reconstruction to an end. But discontent seethed within "the white man's party."

A new avenue for white political protest opened up in the late 1880s, when Ben Tillman took advantage of his reputation as a loyal Democratic partisan to lead a revolt against the party leadership. A wealthy planter whose family had once owned more than a hundred slaves, Tillman was an unlikely champion for poor and middling white men. But Tillman artfully sidestepped the issue of his wealth. He succeeded in defining the political contest as a struggle between "the farmers"—white males employed in agricultural pursuits, whatever their economic position—and their various enemies: aristocratic Democratic leaders, who looked down on them while taking their votes for granted; white northern capitalists, whose monopolistic practices brought agricultural hardship; and black South Carolinians, whose efforts at political power and economic independence threatened the very foundations of agriculturally oriented white supremacy.

Although Tillman attacked both Democratic and Republican policies, his rise to power in 1890 was not based on a reactionary opposition to government as such. To the contrary, Tillman argued that the state government could—and, properly, should—act as the agent and benefactor of "the farmers"; that is, it should safeguard the economic and political independence of poor and middling white men. In Tillman's vision, the state government would provide white farmers and their families with education in the latest farming techniques, enact laws and initiate lawsuits to protect them from corporate exploitation, and defend their racial interests against federal intrusion. Tillman therefore rejected the Populist movement's call for federal intervention in economic affairs: instead, he contrasted the potential benefits of agriculturally oriented state power with the perils of federal intrusion, whether by malevolent Republicans or misguided Populists. Tillman drew support from a broad spectrum of white voters, including those who might have joined the more radical Populist movement as well as those dissatisfied with the status quo but jealous of local autonomy. He won the 1890 Democratic nomination for governor, beat back a conservative-led biracial challenge, and took control of the state.

Tillman's victory over the conservatives was just one phase in an ongoing conflict between two very different conceptions of the state's future.
This conflict, rooted in the broad social and economic geography of South
Carolina, reflected deep divisions and ambivalences regarding the economic transformation of the state. By the standards of industrialized, ur-
banized states to the north, South Carolina was socially and economically
backward, but white Democrats were divided over how to interpret and
respond to that "backwardness." Some Democrats, mainly self-described
conservatives, sought to limit state oversight and corporate taxation in order to attract northern capital to South Carolina and advance its industrialization. Others, including Tillman's farmers' movement, the Farmers'
Alliance, and the Populists, saw agriculture as intrinsically preferable to
industry; they feared that industrialization, subsidized by state tax incen-
tives, would bind white men ever more tightly to a corrupt and oppressive
world market ruled by conspiratorial financial and corporate interests.
Not even the most ardent supporters of either vision of the state's future
could claim perfect consistency, but there were dramatic differences in
outlooks, tactics, and goals between the two viewpoints.[3]

Each vision also included its own set of ideas about the meaning of
white supremacy, the rule of law, and the best way for the state government to help South Carolina prosper. Each claimed to be defending some
concept of "honor," but each meaning of honor implied a different kind of
masculine prerogative. Corporate-oriented white men argued that only
strict adherence to the rule of law would erase South Carolina's bloody
reputation and make the state attractive to northern capital; from this perspective, the most important "reputation" at stake was that of the (argu-
ably feminized) state as a field for outside investment. Agrarian-oriented
white men did not entirely reject the idea that the state's reputation deserved protection, but they were far more concerned with defending
white farmers against corporations that reaped undue profits, political opponents who sought to mobilize black voters, and black people who themselves sought political or economic equality.

But the apparent victory of Tillman's state-oriented program was only
part of the legacy he brought with him to Columbia in 1890. Tillman
sought to protect white men's prerogatives through the operation of the
law, but under certain circumstances he approved of other means and
supported the "unwritten" or "higher law" of vigilante justice. In broad

terms, Tillman and his supporters believed that white men had certain rights beyond those laid out in the law: they expected to be able to police their households and communities and to administer an informal but severe "justice" when circumstances required. In practice, white men decided among themselves which infractions could wait for the law to run its course and which challenged their authority, manhood, and independence and thus their honor.

This localist tradition had governed law enforcement in antebellum South Carolina, and in the years after Reconstruction's overthrow, criminal justice was increasingly understood to mean the enforcement of white supremacy.[4] When writing for northern consumption, white southern officials might deny that this was true, but they protested too much.[5] Even white Democratic newspapers admitted that justice was meted out in a racially discriminatory way.[6] Commenting on the Edgefield Court's session of November 1891, the Charleston *News and Courier* noted that "every criminal [not, the reader will note, suspect or prisoner] is a negro," and "up to this writing, not a single verdict of not guilty has been found."[7]

Frequently, however, white men ignored the forms of law entirely. Violence was a crucial component of white Democratic dominance, from the 1870s through the 1890s, as organized bands of white men broke up Republican and independent political meetings and black laborers' organizations. The threats, beatings, and murders through which white men asserted their dominance over black people violated the law, often brazenly. This readiness to resort to extralegal violence was part of the arsenal of white supremacist rule; it was as much a part of Tillman's white supremacy as the more formal ideas and policies he promoted. The right of white male property holders to a monopoly on violence—with or without recourse to the forms of law—was essential to the "white men's government" for which Tillman had fought in the 1870s and 1880s.

Violence is, of necessity, subject to political interpretation; as historian Drew Gilpin Faust has noted, "Killing is honorable under some circumstances, indictable under others."[8] In the eyes of most white Democrats, the substitution of white supremacist justice for the rule of law was entirely legitimate, and many murders of blacks by whites in postemancipation South Carolina were thereby transformed into "honorable" deeds. The success of white supremacist violence had also made murderers, among them Ben Tillman, into political heroes. This meant that when he came to power in 1890, it was with a history of extralegal violence that took in both his participation in Reconstruction-era massacres and his home county's bloody reputation.[9]

Once he became governor, however, Tillman found himself in the predictably difficult position of representing both the rule of law and the transformative project of white supremacist reform. He was no longer responsible for upholding only the "higher law" of white supremacy; he had sworn to uphold the laws of the state as well. Tillman therefore had both to carry out the intrinsically conservative responsibilities of his office and attempt to use those powers to accomplish the "reform" he had promised.

Further, his agricultural, financial, and educational reform program depended heavily on the state for legitimacy and enforcement. Tillman was already looking toward the national stage, hoping to forge a national coalition of white farmers and industrial workers. The successful exercise of the state's educational and protective functions would, he hoped, demonstrate the national applicability of his reform vision; a reputation for indiscriminate violence would only undermine his ability to attract white men who were neither southerners nor Democrats. Thus, to achieve his short-term and long-term goals, Tillman needed to make it clear that South Carolinians respected the rule of law — at least, the rule of *his* law. Tillmanism in power therefore faced a difficult, perhaps impossible, task: to support the practice of informal white supremacist "justice" without subverting the authority of the state.

The Rape-Lynch Complex

White women's sexuality constituted a crucial defensive perimeter for white supremacy. During the 1890s, southern whites came to understand black people's challenge to white supremacy in sexual terms. If black men and white women married or had children together, more than white men's primacy of sexual access to women would be challenged: "whiteness" itself would be undermined. And since partisans of white supremacy could not admit that any respectable white woman would voluntarily participate in what they called "mongrelization," they saw such interracial liaisons as by definition forced and thus as proof that black men's sexuality was brutal and uncontainable.

This was the culmination of a gradual shift which had been under way since at least Reconstruction, in which white supremacy's archvillain was transformed from a corrupt Republican politician into a brutal black rapist.[10] This "black beast rapist," perpetrating what newspapers and politicians often referred to as "outrageous assaults," or simply "outrages," emerged as the prime embodiment of the forces threatening white supremacy.[11] Many white South Carolinians therefore presented lynching — defined broadly as a group's appropriation of the forms of law to kill without due process — as a defense of white womanhood against a fearsome construction of black men's sexuality.[12] As the 1880s gave way to the 1890s, white southerners increasingly resorted to lynching.

This white supremacist analysis of lynching and its causes did not go unchallenged. During the 1890s, crusaders against lynching such as Ida B. Wells-Barnett and Frederick Douglass frequently pointed out that only a third of all lynchings were even purportedly in retaliation for acts of rape or attempted rape. They pointed to economic conflict, not sexual crimes or liaisons, as the source of most acts of lynching, and they saw apologists' constant references to the "outrageous assault" and the "brute in human form" as cynical, rhetorical sleight-of-hand.[13]

This critique was a well-taken corrective to the mythology of the day, but in focusing on the contradictions and hypocrisies surrounding lynching, it did not fully explain the context and meaning of white supremacist violence.

First, sexual and economic life were not so readily divorced as Victorian proprieties (or analyses of lynching's causes) normally demanded. The separation of public and private spheres was less a reality than an argument; it was therefore in constant danger of contradiction and defeat. In practice, "equality before the law" in a late nineteenth-century southern community meant that black men and women entered physical and social spaces — sites of local commerce, leisure, and government — from which they had formerly been excluded. This social and political movement occurred at precisely the moment that white men faced unprecedented challenges to their economic and local political authority; for many white men, these challenges appeared to constitute one massive, multifaceted assault on their way of life. According to this interpretation, no aspect of white men's authority would remain uncontested, not even their patriarchal sexual authority over their wives and daughters. Black people's movement into workplaces, political arenas, and public accommodations would logically be followed by entry into previously restricted household spaces as well; black men would gain proximity to, authority

over, and finally sexual access to white women.[14] This slippery slope was
the fearsome "social equality" that white supremacists constantly invoked,
and its end result would be not just the end of white-skin privilege but the
end of whiteness itself.[15] The continuing efforts of some southern black
politicians to abolish laws forbidding racial intermarriage, and the marriage of prominent black leaders such as Frederick Douglass to white
women, helped to bolster this perception.

Second, the economic and information structures of the post-
Reconstruction South worked together to increase white paranoia about
black men's sexual predation of white women and girls. Crimes allegedly
committed by black men against white women, chiefly rape and attempted
rape, were held up as justification for nearly half of all lynchings over
most of South Carolina between 1881 and 1895. Rape-related accusations
also drew the largest crowds and were thus perhaps more likely to be seen
and understood as "lynchings" than simply as murders.[16] Many southern
newspapers obsessively repeated reports of rapes and lynchings from all
over the region, creating a kind of journalistic feedback loop that distorted
and disguised social reality. The end result was that a highly disproportionate number of those lynchings about which white southerners read or
heard were committed following allegations of rape or attempted rape. At
the same time, black men looking for seasonal work during a long economic downturn migrated across the South in ever-increasing numbers,
each "stranger" becoming a potential rapist in the eyes of suspicious
whites.[17]

By the early 1890s, white supremacists found a significant audience
for their claim that black and white men were engaged in a war to the
death over white women's sexuality. Lynching's brutal theater of racial
and gender power became an essential white supremacist ritual. But despite their constant claims to be protecting "white womanhood," many in
the lynch mobs knew that this was more the battlefield than the objective
of the war. White women's sexuality was a medium through which some
men sought dominance over others.[18]

A brief example will demonstrate how this could operate. During the
bloody summer of 1893, after three black South Carolina men were accused of raping a white woman, the lynch mob gave special consideration
to the feelings of the man whom the *News and Courier* referred to as "the injured husband." When the third of the accused men was captured, the
sheriff waited for the husband's request before turning the captive over to
the mob. With the husband's consent and cooperation, the lynchers tor-

tured the men before hanging them and shooting repeatedly into their dead bodies, with what one reporter called "a refinement of cruelty and torture that nearly everyone who witnessed it thought deserved."[19]

Lynch mobs operated "behind the mask of chivalry," enforcing white men's economic, political, social, and sexual prerogatives but expressing these primarily in terms of the protection of an idealized white woman-hood. Lynching black men could also work to control which white women were "respectable" and which were not.[20]

When Jake Davis, a black man, was lynched for allegedly attempting to rape the wife of a "respectable" white Abbeville man, a reporter noted that Davis had "committed an assault on a white woman in this community a few years ago, but as her character was questionable he was [on that occasion] allowed to go unpunished." On another occasion, Tillman pardoned a convicted rapist (race unspecified) "on the ground that the woman in the case was of pronounced questionable character."[21] Women who did not conform to white supremacist ideals did not deserve the protection offered either by white supremacist justice or by the rule of law.[22]

White women could not, of course, choose whether or not they wanted this kind of "protection." This was an entirely white male prerogative. Where the defense of sexualized honor was at stake, white men insisted on the right to decide the facts of a case and choose an appropriate punishment for those deemed guilty — in short, the right to take the law into their own hands. Their monopoly on citizenship rights, from jury service to public speech, helped make this possible. In communities where a lynching had just occurred, coroners' juries routinely found that victims had come to their deaths at the hands of "parties unknown." Even papers editorially opposed to lynching, such as the Edgefield *Chronicle,* claimed to be ignorant as to the membership of local lynch mobs.[23]

Political good sense and personal commitment to the social primacy of white men discouraged county officials from taking significant action against lynching. In the last days before Tillman took power in 1890, the Richland County sheriff wrote to Governor Richardson to ask that a prisoner be moved to the state penitentiary before a lynch mob could organize. Otherwise, the sheriff anticipated being placed "in a position of being forced to fire on my friends." Richardson assented. But such defensive steps did not, in the end, make much difference: in 1889 and 1890, under Richardson's administration, a total of seventeen South Carolinians were lynched.[24]

Once Tillman became governor, the onus of upholding "the majesty of the law" fell to him. This might include calling out the militia to prevent lynchings; a former vigilante himself, Tillman found this more than a bit awkward. Tillman's efforts against corporations, biracial movements, the gold standard, and the agricultural status quo gave him credibility with white farmers of all classes, but even he could not afford to get on the wrong side of the emotional issue of lynching, especially when black men were accused of raping white women. At the same time, Tillman's program required a strengthened state apparatus, not one whose laws could be flouted by mob action. The dilemma Tillman faced was therefore partly of his own making, a conflict flowing inevitably from the tension between his violent past and his idealized future, between his role as champion of white supremacist violence and his desire to control, not subvert, the law.

At first, Tillman presented himself as a foe of lynching. His initial litany of grievances against the conservative regime had included "the continued resurgence of horrible lynchings," which followed from "bad laws and their inefficient administration." A few months later, an Edgefield grand jury on which Ben Tillman sat explained lynching as the unfortunate result of an inefficient and overly lenient Supreme Court. Harsher penalties and more rapid prosecutions, apparently, would satisfy the (white male) people. As we have seen, Tillman condemned lynching explicitly and at length in his 1890 inaugural address.[25]

For more than a year, Ben Tillman continued to oppose extralegal violence, using language that referred to the preservation of the reputation of the state and the rule of law. In his public letterbooks he applauded a local sheriff for safeguarding a threatened prisoner and declared that "if all of our peace officers shall act as promptly + decisively, our state will be spared the disgrace of any more lynchings."[26] Like the previous governor, he corresponded with sheriffs throughout the state, giving and receiving warnings of impending lynchings and ordering investigations when they occurred.[27] He sometimes called out the militia to prevent lynchings.[28] As he wrote to the sheriff of Spartanburg County that fall, "It had just as well be understood that the law in South Carolina must be respected + Lynch-law will not be tolerated." This commitment bore fruit: in his first annual address to the legislature in November 1891, he boasted that "during the year the law in the State has been supreme and that no person or prisoner has been lynched."[29]

A few days after Tillman's address, however, a black Edgefield man named Dick Lundy was lynched after being charged with murdering the sheriff's son. Tillman immediately alerted the state solicitor, ordering him to investigate whether the sheriff had acted appropriately and to "see that the majesty of the law is vindicated." Tillman subsequently held a "crafty leader" responsible and found local officials complicit in the lynching. He ridiculed the finding that "parties unknown" had committed the murder, blamed his friend the sheriff for putting personal feelings ahead of the law, and declared that "the law received a wound for every bullet shot into Dick Lundy's body."[30] He wanted the authority to remove sheriffs who did not fulfill their responsibilities, but this would mean unseating locally elected officials.[31]

Reactions to Tillman's policy varied. His conservative opponents remained skeptical. The *News and Courier* editorially blamed the "lawless spirit which prevails among the people of Edgefield County," and did not give Tillman much credit for his condemnation of the event. The paper questioned his ability to stop the mob and suggested that, had he been present, "with true Edgefield instinct, [Tillman] would probably have been hanging around on the edge of the mob." Even after Lundy's murder, though, Tillman received praise for the low incidence of lynching since his inauguration and for his public opposition to lynching. "It is to the credit of Governor Tillman that he has lent the whole influence and power of his office to prevent and to discourage such affairs," admitted the normally hostile newspaper. Some months later, a mass meeting of black activists protesting a second lynching commended Tillman for his "efforts . . . to prevent lynchings in this State."[32]

Tillman faced the same dilemma as the sheriff who had proved reluctant "to fire on my friends."[33] The lynchers and their supporters were the white men whose votes and confidence Tillman sought, and he knew how strongly such men valued their local prerogatives. But over the four years of his governorship, the number of state and regional lynchings (and the amount of attention paid to them) increased dramatically. As the 1880s gave way to the 1890s, mobs more and more often preempted the work of civil authorities, often explicitly claiming the authority of a white supremacist "higher law." Of 170 lynchings committed in South Carolina between 1881 and 1940, nearly a third took place during the 1890s. The proportion was even higher in the white supremacist strongholds of Edgefield, Abbeville, Laurens, and Newberry, and during the 1890s in those counties lynchings actually outnumbered legal executions.[34]

The increasing number and ferocity of lynchings repeatedly forced

Governor Tillman to support both white supremacy and the rule of law at precisely the point where they came into murderous conflict. He recognized the dilemma: as his secretary wrote to a constituent, Tillman was "in sympathy with and will maintain White Supremacy + will enforce the law in that direction but at the same time justice must not be over-ridden."[35] In practice, the conflict between white supremacist justice and the rule of law could not be finessed so easily; Tillman needed both sets of credentials to carry out his programs.

Tillman's solution, as we have seen, was to decry lynching in the abstract but to assert a position of leadership in the case of lynching for rape or attempted rape. Claiming leadership within both systems, Tillman attempted to preserve his personal and professional honor. The authority of his position would render the lynching quasi-official; at the same time, his pledge to *lead* the mob reestablished him as the arbiter of white supremacist justice. Limiting his legitimation of lynching to cases where rape or attempted rape was alleged, Tillman was able violently to defend white supremacy, but without appearing indiscriminately bloodthirsty. The tactic seemed to meet with his supporters' approval: at a campaign meeting later that summer, supporters presented Tillman with a banner hailing him as the "Champion of White Men's Rule and Woman's Virtue."[36]

He took a further step toward "legitimating" his pledge in the eyes of the law by stripping it of its overt racial distinctions: he amended his pledge to include the lynching of "any man of any color who assaults a virtuous woman of any color."[37] This fooled no one. Both friends and foes recognized the white supremacist meaning that lay just beneath these ostensibly neutral words, especially the qualifier "virtuous." Since a well-established tenet of white supremacy was that black sexuality, female as well as male, was inherently degraded, Tillman's pledge would never oblige him to avenge the honor of a black woman. In the white supremacist imagination, no such thing existed or could exist.[38]

The Limits of Opposition

Some South Carolinians fought against the white supremacist "justice" of lynching. Its fiercest opponents, of course, were its principal victims, black South Carolinian agricultural workers. On countless unrecorded occasions, they resisted attempts to humiliate, assault, or murder them; while our sources tell us of the many occasions on which black resistance was crushed, they tell us much less about the times when it was at least partially successful.[39] But there were visible and audible protests as well when lynching began to spread across the country.

High-status black people, usually preachers or politicians, protested frequently that "the rights of the colored people are not respected." In 1885, a group of Charleston ministers asserted that on "any night a band of desperadoes may ride up to the humble cabin of an inoffensive negro, and for some supposed wrong he may be dragged from his home and be cruelly beaten, and perhaps murdered." They identified the rape-lynch complex even as it was forming in the mid-1880s: "If a colored man is accused, through malice, of an insult to a white lady, he is likely to be hung, or shot down like a dog."[40]

Ida B. Wells and Frederick Douglass were not the only black spokespeople attempting to provide alternative analyses of lynching's causes. Congressman Thomas E. Miller, one of South Carolina's last black Republican representatives, noted that lynchings did not occur where black people were politically and numerically strong; he also hinted that "the morals of the white women," not black criminality, might explain some allegations of rape.[41] Others attempted to turn the tables on the lynchers, suggesting that the most common form of interracial rape was that of black women by white men. "Outrages are more aggravating," declared an A.M.E. Zion minister, "when we remember that white men can insult and commit rape upon colored women and very little, if anything, is said about it."[42] White men, he suggested, behaved hypocritically and therefore dishonorably. On at least one occasion during the lynching wave of the late nineteenth century, black South Carolinians lynched a white man accused of raping a black woman. These men were convicted of murder, but they received pardons from Governor Richardson, a conservative, who objected to black men being the first to die when so many white men had committed the same crime and gone unpunished.[43] This event proved exceptional, however, and lynching remained primarily a crime committed by whites against blacks.

Tillman's white conservative opponents faced a dilemma. They opposed the lawless violence and social disruption caused by lynching. And while most conservatives, anxious to establish their opposition to black criminality, agreed that black men who raped white women deserved to die, their approval was far more grudging than Tillman's. The Charleston *News and Courier* embodied the divided mind of the conservative

Democratic opposition. Under editor F. W. Dawson and his successor, J. C. Hemphill, the paper took strong stands against dueling and lynching. In countless headlines and editorial comments, they complained that such "uncivilized" practices "disgraced" the state. Their newspaper was capable of sophisticated (if partial) analyses: it once described lynching as following from "lax administration of the law, the toleration of the pistol bearing habit, the permission of the general sale of liquor, the recognition of a modified 'Code of Honor' that requires a man to avenge an insult or resent the application of an epithet to him, and especially . . . the failure of juries and courts."[44] These men's interests and eyes were trained on how northerners, especially potential investors, perceived them. Lynching struck at their pocketbooks and their notions of modern, "civilized" behavior.

But the *News and Courier*'s position was riddled with ambivalence and contradiction; in both blatant and subtle ways the newspaper subverted its own opposition both to mob rule and to the subordination of due process to honor. It denounced a December 1890 lynching of a black man for allegedly raping a white woman, but it questioned neither the guilt of the victim nor the punishment: having committed "the unpardonable sin," the lynching victim "richly deserved" his fate; the paper simply protested that he should "have been put to death by the law." In this case, as in others, it did not expect that "a fair jury" would convict the lynchers. Reporters covering posses contributed to lynching's momentum by imparting the standard information that "a crowd of men are now scouring the country . . . and if the fiend is caught he will no doubt be disposed of." Like many South Carolina newspapers on both sides of the Democratic conflict, the Charleston daily was obsessed with reports of lynchings, especially of black men accused of raping or attempting to rape white women. During a period when on average one lynching was being perpetrated every three days in the United States, the *News and Courier* apparently reported as many as it could.[45]

Further, while the *News and Courier* editorially decried loose talk of "race war" as dangerous, it routinely used "race war" and "race riot" in headlines for articles which described only tense situations. Decrying "flippant talk" of racial conflict, the paper warned, "The strictly material losses through any such conflict would be terrible enough. The cotton would lie unpicked in the fields. The face of the earth would remain unbroken by the plough." Yet less than a year later, the *News and Courier* starkly headlined dubious "reports" that Mississippi's blacks and whites were arming themselves as "The Mississippi Race War."[46] The habit of thinking of racial conflict in apocalyptic terms overrode the editors' rejections of such language. Perhaps they were caught between their fear of such a conflict and their desire to have done with it, if only to bring the years (indeed, centuries) of periodic anxiety to an end.

As their fears of unpicked cotton and unplowed fields suggested, conservatives and other white critics of lynching were primarily concerned about the harm that Tillman's reputation might do to South Carolina's cotton economy. John C. Sheppard, Tillman's opponent for the governorship in 1892, argued that Tillman's espousal of mob violence meant that northerners "must steer clear of South Carolina for investments and settlement."[47] Concern over the economic effects of lynch law was apparently widespread. In early 1893, the editor of the North Carolina *Southern Progress* wrote to ask Tillman for a "brief letter . . . stating that South Carolina is free from influences that cause investments [to be] unsafe." Tillman replied that there was "nothing whatever in the bugaboo of a possible race conflict to deter immigrants making homes or those who have money to invest," and that South Carolina was not the lawless place some alleged.[48] Clearly, Tillman understood what kind of "influences" caused the North Carolinian his anxiety.

Some white opposition to lynching articulated concern for the state's reputation in less material terms. A few elite white men tried to impress upon their younger male relatives how shamefully the state's white people were acting. "It is the hight of folly to try to convict a white man for killing a poor negro," claimed Alexander M. Salley of Orangeburg in a letter to his son, a student at the Citadel. "A certain class think it is something to be proud of. It was perfectly disgusting to me to see men running after those self-declared murderers. They [the lynchers] had a perfect ovation." James Hemphill privately complained to his nephew, the editor of the *News and Courier*, that lynchings made him doubt "our fitness for government. We should quit boasting that there is no place like South Carolina. We should cover ourselves with sack cloth and ashes."[49]

Indeed, many white South Carolinians who rejected or criticized lynching did so because they believed it caused otherwise civilized white people to behave brutally. By this reckoning, the problem with lynching was not the fact that a mob murdered a person based on accusations but the way in which they committed that murder and the form of theater it became. Lynchings, as I have suggested, became dramas of brutality.[50] The least spectacular were summary hangings that took place at the earliest possible opportunity after the victim had been captured. In these cases, newspapers praised the calmness of the lynch mob, and the murderers were lauded as cool, sober, and determined. One lynch mob carrying its victim on a train was praised for behaving so decorously that white women traveling with them had no idea of their purpose.[51] At the other end of the spectrum were the mass spectacles described so often in the newspapers then and the historiography today, lynchings with elaborate trials and examinations, culminating in grotesque public torture and mutilation of the victim. After death by hanging, shooting, burning, or all three, members of the mob would dismember the bodies and take trophies.[52] Some white southerners thought accounts of these revolting crimes could be turned to good account: they could be used to persuade lynch mobs to behave in a civilized fashion, to act quickly and mercifully, to enforce white supremacy but to do so in a way that did credit to whiteness.

Ultimately, though, most white South Carolinian opponents of lynching were concerned about the moral and economic reputation of their state, not with the rights of the accused or murdered. When Albion Tourgée's National Citizens' Rights Association supported the widow of a lynching victim in a suit against county officials, the *News and Courier* declared that even a successful prosecution would "do more harm than good, . . . irritating the people in the counties in which the lynchers live" and causing further lynchings. Instead, antilynching efforts should focus on ending rape, rather than "championing the cause of the criminals."[53] Many forces had driven conservative opponents of lynching into this corner, but the pivotal event may have been the Denmark lynching.

The Denmark Lynching

The Denmark lynching of April 1893 demonstrated the practical absurdity of Tillman's attempt to reconcile white supremacist justice with the rule of law. It underlined the degree of equivocation required to maintain even a semblance of authority. It also showed how a mob might appropriate state authority and transform the due process of law into a white supremacist spectacle. Denmark, a town in the lowcountry county of Barnwell, played out its rape-lynch drama within a short train ride of the presses of both Charleston and Columbia, and newspapers offered all interested readers the "facts" in the case. As the story reached audiences throughout the state, the true limits of native white opposition to lynching became clear.

In April 1893, Mamie Baxter, a fourteen-year-old from a well-to-do white farm family, alleged that a strange black man had attempted to assault her, presumably with intent to rape. Hastily deputized posses brought more than a dozen suspects before her, black men with no immediate alibi or no regular local employment. All were exonerated and released. Finally, Baxter identified a black suspect named Henry Williams as somewhat resembling the man who had attacked her. After this tentative identification, Williams escaped custody. Tillman offered a $250 reward for Williams being turned over to the sheriff; a group of white citizens matched that sum, conditional only upon Williams's capture. A posse finally caught Williams but did not deliver him to the sheriff.

At least once during these events, a crowd, "composed of many of the best citizens of the town and section," made an effort to lynch Williams, but "prominent citizens" including Barnwell's state senator, a white Democrat named S. G. Mayfield, dispersed the would-be lynchers. While Mayfield held Williams under guard in his office, he wrote to Tillman that the crime warranted death and that if Williams were the guilty man he should be lynched as soon as possible. In response to an ambiguous letter from Tillman, Mayfield announced that he had told the governor that "Barnwell men would protect their women at all hazards."[54] Local honor and white patriarchy were at stake.

Tillman's reply to Mayfield, written while Williams was still at large, was rife with contradiction. Tillman had been "hoping to hear that you have caught and lynched" the "would be ravisher." He agreed with Mayfield that the punishment for "attempt to ravish . . . ought to be death" and that the legal punishment for attempted rape (probably a term of imprisonment) "was inadequate for a case of this kind." Yet he insisted that he would make good on the promised reward only if there were no lynching, for he "would not consider it right to have a man caught by process of law + through the instrumentality of the reward offered by the state, simply to break the law by killing him."

Tillman tried to make his pro-lynching position clear without appearing to use the law itself to further a lynching, but the contradiction could not be papered over with rhetoric. While Tillman saw "very well what the result will be," he looked to Mayfield "to preserve the proprieties." Any lynching, Tillman thought, "ought to be before the officers of the law get possession" of the victim.[55] The thought that the majesty of the law might suffer if a mob seized and lynched yet another imprisoned suspect bothered Tillman considerably. But his sense of "the proprieties" did not prevent the governor from suggesting that a state legislator see to it that the lynching take place preemptively.

White supremacist justice bore the same carnival resemblance to due process that white supremacist politics bore to democracy. A court of the mob told Williams to prove his innocence or be presumed guilty. As a reporter put it, "He was in the hands of the people, and as they said and considered was above and beyond legal interference" by the governor or militia. "The people" sentenced Williams to death, but half an hour before his scheduled lynching, four white farmers (including Alexander Salley, whose letter decrying lynching we have already considered) arrived to verify Williams's alibi. Mayfield, playing the role of judge, allowed these farmers to make statements and to be cross-examined by the crowd. Offering this evidence to the crowd as corroboration of Williams's story, Mayfield declared, "Gentlemen, you have heard the evidence. The case is in your hands. Is he guilty or not guilty?" With some members urging that Williams be lynched and others sobered by the new evidence, a collective decision was somehow reached to keep Williams locked up and pursue other suspects. Bands of men continued to scour the countryside for black men fitting Baxter's description of her assailant.[56]

Tillman's involvement and responsibility became still more direct when another suspect, John Peterson, fled to Columbia. Aided by a Columbia newspaper reporter, Peterson gained an audience with the governor and sought his aid and protection. If newspaper accounts are to be trusted, it appears either that Peterson had run out of other options or that he took Tillman's antilynching rhetoric seriously enough to stake his life on it. Peterson said that he had an alibi and could prove his innocence, but he feared that if he were captured and taken to Denmark by a posse he would certainly be lynched. After receiving Peterson's assurance that his alibi would be corroborated "by white people," Tillman sent him to Denmark but with only a single guard.

Tillman may or may not have believed that this escort would suffice. Perhaps he was collaborating with the lynch mob; perhaps he merely misjudged its temper. In any case, Peterson met precisely the fate that Williams had narrowly avoided—the seizure from state authorities and subsequent lynching that Tillman had said he wanted so badly to avoid. When Peterson arrived, a reporter described the proceeding as "very similar to that in a trial justice's court[:] The prisoner was placed upon the stand and made his statement, evidence was taken on both sides and the prisoner permitted to cross examine the witnesses." Nonetheless, "the jury of public opinion passed upon his case and the verdict was guilty." The mob strung Peterson up in the courthouse square and fired countless bullets into his body. The coroner's jury eschewed the customary formulation of "persons unknown," stating simply that John Peterson "came to his death at the hands of about 500 citizens who intended to inflict the punishment of death . . . for having assaulted Miss Mamie Baxter . . . with intent to commit rape." At Tillman's request, Mayfield sent him a summary of "the lynching and the verdict." [57]

In the wake of Peterson's death, both black and white South Carolinians held mass "indignation meetings," some protesting Peterson's lynching, others denouncing the crime of rape, and all eventually accusing one another of increasing the potential for further violence and of using the event for political gain. Among whites, the loudest and least guarded in his condemnation of the lynching was Columbia editor Narciso Gonzales, whose long hostility toward Tillman reinforced his intolerance of vigilante violence. Gonzales declared that lynching would not end rape or put guards on the road to protect white women; rather, it would inflame black men to work out their rage at such injustice by raping white women.[58]

Others found white protest against lynching most dangerous of all. The Farmers' Alliance newspaper, the *Cotton Plant,* denounced the antilynching indignation meeting in Columbia, attended by some white Democrats, as "an exhibition of blind bitter partisan hate and unscrupulous recklessness of consequences the worst that has ever been seen in South Carolina," promoting "race antagonism" and "embolden[ing]" black men to four subsequent "outrages."[59] A Newberry woman, presumably white, agreed.[60] This was, in a sense, a revival of white supremacist arguments of the Redemption era: black men were the brutish tools through which malevolent outsiders and aristocrats attacked white farmers' households, authority, and independence.

Some black South Carolinians considered organized resistance. A Charleston protest meeting led by black preachers advised African Americans "to be order-loving and law-abiding citizens" but added that "the time is quite at hand for the men of the negro race to make special

provision for the protection of themselves and families against these outrages which may at any time be visited upon them." A few white South
Carolinians interpreted the black ministers' advice to "make special provision" as insurrectionary. Yet black South Carolinians knew the dangers of
even appearing to mobilize in numbers for physical resistance. Such mo-
bilization had led to massively disproportionate white response on many
occasions; black South Carolinians' experiences both before and after
emancipation taught them that taking up arms collectively without reliable legal and military support was a recipe for massacre. Even Tillman
thought this lesson had been sufficiently taught, soothing a subordinate's
fears by informing him that he did "not believe the sensational reports of
negroes trying to rescue Rapists."[61]

For his part, Tillman denied bearing any responsibility for Peterson's
murder. He explained that since Peterson had said he could prove his innocence, and as the mob had released other innocent men, Tillman had
not had any reason to foresee trouble. Tillman validated the court of
Judge Lynch: his words implied that the mob would not have lynched Peterson had he been innocent. But Tillman also declared that the people of
Barnwell had "violated his confidence." He had assumed that "they most
certainly would not hang a man who said he was innocent and was willing
to meet his accusers." Having facilitated a murderous white supremacist
spectacle without unduly dirtying the hands of the state, he went on to defend the state before its northern critics: when the Boston *Transcript* headlined an article on the Denmark lynching "Brute Rule in the South,"
Tillman dismissed the article as "a tissue of falsehoods." Tillman paid little
attention to those who condemned his role in the Denmark lynching.[62]

Nor did Tillman subscribe to the position of white "moderates" who
sought merely to decrease lynching's brutality. As his letter to Mayfield
suggested, Tillman was perfectly satisfied with the murderous results of
most lynchings; his objection was political and philosophical and concerned the threat that lynching posed to state authority. Spectacular
lynchings such as that at Denmark emphasized the weakness of the state's
powers, robbed the state of its authority, and made a mockery of due process. They robbed the state government of power and respect of its honor.

Some of Tillman's opponents began to move toward this position. After lynchings in Laurens and Williamsburg in the weeks after Denmark,
the conservative *News and Courier* proposed a system of special courts that
would travel to areas where lynchings seemed imminent and lend the proceedings a veneer of legality. The question was not the punishment — only

death would suffice — but the forms preceding its administration. "If the Legislature will not provide a special Court for the 'prompt' trial and punishment of rapists, the people will," declared the paper, echoing the words of the defenders of the Denmark lynching. After all, "a hasty trial is better than none."[63] Adherence to the *forms* of law would help protect the state's reputation.

The *News and Courier,* passing on the unwelcome news that the Chicago *Inter-Ocean* had hired "an educated young colored woman" to investigate lynchings in the South — Ida B. Wells-Barnett, although the paper did not identify her by name — focused on the "devilish propensities" of black criminals, not the rule of white mobs, as the essential threat to civilized order. As nonsouthern criticism of lynching increased over the next few years, the *News and Courier* closed ranks against the protesters, assenting to a system of "justice" that focused on the crime of rape rather than the crime of lynching, a system in which black men's guilt was presumed and the ultimate authority of local white men was a given.[64] The editor's only reservation concerned the form of the execution, not the guilt or innocence of the victim.

Some whites tried to blunt the brutal racial edge of spectacular lynchings by implicating black South Carolinians. At several lynchings of black men accused of assaulting white women during the early 1890s, Democratic newspapers took pains to highlight the participation of black men and women. Black women were said to have given evidence against lynching victims, and black men were noted in the crowds, among the executioners, and even on coroner's juries that reached the verdicts of "persons unknown."[65] Such reports of black cooperation or participation became relatively common, perhaps revealing the underlying white insecurity manifested in the recurrent fear of an impending "race war." By implicating black people in lynchings, these whites did more than try to convince outsiders that lynching was not about race; they sought to reassure themselves that black people were not the monolith posited by white supremacy, not a New World golem needing only one more violent provocation to set it in murderous, retaliatory motion. Accepting that black people were human individuals — confused, brave, fearful, and the rest — dismantled the monster, though potentially at the cost of some of white supremacy's ordering assumptions.

While spectacular lynchings defined white supremacist justice, they also revealed the limitations of white supremacy as a mode of governance. Tillman, especially, felt the tension between lynching and the law because he had attempted to lead and represent both. By talking out of both sides of his mouth, Tillman had learned to negotiate the conflicting imperatives of white supremacist justice and the rule of law. But these tactical successes should not mislead us into thinking that Tillman had found a formula which would reconcile lynching with state-building. In fact, Tillman had stretched himself across a political chasm that even his artful demagoguery could not long bridge.

In the aftermath of the Denmark lynching, less than a year after Tillman's famous pledge to lead the mob, his words came back to haunt him. After Peterson's lynching, mass meetings of white men echoed the language of Tillman's 1892 promise, declaring their intention to lynch any man, "white or black," who "makes an assault upon our wives, daughters or sisters." Some went further, suggesting that the lynchers' examination had been a legitimate substitute for what they derided as overly restrictive "forms of law." As one meeting resolved, "The whole people are a law unto themselves," that "justice is more essential than mere forms of justice," and that "the verdict of a jury of five hundred men . . . is entitled to as much respect as a verdict of twelve of the men in a Court room." "It makes no difference," agreed another paper, "whether the people of Columbia believed Peterson to be innocent or guilty, [for] the people of Denmark and Barnwell county, white and colored, by an overwhelming majority believed him to be guilty; and in this matter they were, by common consent in such cases, the sole judges of his guilt or innocence." White men's honor continued to depend on their right to determine the means and ends of justice in their localities.[66]

Spectacular lynchings demonstrated white supremacy's power, but they also made the actual achievement of Tillman's vision more remote by weakening the authority of the state government. If there were to be show trials, he wanted the state, not the mob, to be in charge. White mobs, however, continually refused to recognize the importance of strong and credible state authority. In the end, Tillman's attempt to reconcile spectacular lynching with the appearance of state authority left him fatigued and annoyed. While he continued to assert that accused rapists should be lynched, at the end of 1893 he told reporters that "everybody would have been much better satisfied" if a recent lynching victim could have been "hanged according to law."[67] The spectacle would perhaps have lacked the bloodthirsty catharsis of a lynching, but as long as a man had to die, Tillman preferred it to be at the hands of the state.

In the end, not even Ben Tillman could persuade white men that their interests lay with a strengthened state government, at least not if that meant surrendering local freedom. After further skirmishes over lynching and an unpopular liquor law, Tillman gave up that fight for a seat in the U.S. Senate. There, as a sectional leader of a national party, he could afford to indulge in broader, more programmatic statements of his white supremacist principles without worrying about the effect on local government in South Carolina. This was, however, a retreat, an admission of failure. Tillman had envisioned a white supremacist project far more ambitious than punishing individual transgressors; he had wanted to build a world in which whites and blacks, men and women, knew their political, economic, social, and sexual places and kept to them. He had been prepared for resistance from black southerners and even from white conservatives; he had not expected to have such a hard time convincing white farmers that to accept a degree of state authority was in their own long-term interest.

Despite his inability to establish the world of his dreams, Tillman did help shape regional and national life. His and others' legislative efforts resulted in disfranchisement and segregation. Just as important, his commitment to white patriarchal control led directly to the grotesque racial violence that defined the South in many Americans' eyes for decades to come. Together, racial legislation and terrorism all but destroyed dissent within the South. Tillman offered white men a vision of a world where they were the undisputed and beloved rulers and where the preservation of their honor took primacy over the formalities of law. He insisted that the state's power be respected, but he also told these white men that, for all practical purposes, they *were* the state. State government came to represent the same race, class, and gender prerogatives as local government, and the violent assertion of this newly expansive notion of white men's honor became a common feature of American life.

Notes

1. Benjamin Ryan Tillman (hereinafter BRT) at Barnwell campaign meeting, 7 June 1892, quoted in Edgefield (S.C.) *Advertiser,* 16 June 1892; also quoted without comment in Charleston *News and Courier,* 14 June 1892; BRT, inaugural address (Columbia, S.C., 1890),

pamphlet at the South Carolina Library, University of South Carolina, Columbia (hereinafter SCL).

2. This and succeeding paragraphs draw on my doctoral thesis: Kantrowitz 1995.

3. Randolph Dennis Werner's (1977) interpretation of Tillman, his opponents, and South Carolina politics in this period makes a similar argument about the relationship between economic interest and ideology, but it leaves little room for conflicts within groups and within individuals themselves.

4. See McCurry 1995 and Ayers 1984. For particularly wrenching examples of black southerners' growing understanding of judicial discrimination after Reconstruction ended, see L. Edwards 1991.

5. See, for example, J. M. Stone 1894. See also BRT to Lyles, editor of *Southern Progress*, 16 May 1893, Gov. BRT Letterbooks, South Carolina Department of Archives and History (hereinafter DAH). On this subject generally, see Ayers 1984.

6. Edgefield (S.C.) *Monitor*, quoted in Edgefield (S.C.) *Chronicle*, 18 January 1884.

7. *News and Courier*, 17 November 1891.

8. Faust 1985.

9. Edgefield County has long been seen as a uniquely violent American place: see, for example, Davis to Laughlin, 21 March 1887, Robert Means Davis Papers, SCL; R. M. Brown 1975, chap. 3; Butterfield 1995. For some countervailing data on the geographical distribution of lynchings, see Finnegan 1992, 172.

10. Hodes 1993; Dailey 1995; Painter 1988; G. Gilmore 1996.

11. See Hall 1983 and 1993.

12. W. Fitzhugh Brundage (1993, 18–19) has proposed a "taxonomy of mob violence" and identified four distinct types: small "private" mobs, larger "terrorist" mobs, posses, and mass mobs of more than fifty people.

13. *Southern Horrors* and *A Red Record*, pamphlets collected in Wells-Barnett 1991.

14. Jane E. Dailey's (1995) work shows how in 1880s Virginia the ideology of separate spheres enabled white supremacists to claim that Readjuster efforts to desegregate teaching in public schools were intended to give black men sexual power over white girls. Martha Hodes (1993) has suggested that this prohibition was not as clear-cut as has usually been thought during the antebellum. As we will see, in the South of the 1880s and 1890s, sexual relations between black men and white women generated considerable hostility among white men.

15. See Painter 1988.

16. Finnegan 1992, 168, 319.

17. Ayers 1984 and 1992. See also Brundage 1993.

18. Jacquelyn Dowd Hall (1983, 332), paraphrasing Claude Lévi-Strauss, writes that men use women as verbs with which to communicate with one another.

19. *News and Courier*, 1 August 1893. Sharon Block tells me that, in her research on rape in eighteenth- and nineteenth-century America, including South Carolina, she has found that legal and social opinion treated rape as an offense against the household and especially against its male head.

20. MacLean 1994, esp. 98–148; Hall 1983; Painter 1988.

21. *Advertiser*, 24 August 1893; *News and Courier*, 14 June 1894.

22. Tillman was not the most extreme defender of lynching. Many correspondents applauded Tillman's position and his harsh responses to northern critics of southern lynching. One writer suggested repealing both mob violence and rape laws in Georgia, the effect of which would be to deny accused rapists the protection of the law and weaken the ability of the state to punish their lynchers. This proposal demonstrated how earnestly some white supremacists believed that black-on-white rape was to be regarded less as a violation of law than as a blow against white civilization. Townsend to BRT, 18 October 1894; also Sundberg to BRT, 13 August 1894, Hall to BRT, 29 May 1894, Gov. BRT Letters, DAH.

23. *Chronicle*, 16 December 1891. Although its own list of those examined by the circuit solicitor during his investigation included many prominent white Edgefield Democrats, the paper professed ignorance of any specific knowledge. The fears and pressures working on the *Chronicle*'s editor, himself a white Democrat with a local business, are not difficult to imagine.

24. Roman to Richardson, 17 November 1890, Governor Richardson Letters, DAH; Neal 1976, 307.

25. *News and Courier*, 23 January 1890; *Chronicle*, 12 March 1890; BRT, Message to the General Assembly (Columbia, 1891), pamphlet at SCL.

26. BRT to Lenore, 17 December 1890, Gov. BRT Letterbooks, DAH.

27. See *News and Courier*, 3 January 1890; Richardson to McDonald, 13 March 1890, Roman to Richardson, 17 November 1890, Gov. Richardson Letters, DAH.

28. 12 February, 23 October, 7 December 1891; 7, 30 November, 17 December 1892, Gov. BRT Telegrams, DAH. See also Tompkins to Hanston, 1 September 1891, Gov. BRT Letterbooks, DAH.

29. BRT to Nichols, 29 September 1891, BRT Letterbooks, DAH; BRT, Message to the General Assembly, 1891, 29.

30. BRT to Nelson, 7 December 1891, Gov. BRT Letterbooks, DAH; *News and Courier*, 15 December 1891.

31. Tillman had to be careful how he justified such an intrusion: "The Anglo-Saxon race has ever been jealous of the prerogatives of the King. Their descendants in America are equally watchful against official tyranny, but it is easy to show that there is no possibility of the Executive having the laws 'faithfully executed' unless his hands are strengthened." Message of B. R. Tillman to the General Assembly, 1891, 22.

32. *News and Courier*, 15 December 1891, 25 May, 1 June 1892.

33. Roman to Richardson, 17 November 1890, Gov. Richardson Letters, DAH.

34. Finnegan 1992, 11, 15, 61.

35. Tompkins to Heyward, 27 May 1892, Gov. BRT Letterbooks, DAH.

36. *News and Courier*, 18 August 1892.

37. McPherson to BRT, 29 June 1892, Tompkins to McPherson, 1 July 1892, Gov. BRT Letters, DAH.

38. Deborah Gray White argues that black women have historically been presented either as Mammy (a desexualized surrogate mother) or as Jezebel (a libidinally driven temptress); see White 1985, esp. 27–61. See also Guy-Shetfall 1990 and, for some black women's struggles against such representations, Brooks-Higginbotham 1993, esp. 185–211.

39. Local black resistance to lynching following Reconstruction demands further study. Useful models for such a project include Timothy Tyson, *Radio Free Dixie* (Chapel Hill, forthcoming) and Kelley 1990.

40. *News and Courier*, 25 November 1885.

41. Rep. Thomas E. Miller in Congress, 14 February 1891, quoted in Columbia *State*, 24 February 1891. A similar suggestion, phrased somewhat less elliptically, led to Ida B. Wells-Barnett's exile from Memphis and to the destruction of her newspaper and many other black publications in the South during the 1890s. For corroboration of Miller's hypothesis that black political power discouraged lynching, at least in South Carolina during the 1880s and 1890s, see Finnegan 1992, 108, 165.

42. *Star of Zion* (Salisbury, N.C.), 4 October 1894.

43. *News and Courier*, 3 and 6 January 1888; Finnegan 1992, 258–60.

44. *News and Courier*, 18 September 1894.

45. *News and Courier*, 16 December 1890, 15 September 1891. For one five-week period in early 1892, the paper recorded six incidents in five states that claimed nine black victims. *News and Courier*, 13, 14, 17, and 22 February, 10 and 22 March 1892. Weekly papers such as the *Advertiser* often reported at least one lynching in each issue for long stretches during the early 1890s. Some white readers may have come to see these, like reports of sermons or campaign meetings, as regular features of the social landscape.

46. *News and Courier*, 19 December 1888, 15 September 1889.

47. *News and Courier*, 1 and 6 July 1892.

48. Lyles to BRT, 4 April 1893, Gov. BRT Letters, DAH; BRT to Lyles, 16 May 1893, Gov. BRT Letterbooks, DAH.

49. A. M. Salley to A. S. Salley, 26 January 1889, Alexander Samuel Salley Jr. Papers, SCL; J. Hemphill to Calvin, 24 January 1890, Hemphill Family Papers, Special Collections, Perkins Library, Duke University.

50. On this subject, I am indebted to comments made by David Roediger at a roundtable discussion, Contemporary Historical Approaches to Race and Racism, at the Havens Center, University of Wisconsin-Madison, 10 November 1995.

51. See, e.g., reports and comments in *Advertiser*, 3 and 24 August 1893, *News and Courier*, 16 December 1890, 25 May 1892, 1 August 1893.

52. See Brundage 1993.

53. *News and Courier*, 15 July 1893.

54. *News and Courier*, 20–25 April 1893; Finnegan 1992, 131–35.

55. Tompkins to Mayfield, 18 April 1893, BRT Papers, Special Collections, Cooper Library, Clemson University [hereinafter CSC]; Mayfield to BRT, 22 April 1893, Gov. BRT Letters, DAH.

56. *News and Courier*, 20–23, 26–28, 29 April 1893.

57. Augusta (GA) *Chronicle*, quoted in *Advertiser*, 4 May 1893; *News and Courier*, 26–28 April 1893.

58. *News and Courier*, 2 May 1893.

59. *Cotton Plant* (S.C.), 20 May 1893.

60. Unidentified clipping, 10 May 1893, in BRT Papers, CSC.

61. *News and Courier*, 13 May 1893; BRT to Farley, 28 July 1893, Gov. BRT Telegrams, DAH.

62. *News and Courier*, 26–28 April, 2 May 1893; BRT to editor, 20 May 1893, BRT Papers, CSC.

63. *News and Courier*, 12 May 1893. Details in *Advertiser*, 18 May 1893; *News and Courier*, 10 and 18 July 1893. These special courts were never created. But later that year some members of the House supported public executions as a means of deterring violent offenders. *News and Courier*, 16 December 1893.

64. *News and Courier*, 26 July 1893, 11 and 12 September 1894.

65. See *Advertiser*, 4 May, 24 August 1893; *News and Courier*, 12 May 1893.

66. *News and Courier*, 2 and 17 May 1893; *Advertiser*, 4 May 1893.

67. *News and Courier*, 3 October 1893.

9

"The Equal of Some White Men and the Superior of Others": Masculinity and the 1916 Lynching of Anthony Crawford in Abbeville County, South Carolina

TERENCE FINNEGAN

"The black must submit to the white or the white will destroy," wrote William P. Beard, the racist, iconoclastic editor of the Abbeville *Scimitar*. Beard was commenting on the October 1916 lynching of the wealthy African American landowner Anthony Crawford and the subsequent efforts of the state of South Carolina to convict eight white men for Crawford's murder. Beard believed that the doctrine of white supremacy, which demanded that the "LOWEST white man in the social scale is above the negro who stands HIGHEST by the same measurement," was the root cause and justification for Crawford's murder. Beard scoffed at the hypocritical and mawkish appeals of white elites for "law and order" and insisted that the "best people" of South Carolina know that "when white men cease to whip, or kill negroes who become obnoxious, that they will take advantage of the laxity, and soon make this state untenable for whites of ALL kinds, and that under such conditions the 'best' will be like the worst, and the worst like the best." Who actually killed Crawford mattered little, according to Beard, because all whites shared in the blame. Whites of all classes taught their children to "keep nigger in his place," said Beard, and the failure of elite whites to legally assign blacks to a subordinate caste made interracial violence a necessity.[1]

Beard viewed lynching primarily as an instrument of racial oppression, and most modern scholars of lynching would agree with this interpretation.[2] But Beard's perceptions about the causes of lynching also acknowledge the importance of interpersonal conflict as a cause of racial violence. Indeed, many lynchings (Crawford's included) share striking similarities with "scenarios of violence" that sociologists associate with models of masculine homicide, especially those involving honor conflicts and personal disputes. The problem with viewing lynching as primarily a mechanism of white social control is that such a perspective tends to obscure the reactive nature of lynching violence. Rarely was lynching something that whites deliberately planned to inflict on a black victim. Rather, lynching, like masculine homicide, was often "the outcome of a dynamic interchange between an offender, victim, and . . . bystanders."[3] Models of masculine homicide emphasize the importance of honor altercations and conflict resolution as catalysts for male homicidal violence, and the same kinds of interpersonal dynamics were also the precipitating cause of many lynchings.[4]

Lynching Victims

The typical black lynching victim was far from an outcast in southern society. Most black lynching victims in Mississippi and South Carolina, for example, were agricultural workers, primarily tenants, who had lived and worked in the same area for years. Black tenants and white landlords often had a mercurial relationship because black tenants routinely resisted the attempts of white landlords to impose their will on work arrangements, crop settlements, monetary matters, freedom of movement, and interpersonal relations. The violent conflict that these disputes could engender often precipitated lynching, especially when whites interpreted such resistance as an affront to their personal honor and the continued political and social hegemony of white males.[5]

Black tenant Major Clark, for instance, was lynched near Shubuta, Mississippi, in 1918 because he dared to oppose the sexual relationship that his employer was having with Clark's fiancée and her sister. (The two women and Clark's brother were also lynched.)[6] Clark's employer, E. L. Johnston, was a thirty-five-year-old alcoholic dentist from Mobile, Alabama. Johnston failed as a dentist in Mobile and then decided to become an itinerant dentist in the Red Hills region of Mississippi, where his father owned a profitable farm. During one of his trips through the country, Johnston apparently seduced a twenty-year-old black woman named Maggie Howze. Johnston's country practice also collapsed, which prompted him to take over his father's farm. Later the philandering dentist invited Maggie and her younger sister, Alma, to live and work on his farm so that "he could have [Maggie] at his disposal whenever he wished."[7] Although Johnston was married and had a child, he apparently felt no remorse over his many extramarital affairs.

When the Howze sisters arrived on the farm, Clark and his brother Andrew were working for Johnston to pay a debt on a mule that their father had purchased from the dentist. Major Clark began courting Maggie Howze, and the two eventually decided to marry. Johnston became enraged over the relationship, however, and bluntly told Clark that he would kill him if he did not stop seeing Maggie. The animosity between Clark and Johnston grew worse when Clark learned that both Maggie and Alma were pregnant and that Johnston was the father in both instances.

One morning in mid-December 1918, Johnston was shot in his barn while milking a cow. Suspicion immediately focused on Major Clark, who had carried the mortally wounded dentist to his house. Johnston's father, however, a former member of the Mississippi state legislature, did not believe that Clark had killed his son and later even pleaded for Clark's life before a mob. Many whites in Shubuta, moreover, believed that a white man had killed Johnston because of another sexual affair in which the dentist was involved. But the private beliefs of whites mattered little in this instance because of the widespread perception that Clark had killed Johnston because he was Clark's sexual rival. White anger over Clark's alleged actions was no doubt intensified because Clark was Johnston's employee and because the dentist was killed without warning. These circumstances transformed Johnston's death into a public challenge to the collective manhood of local white males, similar to the individual provocations that constitute the basis for many honor-related homicides.[8]

A week and a half elapsed between the killing of Johnston and the preliminary hearing to arraign Clark, his brother Andrew, and the Howze sisters on murder charges. To prevent a lynching, all four were held outside Shubuta. Major Clark was held in Meridian, some forty miles from Shubuta, where authorities extracted a confession from him by smashing his testicles in a vice. When the defendants were returned to Shubuta for their hearing, it was a foregone conclusion that they would be lynched. The day of the arraignment, scores of cars and people began pouring into Shubuta after dark, prompting the chief of police to leave town for Meridian. When a mob arrived to remove the prisoners from jail, the deputy sheriff in charge allowed himself to be handcuffed at the mob's request. Shortly thereafter, the well-orchestrated mob cut all power to the town.

The mob drove the four victims to a covered bridge over the Chickasawha River, a short distance from Shubuta. Four ropes were tied to a girder under the bridge and placed around the victims' necks. To their dying breaths the victims insisted that they were innocent and begged for mercy. When Maggie Howze screamed for her life, a mob member silenced her with a monkey wrench to the mouth, which knocked out some of her teeth. He then bashed Maggie in the head, leaving a half-inch-wide gash in her skull. The mob threw each of the victims over the bridge with the ropes around their necks. The Clark brothers and Alma Howze each died instantly, but Maggie twice caught herself on the side of the bridge before finally succumbing. The next day mob members laughed about how that "big black Jersey woman" had desperately clung to life.

When the bodies were "discovered," local African Americans refused to retrieve them, saying, "The white folks lynched them, and they can cut them down." After the bodies were brought to a white funeral home, some witnesses claimed to see Alma Howze's child still moving in her womb. The victims were eventually buried, without the benefit of religious services, just outside the white cemetery. (African Americans in Shubuta refused to accept the bodies into the black cemetery.) The lynching prompted many black tenants to flee, leaving crops to decay in the fields. The brutal lynching was done in defense of a white man's "right" to treat African Americans in any way that he pleased. The mob, which was led by a prominent local merchant, felt compelled to act not because they wanted to avenge the honor of a known philanderer but because Major Clark's aggressive behavior had created the fear among whites that "no white man who had wronged a Negro would be safe" from future acts of violent retribution.

The Clark-Howze lynching was precipitated by a specific event that was interpreted (rightly or wrongly) by the white community as a direct challenge to the continued hegemony of white males, but many other southern lynchings grew out of social tensions that developed between a particular black male and the larger white community. This sort of lynching can be compared to "conflict-resolution" homicides, which typically develop over an extended period of time, exhibit evidence of premeditation, and involve persistent disputes that one or more of the major actors in a homicide comes to believe has to be resolved through violence.[9]

A "conflict-resolution" lynching often involved an individual who persistently opposed the oppressive nature of the southern racial system. Wilder McGowan, for instance, was a young, industrious black entrepreneur, whom whites lynched near Wiggins, Mississippi, in November 1938. Whites accused McGowan of raping and robbing a seventy-four-year-old white woman, but an NAACP investigator claimed that McGowan's innocence was well known throughout Wiggins and that the alleged crime was merely used as an excuse to lynch McGowan because he "did not know his place."

The twenty-four-year-old McGowan owned a prosperous moving and hauling business and lived with his aged grandmother. McGowan was a marked man in Wiggins apparently because he had repeatedly resisted the violent intimidation of local whites. On one occasion, a mob of drunken whites attacked McGowan after he refused to flee when some white hoodlums tried to run some blacks down with a car. McGowan fought the ruffians off and took a revolver from one white man, whereupon the miscreants left him alone. On another occasion, McGowan wounded a white man with a knife after a mob tried to enter an African American dance hall in search of some "good-looking nigger women."[10]

The unsuspecting McGowan was lynched one morning while working on his truck. A mob that included the local sheriff and his deputies forced McGowan at gunpoint to a wooded area and "hanged him without any investigation or consideration."[11] A white merchant drove McGowan's body back to Wiggins, where white residents viewed it with merriment. In the meantime, a group of white law officers, merchants, laborers, and others severely beat a black woman and a young black man in separate incidents, bringing the day's activities to a suitable conclusion.[12]

Anthony Crawford

The social tension that resulted from the desire of African Americans for equality with whites was a primary cause of violent racial conflict in the

South, and this was no more evident than in the case of Anthony Crawford. Similar to Wilder McGowan's lynching, the Crawford lynching has
many of the same characteristics as a "conflict-resolution" male homicide.
Crawford was a longtime resident of his community, with a history of
challenging white sensibilities about blacks. Although Crawford's lynching was precipitated by a specific racial incident, it was clearly the result
of years of tension between Crawford and the Abbeville white community. Finally, both Crawford and the whites who lynched him were willing to use violence to resolve the racial disputes that Crawford's behavior
engendered.[13]

Crawford was lynched in Abbeville, which prided itself on being the
home of John C. Calhoun and claimed to be the site of both the birth and
the death of the Confederacy. Abbeville was an attractive town, filled with
majestic oaks, stately mansions, and manicured lawns reminiscent of its
storied past. The elegant facade of Abbeville's genteel elite, however, was
but a thin veneer that covered a virulent and pervasive racism. Working-
class whites around Abbeville's mill district, for instance, had formed an
armed club of some one hundred men that had regular contact with the
Josh Ashley clan from Anderson County, another group of violent racists
that was responsible for several lynchings.[14]

The "best people" of Abbeville, moreover, routinely gave their bless-
ing to violence against African Americans, which they regarded as a necessary evil. J. Allen Smith, the president of the National Bank of Abbeville, for example, claimed that he only wanted Crawford beaten, but he
insisted that "Crawford was insolent to a white man and he deserved a
thrashing." W. P. Greene, a lawyer and editor of the Abbeville *Press and
Banner,* described Crawford as a "vicious Negro" who was "too eager to
curse and abuse a white man and assert his manhood." Violence against
"uppity" African Americans was commonplace in Abbeville. "When a nigger gets impudent," commented a local gin manager, "we stretch him out
and paddle him a bit."[15] Anthony Crawford earned the animosity of
whites of all classes because he was prosperous and because he had a
confident, aggressive posture that was unsettling to the prevailing racial
orthodoxy.

An important contributing factor in the Crawford lynching, moreover,
was the desire of some disgruntled local white politicians to embarrass
Sheriff R. M. Burts and Governor Richard Manning. Burts came from
a wealthy, well-connected Abbeville family, and the genteel Manning

unexpectedly appointed Burts sheriff despite his lack of qualifications. This angered those who felt that Police Chief Joe Johnson should have been given the job. Burts was subsequently elected to a four-year term after defeating Jess Cann and George White, two men who would later play a central role in the lynching of Crawford.[16]

In the 1916 August gubernatorial primary, Manning ran against former governor Coleman Blease and Abbeville county solicitor Robert Cooper. The candidates held a debate in Abbeville in July, at which Blease decried Manning's progressive attitude toward race relations and claimed that this had encouraged an outbreak of murderous assaults by blacks against white men and women. In the first primary Blease swamped Manning and Cooper in Abbeville County, and in the runoff Blease again defeated Manning in Abbeville County, even though Manning narrowly won the statewide election. A young Bleasite attorney named Sam Adams also ran a strong race for the state legislature but lost by a narrow margin. Perhaps hoping to boost his political stature, Adams took an active role in the Crawford lynching and bragged that he had placed the rope around Crawford's neck and had fired the first shot. Hoping to ride such heroics to new heights of popularity, the firebrand Adams asked editor Beard to prominently feature him in a story about the lynching and to name him as one of the ringleaders.[17]

The racial hatred that Abbeville whites felt toward Anthony Crawford was due in large part to his remarkable material success. Crawford was a literate, fifty-six-year-old former slave, who owned some 427 acres of prime cotton land on the Little River about seven miles west of Abbeville.[18] As a boy Anthony Crawford helped his father farm a small cotton patch. He was an ambitious lad who routinely walked seven miles to and from Abbeville to attend school. Over the years the dapper and determined Crawford transformed the ambition and perseverance of his youth into a considerable fortune. In his early twenties Crawford purchased nearly 200 acres of land for $830. Just five years later, in 1888, Crawford bought about 100 acres of land for $670 that bordered on the farms of his father and his brother. By the mid-1890s Crawford had achieved enough prominence to help found the Industrial Union of Abbeville County, which was dedicated to promoting the "material moral and intellectual advancement of the colored people." Around the turn of the century, Crawford completed his land holdings, acquiring about 170 acres of land for $700 in 1899 and then another 113 acres of land for $800 in 1903. At the time of his death in 1916, Crawford's estate was worth approximately $25,000.[19]

Crawford's prosperity was well known in the white community. On at least two occasions one of the local papers ran a story about the success of Crawford's farming operations. In November 1904, for instance, the Abbeville *Medium* reported that Crawford had raised a "splendid" 1,000-bushel crop of corn along with forty-eight bales of cotton. The paper also reported, somewhat enviously, that Crawford owned six horses, twelve head of cattle, eighteen hogs, two wagons, a McCormick rake, a new top buggy, and a substantial bank account.[20]

Anthony Crawford was not a humble man, and material success only bolstered his self-confidence. For nearly two decades he was the chief benefactor and secretary of the Chapel A.M.E. Church, which he dominated as completely as any bishop. On one occasion, for example, Crawford opposed a preacher who wanted to expel one of the church members. The next Sunday the irate pastor addressed the congregation about "boss-ridden" institutions. Crawford leapt to his feet, slapped the preacher, and fired him on the spot. The self-assured Crawford deferred to no man, black or white. According to a contemporary, success had convinced Crawford that he was both "the equal of some white men and the superior of others."[21]

Crawford passed this confidence along to his twelve sons and four daughters. He tried to provide his children with all the advantages of wealth. Some of his sons attended college, and all of the children had farms in close proximity to their father.[22] In late December of 1905, several of Crawford's sons had an altercation with some white men, one of whom, James Rodgers, suffered a gunshot wound. Four of Crawford's sons were eventually convicted of aggravated assault, but Crawford hired an attorney to appeal the decision. (Crawford eventually paid a $500 fine on behalf of his sons.) Later he tried to settle the dispute when, in September of 1908, he wrote an open letter to a local paper in which he assured whites "that no one deplores the matter more than I." Crawford promised that both he and his family would "strive to make as good citizens in the future as we have in the past" and said that he had "nothing but a friendly feeling" for his opponents.[23] Years later when Crawford was lynched, the mayor of Abbeville, C. C. Gamble, happened to be a relative of James Rodgers, and although Gamble witnessed much of the lynching, he predictably did nothing to stop it.

Although Crawford hoped that in the future whites and blacks could "settle their differences, legally and amicably," such apologies did not mollify those whites who "had been figuring on giving him [Crawford] a licking for a long time."[24] Whites resented that Crawford sometimes hired black laborers, who were already under contract with white farmers, and that he usually had plenty of help even when labor was scarce.[25]

In the years preceding the Crawford lynching, moreover, race relations in Abbeville County were far from congenial. In March 1910, for instance, whites burned a local black college to the ground and three black male students were killed in the fire.[26] Three years later, some Abbeville whites castrated a black youth because a young white woman thought the boy was going to insult her. One of the perpetrators of this atrocity took an active part in the Crawford lynching, bragging about his exploits and encouraging those present to lynch that "damn nigger Crawford."[27] Fifteen months before Crawford's death, whites lynched a black man named Will Lozier, after Lozier mortally wounded the son of a well-known white farmer during an argument on a public road.[28] Finally, just a few weeks before Crawford was killed, a young black man was severely whipped for allegedly insulting a white store clerk. A more circumspect man might have modified his behavior in light of such atrocities—but not Anthony Crawford. Crawford feared no one; he once told a friend, "The day a white man hits me is the day I die."[29]

Crawford's Death

The day that Crawford died was Saturday, October 21, 1916, when he came to Abbeville with two loads of cotton and a load of seed. While waiting in line for the cotton gin, Crawford went to sell his seed at the store of W. D. Barksdale. Crawford knew that cottonseed was selling for ninety cents a pound, so when Barksdale offered only eighty-five cents Crawford told him that he had already received a better offer. Barksdale called Crawford a liar, which incensed the proud farmer, who cursed Barksdale for trying to cheat him. After Barksdale retreated inside his store, Crawford continued his tirade, saying he would not sell "to any damn white man only at his [Barksdale's] price." Two of Barksdale's clerks, one of whom was the son of the president of the People's Bank of Abbeville, then armed themselves with axe handles and attempted to beat Crawford, but he fended them off. As Crawford fled across the town square, Sheriff Burts arrested him. Before Burts could escort Crawford to the municipal

building, however, a crowd intent on whipping Crawford for his animad-
versions gathered quickly, but the men were easily dispersed. After the
crowd had gone, Police Chief Johnson released Crawford on fifteen dol-
lars bail. Johnson then went home, allegedly sick, and did nothing to prevent the subsequent lynching.[30]

While Crawford was arranging his bail, Barksdale talked with McKinney Cann, a local strongman who belonged to the same Baptist church as
Barksdale. Barksdale asked Cann to organize a mob to whip Crawford
and "cure him if possible," but the pusillanimous merchant wanted no direct role in the beating.[31] When Crawford began to make his way back to
the cotton gin, someone alerted the mob while another man blocked the
jail door from the outside and prevented Sheriff Burts from leaving. Real-
izing the danger, Crawford fled for the gin and hid in a partially covered
pit in the boiler room. There he found a four-pound hammer and waited.
When McKinney Cann peered into the pit, Crawford smashed his skull
with the hammer and would probably have killed Cann if someone had
not restrained his arm. Someone in the mob then crushed Crawford's head
with a rock and he collapsed. The mob, which included three brothers of
McKinney Cann, took Crawford outside to the street, where he regained
consciousness and tried to escape. Fighting his way some fifty feet, Crawford beat six of the mob rather badly before being stabbed in the back
with a knife. The gin superintendent and two furniture dealers tried to
prevent the beating, but as Crawford lay in the street, two hundred men
kicked and beat him unconscious.

Crawford probably would have been lynched then and there had it
not been for Sheriff Burts, who pleaded with the mob to release Crawford
to his custody. For forty-five minutes Burts implored his constituents not
to tarnish his reputation and violate his oath of office by lynching Crawford. Finally after promising Lester and Jack Cann that Crawford would
not be moved until their brother's condition had stabilized, Burts was allowed to remove the bloodied Crawford to the county jail. At the jail
Mayor Gamble, who was also a doctor, treated Crawford and declared
that he would probably die.

Around 3:45 P.M. a rumor started that Sheriff Burts was going to put
Crawford on the 4 o'clock train. This rumor, coupled with the fear that
Crawford would die before he could be lynched, prompted the now
drunken mob to storm the jail. Neither the sheriff nor the jailer resisted as
the mob took their guns and keys. The beaten and broken Crawford was
quickly dragged down three flights of stairs and thrown into the street

amidst a chorus of cheers. Some men, including the grandson of the county coroner, pummeled Crawford with rocks while others beat him with wagon boards. The mob repeatedly lifted Crawford by the shoulders and feet, threw him on the ground, and jumped, spit, and beat on him. A white woman, named Mrs. D. A. Dewey, phoned Mayor Gamble to stop the violence, but he replied that his hands were tied. The mob then dragged Crawford through the black district as a warning to "good niggers." Such diversions were not appreciated in the more elegant part of town, however, so the mob threw Crawford's lifeless body onto a passing load of slabs so as not to unduly offend the "better class of people," who lived in their august and princely homes and were "strongly opposed to work of this character, but . . . were all helpless before the frenzied mob." [32]

When the mob reached the fairgrounds, Crawford was surely dead, but they hanged him anyway and then emptied several hundred rounds into his body. At sunset Coroner F. W. R. Nance led a jury up the lynching hill. Knowing that his grandson had taken an active part in the lynching, Nance appointed two members of the lynch mob to the jury, which decided without taking any evidence that Crawford had been killed by parties unknown. [33] That night, with liquor flowing freely, a drunken and unruly mob decided to drive the Crawford children and their families from the area. Upon seeing the mob, one prominent citizen commented, "If they ever started they'd shoot every nigger along that seven miles of road." Fearing a bloodbath, three or four leading businessmen convinced the mob to forgo further violence by arranging a meeting on the next Monday, October 23, to decide what to do about the Crawford family. [34]

The Monday meeting was well attended and attracted persons from as far away as Anderson County, twenty miles to the north. The Cann faction wanted to take immediate action, but again the town's "better" element, led by court clerk Jack Perrin, bank president J. Allen Smith, and merchant J. S. Stark, prevailed and agreed to convince the Crawfords to leave the state by November 15. When Perrin, Smith, and Stark returned, they told the meeting of several hundred persons that the Crawfords were good "niggers" and that they had agreed to leave the state at any time but preferred to stay on their father's farm. The committee's report was interrupted, however, by a revolver shot and shouts of "Run 'em out today!" and "Lynch the black bastards!" A vote was then taken and the meeting unanimously decided that the Crawfords should be gone by November 15.

But Abbeville's elites had once again lost control of the situation, and the terror began anew when a mob forced all the black businesses in

Abbeville to close. The only black business to remain open was the blacksmith shop and that only because Jack Perrin faced down the mob when they came to close it. The mob also engaged in "some shooting to impress the negroes that they meant business." When one group of terrified blacks fled to the house of the aforementioned Mrs. Dewey during the pogrom, the courageous woman appeared with a rifle and drove the mob from her lawn. Later Mrs. Dewey's husband asked her why she had not fired at the mob, and she replied that she felt reluctant to shoot "dogs in the back as these people were dogs of the lowest type."[35]

African Americans refused to shop at the stores of white merchants in response to these outrages. Mayor Gamble, who had done nothing to stop the lynching, now admitted that business had fallen off frightfully and that black laborers were leaving fast. The refusal of blacks to purchase goods from white merchants and the exodus of black labor prompted white businessmen to publicly condemn those who wanted the Crawford children to leave the county. In mid-November a twelve-man "reconciliation committee" was formed, and the Crawfords were allowed to remain on their land.

The Crawford lynching had far-reaching consequences for Abbeville County. Whites were unable to stem the migratory flow of black labor. One prescient white paper, the Columbia *State*, hoped that the migration and economic boycott might finally convince whites to refrain from lynching. Whites had "lynched their own pocketbooks," said the *State* on October 23, and with the coming of the boll weevil the situation could only get worse. Unless mobs ceased, the *State* feared that lynching and boll weevils would "drive away the labor from farms and bankrupt this Southern country." White farmers needed more black labor, in the *State*'s opinion, not less, and the paper reminded its readers that the "flight of the Israelites from Egypt still has its lessons." From the perspective of white landowners, at least, the *State* claimed that the deleterious effects of mobs were "hard facts [that] are unlynchable." The 1920 census confirmed this assessment: Abbeville County lost over 30 percent of its black population in the 1910s compared with an average of less than 1 percent for all South Carolina counties.

"Property ownership," said one prominent white South Carolina newspaper editor, "always makes the Negro more assertive, more independent, and the poor whites can't stand it." But the success of a man like Anthony Crawford was offensive to both rich and poor whites alike.[36]

A bank president from Abbeville told a state investigator that he believed Crawford should have been lynched, since lynching was the only way to handle such matters in the South. A Dr. Harrison, president of the Farmers' Bank, commented that Crawford was insolent to whites and got what he deserved. Although Harrison wanted the law upheld, he did not want "a white man's right to whip a negro once in a while interfered with." After interviewing many of Abbeville's most prominent citizens, New York investigative reporter Roy Nash concluded that Crawford had been lynched simply because "he lacked the humility becoming a 'nigger.'" In the end Crawford was lynched because he lived as if he could be both black and the social equal of white men at the same time. But for black men in the South "to exercise manhood, as white men displayed it," was, according to South Carolina native Benjamin E. Mays, "to invite disaster."[37]

The desire among many whites to strip blacks of every vestige of equality allowed the more vicious members of the white community to use violence with impunity. Despite the well-intentioned efforts of Governor Manning to bring Crawford's murderers to justice, the bloodletting in Abbeville County continued. Amazingly, just three years after Crawford's death, the Cann family figured prominently in another Abbeville lynching, which again stemmed from a violent confrontation between a black man and a white man. Lester Cann, who by this time had become an Abbeville sheriff's deputy, was allegedly shot and killed by a black man named Mark Smith. Shortly after Smith was acquitted of murder, however, a mob riddled Smith with bullets in the presence of his wife and mother.[38]

The lynching of Anthony Crawford was due in part to the desire among a few whites to eliminate a rather unsettling exception to the doctrine of white supremacy. But the Crawford lynching was, as William Beard noted, an extension of the "spirit of [18]76" when the "TRUE white people of South Carolina arose en masse . . . armed themselves and in defiance of every law, trampled the authority of the federal government in the dust, shot, hung, beat and bullied negroes out of their constitutional rights, and to make sure of their position, stole the state government from them through a fraudulent election, in order to save the state of civilization." Only "fools and cowards" tampered with sentiments that were stronger than any law, opined Beard.[39] African Americans, of course, saw things otherwise, and many "fools" like Major Clark, Wilder McGowan, and Anthony Crawford refused to endure the indignities of white ascendancy at the cost of their very lives.

Notes

1. Abbeville *Scimitar*, 1 February 1917. The information on Anthony Crawford and his lynching is taken from many sources, the two most important being Roy Nash, "The Lynching of Anthony Crawford: South Carolina Declares an End to Mob Rule," New York *Independent*, 11 December 1916; and a series of investigative reports from detective J. B. Eagan to Governor Richard I. Manning, Manning Papers, 1915–1919, South Carolina Department of Archives and History (SCDAH), box 15, miscellaneous—lynching. Other sources that were consulted include *Papers of the NAACP*, microfilm, *Series A: The South* (Bethesda, Md.: University Publications of America, 1991), reel 15, frames 360–404; Tuskegee Newsclipping files, microfilm edition, roll 221, frames 376–403; Garris 1973, 14–24; and Devlin 1989, 171–88. The story of Crawford's lynching is also told in Schweninger 1990, 233–35.

2. Tolnay and Beck 1995, 18–19; Brundage 1993, 17–19.

3. Luckenbill 1977, 185.

4. Polk 1994, 85–92, 127–35.

5. Finnegan 1996.

6. The sordid details surrounding the Howze-Clark lynching can be found in *Papers of the NAACP*, reel 13, frames 1128–63. The famed Walter White was the NAACP's primary investigator in the case.

7. Walter White, "An Example of Democracy in Mississippi," *Papers of the NAACP*, reel 13, frames 1155–63.

8. Polk 1994, 91.

9. Ibid., 129, 133.

10. Letter from Thurgood Marshall, assistant special counsel for the NAACP, to U.S. Attorney General Frank Murphy, 15 April 1939, Department of Justice, Record Group 60, file 158260, box 1230xg, sec. 45, National Archives; *St. Louis Argus*, 16 December 1938.

11. Letter from George Baldwin, Wiggins, Mississippi, to Joseph Gelders, chairman of the National Committee for People's Rights, Birmingham, Alabama, 21 November 1938, Department of Justice, Record Group 60, file 158260, box 1230xg, section 45, National Archives.

12. Marshall to Murphy, 15 April 1939.

13. Polk (1994, 129) identifies three general characteristics of conflict-resolution homicides: the victim and offender must know one another for a considerable period of time; the conflict between the parties must be the result of a dispute that builds over time; and one of the parties must finally decide to use violence to resolve the matter.

14. Eagan, report of 25 November 1916, SCDAH.

15. Nash 1916; Ware n.d., 186.

16. Eagan, report of 21 November 1916, SCDAH; Garris 1973, 22; Nash 1916.

17. Ware n.d., 186; Eagan, reports of 10 November 1916 and 20 November 1916, SCDAH.

18. Letter from W. C. Crawford to R. I. Manning, 25 November 1916, SCDAH.

19. Ware n.d., 184; Eagan, report of 11 November 1916, SCDAH.

20. Ware n.d., 185.

21. Nash 1916; Eagan, report of 11 November 1916, SCDAH.

22. Nash 1916.

23. Charleston *News and Courier,* 10 December 1905, 13 September 1906; Ware n.d., 185.

24. Eagan, report of 19 November 1916, SCDAH.

25. Garris 1973, 17.

26. Helsley 1988.

27. Eagan, report of 20 November 1916, SCDAH.

28. Charleston *News and Courier,* 15 July 1915.

29. Eagan, report of 11 November 1916, SCDAH; Nash 1916.

30. Eagan, report of 28 November 1916, SCDAH; Nash 1916.

31. Eagan, report of 11 November 1916, SCDAH.

32. Eagan, report of 9 November 1916, SCDAH.

33. Eagan, reports of 18 and 23 November 1916; letter from J. Howard Moore to R. I. Manning, 1 November 1916, SCDAH.

34. Nash 1916; Columbia *State,* 9 November and 23 October 1916.

35. Eagan, report of 23 November 1916, SCDAH.

36. Nash 1916.

37. Eagan, report of 11 November 1916, SCDAH; Nash 1916; Mays 1987, 26.

38. Abbeville *Medium,* no date; Tuskegee Newsclipping files, roll 221, frame 835.

39. Abbeville *Scimitar,* 15 February 1917.

REFERENCES

About, Edmond. 1861. *Rome contemporaine.* 4th ed. Paris.

Adler, Jeffrey Scott. 1991. *Yankee merchants and the making of the urban west: The rise and fall of antebellum St. Louis.* Cambridge.

Allen, Judith. 1989. Men, crime and criminology: Recasting the questions. *International Journal of the Sociology of Law* 17:19–39.

———. 1990. *Sex and secrets: Crimes involving Australian women since 1880.* Melbourne: Oxford University Press.

Allgemeines Landrecht für die preußischen Staaten von 1794. 1970. Frankfurt.

Amussen, Susan Dwyer. 1988. *An ordered society: Gender and class in early modern England.* Oxford: Oxford University Press.

Andrew, Donna T. 1980. The code of honour and its critics: The opposition to duelling in England, 1700–1850. *Social History* 5:409–34.

Armstrong, Nancy. 1987. *Desire and domestic fiction: A political history of the novel.* New York.

Aschenbrenner, M. 1804. *Über das Verbrechen und die Strafe des Zweikampfs.* Würzburg.

Atti costitutivi dell' Associazione della Stampa Periodica in Italia. 1877. Rome: Popolo Romano.

Atti della Commissione Parlamentare chiamata a dare il proprio parere sul progetto di un nuovo codice penale. 1930. Rome: Senato.

Audoin-Rouzeau, Stéphane. 1992. *Men at war, 1914–1918: National sentiment and trench journalism in France during the First World War.* Trans. Helen MacPhail. Oxford: Berg.

———. 1993. *La Guerre des enfants: Essai d'histoire culturelle.* Paris: Armand Colin.

Auspitz, Katherine. 1982. *The radical bourgeoisie: The Ligue de l'Enseignement and the origins of the Third Republic.* Cambridge: Cambridge University Press.

Ayers, Edward L. 1984. *Vengeance and justice: Crime and punishment in the nineteenth-century American South.* New York: Oxford University Press.

———. 1992. *The promise of the New South: Life after Reconstruction.* New York: Oxford University Press.

Backhouse, Constance. 1984. Desperate women and compassionate courts: Infanticide in nineteenth-century Canada. *University of Toronto Law Journal* 34:447–78.

——. 1985. Nineteenth-century Canadian prostitution law. *Social History* [Canada] 18:387–424.

——. 1986. The tort of seduction: Fathers and daughters in nineteenth-century Canada. *Dalhousie Law Journal* 10:45–80.

Bahr, Hermann. 1918. *1917*. Innsbruck.

Baker, Benjamin A. 1857. *A Glance at New York . . . as performed at the principal English and American theaters.* New York.

Baker, Jean. 1977. *Ambivalent Americans: The Know-Nothing Party in Maryland.* Baltimore.

Balduin, F. 1621. *Christlicher Unterricht vom Balgen auß Heiliger Göttlicher Schrifft genommen.* Wittenberg.

Barker-Benfield, G. J. 1992. *The culture of sensibility: Sex and society in eighteenth-century Britain.* Chicago: University of Chicago Press.

Baronti, G. 1986. *Coltelli d'Italia: Rituali di violenza e tradizioni produttive nel mondo popolare.* Padua.

Bartoccini, F. 1985. *Roma nell' Ottocento.* 2 vols. Bologna.

Bartunek, J. 1912. *Die Austragung von Ehrenangelegenheiten.* Vienna.

Basevi, P. 1954. *Introduzione a Roma contemporanea.* Rome.

Beattie, John M. 1985. Violence and society in early modern England. In *Perspectives in Criminal Law,* ed. A. N. Doob and E. L. Greenspan, 36–61. Aurora, Ont.

——. 1986. *Crime and the courts in England, 1660–1800.* Oxford: Oxford University Press.

Becker, Marvin B. 1976. Changing patterns of violence and justice in fourteenth- and fifteenth-century Florence. *Comparative Studies in Society and History: An International Quarterly* 18 (3): 281–96.

Behlmer, George. 1982. *Child abuse and moral reform in England, 1870–1908.* Stanford: Stanford University Press.

Bennassar, Bartolomé. 1975. *L'Homme espagnol: Attitudes et mentalités du 16e au 19e siècle.* Paris.

Billacois, François. 1986. *Le duel dans la société française des 16e–17e siècles: Essai de psychosociologie historique.* Paris. English translation: *The duel: Its rise and fall in early modern France.* New Haven: Yale University Press, 1990.

Blengini-di-San-Grato, C. A. 1868. *Duello e sue norme principali per effettuarlo.* Padua: Prosperini.

Blok, Anton. 1974. *The mafia of a Sicilian Village, 1860–1960: A study of violent peasant entrepreneurs.* New York: Harper and Row.

——. 1980. Eer en de fysieke persoon. *Tijdschrift voor Sociale Geschiedenis* 18:211–30.

——. 1991. Zinloos en zinvol geweld. *Amsterdams Sociologisch Tijdschrift* 18 (3): 189–207.

Bodio, L. 1885. Relazione sullo studio retrospettivo della delinquenza secondo le statistiche degli undici anni 1873–1883. *Annali di statistica,* ser. 3, vol. 15, *Atti della*

Commissione per il riordinamento della statistica giudiziaria civile e penale, February 1885, 45–81. Rome.

Boritch, Helen, and John Hagan. 1990. A century of crime in Toronto: Gender, class, and patterns of social control, 1859–1955. *Criminology* 28:567–99.

Boschi, Daniele. 1996. L'omicidio a Roma fra la metà dell' Ottocento e la prima guerra mondiale, 1841–1914. Diss., University of Rome.

Bosco, A. 1898. *L'omicidio in Italia.* Rome.

Bourdieu, Pierre. 1972. *Esquisse d'une théorie de la pratique, précédé de trois études d'ethnologie Kabyle.* Geneva.

———. 1980. *Le Sens pratique.* Paris.

Boyd, William H. 1858. *The Baltimore city directory: Containing the names of the citizens, a subscriber's business directory, state and city records, a street directory, (never before published) and an appendix of much useful information.* Baltimore.

Breittmayer, Georges. 1918. *Code de l'honneur et du duel.* Paris: Privately printed.

Brennan, Thomas. 1988. *Public drinking and popular culture in eighteenth-century Paris.* Princeton: Princeton University Press.

Bresciani, A. 1862. *Edmondo o dei costumi del popolo romano.* 2d ed. Milan.

Broers, Michael. 1990. Revolution as vendetta: Napoleonic Piedmont, 1801–1814. *Historical Journal,* 573–97, 787–809.

Brooks-Higginbotham, Evelyn. 1993. *Righteous discontent: The women's movement in the black Baptist church, 1880–1920.* Cambridge: Harvard University Press.

Brown, Keith M. 1986. *Bloodfeud in Scotland, 1573–1625: Violence, justice, and politics in an early modern society.* Edinburgh.

Brown, Richard Maxwell. 1975. *Strain of violence: Historical studies of American violence and vigilantism.* New York.

———. 1991. *No duty to retreat: Violence and values in American history and society.* New York: Oxford University Press.

Browne, Gary L. 1980. *Baltimore in the nation.* Chapel Hill: University of North Carolina Press.

Bruce, Dickson D., Jr. 1979. *Violence and culture in the Antebellum South.* Austin: University of Texas Press.

Brüdermann, Stefan. 1991. *Der göttinger Studentenauszug 1790: Handwerkerehre und akademische Freiheit.* Göttingen.

Brundage, W. Fitzhugh. 1993. *Lynching in the New South: Georgia and Virginia, 1880–1930.* Urbana: University of Illinois Press.

Burke, Peter. 1978. *Popular culture in early modern Europe.* New York: New York University Press.

———. 1987. *The historical anthropology of early modern Italy: Essays on perception and communication.* Cambridge: Cambridge University Press.

Bushman, Richard L. 1992. *The refinement of America: Persons, houses, cities.* New York: Knopf.

Butterfield, Fox. 1995. *All God's children: The Bosket family and the American tradition of violence.* New York: Knopf.

Bynum, Caroline Walker. 1987. *Holy feast and holy fast: The religious significance of food to medieval women.* Berkeley: University of California Press.

———. 1991. *Fragmentation and redemption: Essays on gender and the human body in medieval religion.* New York: Zone Books.

Bynum, Victoria E. 1992. *Unruly women: The politics of social and sexual control in the Old South.* Chapel Hill: University of North Carolina Press.

Cadden, Joan. 1993. *Meanings of sex difference in the Middle Ages: Medicine, science and culture.* Cambridge: Cambridge University Press.

Cafagna, L. 1952. Anarchismo e socialismo a Roma negli anni della "febbre edilizia" e della crisi 1882–1891. *Movimento Operaio,* 729–71.

Cain, Maureen, ed. 1989. *Growing up good: Policing the behaviour of girls in Europe.* London.

———. 1990. Towards transgression: New directions in feminist criminology. *International Journal of the Sociology of Law* 18:1–18.

Cajani, Luigi. 1991. Pena di morte e tortura a Roma nel '700. In *Criminalità e società in età moderna,* ed. Luigi Berlinguer, 517–47. La Leopoldina, vol. 12. Milan.

Camporesi, Piero. 1988. *The incorruptible flesh: Bodily mutation and mortification in religion and folklore.* Cambridge: Cambridge University Press.

Caracciolo, A. 1984. *Roma capitale: Dal Risorgimento alla crisi dello stato liberale.* 3d ed. Rome.

Carnes, Mark C., and Clyde Griffen, eds. 1990. *Meanings for manhood: Constructions of masculinity in Victorian America.* Chicago: University of Chicago Press.

Carrasco, Raphaël. 1990. La violence physique d'après les archives judiciaires: Le cas de Cuenca, 1535–1623. In *Le corps dans la société espagnole des 16e et 17e siècles,* ed. Augustin Redondo, 165–71. International Colloqium, Sorbonne, 5–8 October 1988. Paris.

Carrington, Kerry. 1990. Feminist readings of female delinquency. *Law in Context* 8:5–31.

Cassedy, J. Albert. 1891. *The firemen's record.* Baltimore.

Castracane Mombelli, M. 1979. Le fonti archivistiche per la storia delle codificazioni pontificie, 1816–1870. *Società e Storia* 6:839–64.

Cavallo, Sandra, and Simona Cerutti. 1990. Female honor and the social control of reproduction in Piedmont between 1600 and 1800. In *Sex and gender in historical perspective,* ed. Edward Muir and Guido Ruggiero, 110–40. Selections from *Quaderni Storici.* Baltimore: Johns Hopkins University Press.

Cerroni, A. M. 1995. La criminalità comune a Roma fra il 1849 ed il 1859 attraverso le fonti del Tribunale criminale. Thesis. Rome.

Cesana, Giuseppe Agosto. 1874. *Il primo duello (dalle memorie di un giornalista): Almanacco di Fanfulla.* Rome: Dell'Italie.

Chadwick, Roger. 1992. *Bureaucratic mercy: The Home Office and the treatment of capital cases in Victorian Britain.* New York.

Chauchadis, Claude. 1984. *Honneur morale et société dans l'Espagne de Philippe II.* Paris.

Clark, Anna. 1987. *Women's silence, men's violence: Sexual assault in England, 1770–1845.* London.

Cloutier, Daniel. 1896. *Deux Ecoles d'armes: L'Escrime et le duel en Italie et en France.* 4th ed. Paris: Charles Lavauzelle.

Cockburn, J. S. 1991. Patterns of violence in English society: Homicide in Kent, 1560–1985. *Past and Present* 130 (February): 70–106.

Cohen, Elizabeth S. 1992. Honor and gender in the streets of early modern Rome. *Journal of Interdisciplinary History* 22 (4): 597–625.

Cohen, Thomas V. 1992. The lay liturgy of affront in sixteenth-century Italy. *Journal of Social History* 25 (4): 857–77.

Cohen, Thomas V., and Elizabeth S. Cohen. 1993. *Words and deeds in Renaissance Rome: Trials before the papal magistrates.* Toronto: University of Toronto Press.

Conley, Carolyn A. 1991. *The unwritten law: Criminal justice in Victorian Kent.* New York: Oxford University Press.

Coombe, Rosemary. 1988. "The most disgusting, disgraceful and inequitous proceeding in our law": The action for breach of promise of marriage in nineteenth-century Ontario. *University of Toronto Law Journal* 38:64–108.

Counts, Dorothy Ayers, Judith K. Brown, and Jacquelyn C. Campbell, eds. 1992. *Sanctions and sanctuary: Cultural perspectives of the beatings of wives.* Boulder, Colo.: Westview Press.

Croabbon, A. 1894. *La Science du point d'honneur.* Paris: Libraries-Imprimeries Réunies.

Cuénin, Madeleine. 1982. Le Duel dans la société française des XVIe–XVIIe siècles. Paris: Presses de la Renaissance.

Culianu, Ioan P. 1991. A corpus for the body (review article). *Journal of Modern History* 63 (1): 61–80.

Czeipek, F. 1899. *Ehren-Notwehr und Winke für die günstige Austragung des Zweikampfes.* Vienna.

Dailey, Jane Elizabeth. 1995. Race, sex, and citizenship: Biracial democracy in re-adjuster Virginia, 1879–1883. Ph.D. diss., Princeton University.

Dana, David. 1858. *The fireman.* Boston.

Da Passano, M. 1984. *Delitto e delinquenza nella Sardegna sabauda, 1823–1844.* Milan.

Daumas, Maurice. 1987. Les Conflits familiaux dans les milieux dominants au 18e siècle. *Annales ESC* 42 (4): 901–23.

Davidoff, Leonore, and Catherine Hall. 1987. *Family fortunes: Men and women of the English middle class, 1780–1850.* Chicago: University of Chicago Press.

Davis, J. 1964. Passatella: An economic game. *British Journal of Sociology* 15 (3): 191–206.

Davis, Jennifer. 1989. Prosecutions and their context: The use of the criminal law in later nineteenth-century London. In *Policing and prosecution in Britain, 1750–1850*, ed. Douglas Hay and Francis Snyder, 397–426. Oxford: Oxford University Press.

Davis, Natalie Zemon. 1987. *Fiction in the archives: Pardon tales and their tellers in sixteenth-century France*. Stanford: Stanford University Press.

Davis, Robert C. 1994. *The war of the fists: Popular culture and public violence in late Renaissance Venice*. New York: Oxford University Press.

Davis, Susan. 1986. *Parades and power: Street theater in nineteenth-century Philadelphia*. Berkeley: University of California Press.

Deák, István. 1992. *Beyond nationalism: A social and political history of the Hapsburg Officer Corps, 1848–1918*. Oxford: Oxford University Press.

Della Peruta, F. 1952. L'Internazionale a Roma dal 1872 al 1887. *Movimento Operaio*, 5–32.

Demeter, K. 1965. *Das deutsche Offizierkorps in Gesellschaft und Staat, 1650–1945*. 4th ed. Frankfurt.

Desjardins, Emile Ferreus. 1891. *Annuaire du duel*. Paris: Perrin.

Devlin, George A. 1989. *South Carolina and black migration, 1865–1940: In search of the promised land*. New York: Garland.

Digeon, Claude. 1959. *La Crise allemande de la pensée française, 1879–1914*. Paris: P.U.F.

Dinges, Martin. 1991. Weiblichkeit in Männlichkeitsritualen? Zu weiblichen Taktiken im Ehrenhandel in Paris im 18. Jahrhundert. *Francia: Forschungen zur westeuropäischen Geschichte* 18 (2): 71–98.

——. 1994. *Der Maurermeister und der Finanzrichter: Ehre, Geld, und soziale Kontrolle im Paris des 18. Jahrhunderts*. Göttingen.

Dorson, Richard M. 1943. Mose the far-famed and world-renowned. *American Literature* 15:288–300.

Dossena, C. Luigi. 1861. *Il pregiudizio del duello, racconto seguito da riflessi morali e notizie storiche sulla monomachia*. Milan: Francesco Sanvito.

Doyle, Don. 1977. The social functions of voluntary associations in a nineteenth-century American town. *Social Science History* 1:333–55.

Dubinsky, Karen. 1993. *Improper advances: Rape and heterosexual conflict in Ontario, 1880–1929*. Chicago: University of Chicago Press.

Dupont-Bouchat, Marie-Sylvie. 1994. L'Homicide malgré lui: Les Transformations dans la gestion de l'homicide à travers les lettres de rémission, 16e–18e siècle. Unpublished ms.

Düsterlohe, A. von. 1896. Ein Beitrag zur Duellfrage. *Deutsches Adelsblatt* 14:358.

Dukehart, Albert. 1877. Baltimore reminiscences. *New York Fireman's Journal* 1:69.

Dykstra, Arlen R. 1974. Rowdyism and rivalism in the St. Louis fire department, 1850–1857. *Missouri Historical Review* 69 (1): 49–64.

Edwards, Edward. 1906. *History of the volunteer fire department of St. Louis*. St. Louis.

Edwards, Laura. 1991. Sexual violence, gender, reconstruction, and the extension of patriarchy in Granville County, North Carolina. *North Carolina Historical Review* 68:237–60.

Egmond, Florike. 1993. *Underworlds: Organized crime in the Netherlands, 1650–1800.* Cambridge: Cambridge University Press.

———. 1994. Erezaken: Rond een echtelijk conflict in het 16e eeuwse Haarlem. *Tijdschrift voor Geschiedenis* 107:3–22.

Elias, Norbert. 1978. *The Civilizing Process.* 2 vols. Oxford.

———. 1983. *Die höfische Gesellschaft.* Frankfurt.

———. 1992. *Studien über die Deutschen: Machtkämpfe und Habitusentwicklung im 19. und 20. Jahrhundert.* Frankfurt a.M.

Emmerichs, Mary Beth Wasserlein. 1991. Five shillings and costs: Petty offenders in late Victorian Northampton. Ph.D. diss., University of Pennsylvania.

———. 1993. Trials of women for homicide in nineteenth-century England. *Women and Criminal Justice* 5:99–109.

Emsley, Clive. 1987. *Crime and society in England, 1750–1900.* London.

Ernsthausen, A. E. von. 1894. *Erinnerungen eines preußischen Beamten.* Bielefeld.

Ettore, Giuseppe. 1928. *Questioni d'onore.* Milan: Hoepli.

Fabricius, W. 1898. *Die deutschen Corps.* Berlin.

Fambri, Paolo. 1869. *Della giurisprudenza e della tecnica del duello.* Florence: G. Barbèra.

Farr, James R. 1988. *Hands of honor: Artisans and their world in Dijon, 1550–1650.* Ithaca: Cornell University Press.

———. 1991. The pure and the disciplined body: Hierarchy, morality, and symbolism in France during the Catholic Reformation. *Journal of Interdisciplinary History* 21 (3): 391–414.

Faust, Drew Gilpin. 1985. Southern violence revisited (review of Ayers 1984). *Reviews in American History* (June): 205–10.

Feeley, Malcolm M., and Deborah L. Little. 1991. The vanishing female: The decline of women in the criminal process, 1687–1912. *Law and Society Review* 25 (4): 719–57.

Feher, Michel, Ramona Naddaff, and Nadia Tazi, eds. 1989. *Fragments for a history of the human body.* 3 vols. New York.

Fehr, Hans. 1908. *Der Zweikampf.* Berlin.

Feldberg, Michael. 1980. *The turbulent era: Riot and disorder in Jacksonian America.* Oxford: Oxford University Press.

Ferri, E. 1895. *L'omicidio nell' antropologia criminale: Omicida nato e omicida pazzo.* Turin.

Finnegan, Terence Robert. 1992. "At the hands of parties unknown": Lynching in Mississippi and South Carolina, 1881–1940. Ph.D. diss., University of Illinois at Urbana-Champaign.

———. 1995. Lynching and political power in Mississippi and South Carolina. In *Under sentence of death: Essays on lynching in the South,* ed. W. Fitzhugh Brundage. Chapel Hill: University of North Carolina Press.

———. 1996. Who were the victims of lynching? Evidence from Mississippi and South Carolina. In *Varieties of southern history: New essays on a region and its people,* ed. Bruce Clayton and John Salmond, 79–95. Westport, Conn.: Greenwood Press.

Fiume, Giovanna. 1990. *La vecchia dell' aceto: Un processo per veneficio nella Palermo di fine Settecento.* Palermo.

Flach, J. 1887. *Der deutsche Student der Gegenwart.* Berlin.

Folin, M. 1990–91. I "disgusti" della villeggiatura: I nobili poveri nella campagna veronese del Settecento. *Atti dell' Istituto Veneto di Scienze, Lettere, ed Arti* 149: 17–56.

Forrest, Clarence H. 1898. *Official history of the fire department of the city of Baltimore.* Baltimore.

Fosi, I. Polverini. 1992. Signori e tribunali: Criminalità e giustizia pontificia nella Roma del Cinquecento. In *Signori, patrizi e cavalieri nell' Italia moderna,* ed. M. A. Visceglia, 214–30. Bari.

Foucault, Michel. 1976. *Histoire de la sexualité,* vol. 1: *La volonté de savoir.* Paris.

Freeman, Joanne B. 1996. Dueling as politics: Reinterpreting the Burr-Hamilton duel. *William and Mary Quarterly* 53 (2): 289–318.

Frevert, Ute. 1991. *Ehrenmänner: Das Duell in der bürgerlichen Gesellschaft.* Munich.

———. 1993. Honour and middle-class culture: The history of the duel in England and Germany. In *Bourgeois Society in Nineteenth-Century Europe,* ed. Jürgen Kocka and Allan Mitchell, 207–40. Oxford: Oxford University Press.

———. 1995a. *Men of honour: A social and cultural history of the duel.* Oxford: Oxford University Press.

———. 1995b. *"Mann und Weib, und Weib und Mann": Geschlechter-Differenzen in der Moderne.* Munich.

Fries, J. F. 1818. *Handbuch der praktischen Philosophie oder der philosophischen Zwecklehre,* vol. 1. Heidelberg.

Fritschius, A. 1686. *Ohnvorgreiffliches Bedencken Wie denen Duellen und Balgereyen derer Studenten auf Academien mit mehrerem Nachdruck zu steuren seyn möchte?* Regensburg.

Friz, G. 1974. *La popolazione di Roma dal 1770 al 1900.* Rome.

———. 1980. *Consumi, tenore di vita e prezzi a Roma dal 1770 al 1900.* Rome.

Frost, Ginger. 1991. Promises broken: Breach of promise of marriage in England and Wales, 1753–1970. Ph.D. diss., Rice University.

Fusco, Giovanni Scalfati. 1930. *Il duello nel progetto definitivo del nuovo codice penale.* Naples: Gip. Majolo.

Gabelli, A. 1881. Roma e i Romani. Introduction to *Ministero di Agricoltura, Industria e Commercio, Monografia della città di Roma e della campagna Romana.* Rome.

Gallagher, Catherine, and Thomas Laqueur, eds. 1987. *The making of the modern body: Sexuality and society in the nineteenth century.* Berkeley: University of California Press.

Garris, Susan Page. 1973. The decline of lynching in South Carolina. Master's thesis, University of South Carolina.

Garve, Christian. 1794. Über die Maxime Rochefaucaults: Das bürgerliche Air verliehrt sich zuweilen bey der Armee, niemahls am Hofe. In *Popularphilosophische Schriften über literarische, ästhetische und gesellschaftliche Gegenstände*, 1:559–716. Stuttgart.

Gatrell, V. A. C. 1980. The decline of theft and violence in Victorian and Edwardian England. In *Crime and the law: The social history of crime in western Europe since 1500*, ed. V. A. C. Gatrell, Bruce Lenman, and Geoffrey Parker, 238–370. London.

——. 1994. *The hanging tree: Execution and the English people, 1770–1868.* Oxford: Oxford University Press.

Gatrell, V. A. C., and T. B. Hadden. 1972. Nineteenth-century criminal statistics and their interpretation. In *Nineteenth-century society: Essays in the use of quantitative methods for the study of social data*, ed. E. A. Wrigley, 336–96. Cambridge: Cambridge University Press.

Gauvard, Claude. 1991. *"De grace especial": Crime, état et société en France à la fin du Moyen Age.* 2 vols. Paris.

Gay, Peter. 1993. *The bourgeois experience: Victoria to Freud*, vol. 3: *The cultivation of hatred.* New York: Norton.

Gelli, Iacopo. 1901. Il duello nell'ultimo ventennio. *Nuova Antologia* (January): 3–12.

——. 1926. *Codice cavalleresco italiano.* 15th ed. Milan: Hoepli.

——. 1928. *Duelli celebri.* Milan: Hoepli.

——. n.d. *Statistiche del duello: Italia 1879–1895, Francia 1879–1889.* Milan: Lombardi Fioni Oscuri.

Gerbod, Paul. 1982. L'Ethique héroïque en France. *Revue historique* 544 (Oct.–Dec.): 409–29.

Gilmore, David D. 1990. *Manhood in the making: Cultural concepts of masculinity.* London.

Gilmore, Glenda Elizabeth. 1996. *Gender and Jim Crow: Women and the politics of white supremacy in North Carolina, 1896–1920.* Chapel Hill: University of North Carolina Press.

Goblot, Edmond. 1925. *La Barrière et le niveau: Etude sociologique sur la bourgeoisie française moderne.* Paris: Alcan.

Gorn, Elliot J. 1986. *The manly art: Bare-knuckle prize fighting in America.* Ithaca: Cornell University Press.

——. 1987. "Good-bye, boys, I die a true American": Homicide, nativism, and working-class culture in antebellum New York City. *Journal of American History* 74 (2): 388–410.

Gottfredson, Michael R., and Travis Hirschi. 1990. *A general theory of crime.* Stanford: Stanford University Press.

Gowing, Laura. 1994. Language, power, and the law: Women's slander litigation in early modern London. In *Women, crime, and the courts in early modern England*, ed. Jenny Kermode and Garthine Walker, 26–47. London.

Graeser, K. 1902. *Für den Zweikampf.* Berlin.

Greenberg, Amy. 1995. Cause for alarm: The volunteer fire department in the nineteenth-century city. Ph.D. diss., Harvard University.

Greenberg, Kenneth S. 1990. The nose, the lie, and the duel in the Antebellum South. *American Historical Review* 95 (1): 57–74.

Greveniz, F. A. F. von. 1808. *Unterricht zur Kenntniß der vorzüglichsten und wichtigsten Abweichungen der gesetzlichen Vorschriften des Code Napoleon von den in den neuerlich abgetretenen preußischen Provinzen sowohl den deutschen, als polnischen, bisher gültig gewesenen.* Leipzig.

Grimsted, David. 1972. Rioting in its Jacksonian setting. *American Historical Review* 77:365–97.

Gurr, Ted Robert. 1981. Historical trends in violent crime: A critical review of the evidence. *Crime and Justice: An Annual Review of Research* 3:295–353.

Guttandin, Friedhelm. 1993. *Das paradoxe Schicksal der Ehre: Zum Wandel der adeligen Ehre und zur Bedeutung von Duell und Ehre im monarchischen Zentralstaat.* Berlin.

Guy-Shetfall, Beverly. 1990. *Daughters of sorrow: Attitudes toward black women, 1880–1920.* Brooklyn.

Halkin, Léon-E. 1949. Pour une histoire de l'honneur. *Annales ESC* 4:433–44.

Hall, Jacquelyn Dowd. 1983. The mind that burns in each body: Women, rape, and racial violence. In *Powers of desire: The politics of sexuality*, ed. Ann Snitow et al., 328–49. New York.

———. 1993. *Revolt against chivalry: Jesse Daniel Ames and the women's campaign against lynching.* Rev. ed. New York.

Halttunen, Karen. 1982. *Confidence men and painted women: A study of middle-class culture in America, 1830–1870.* New Haven: Yale University Press.

Hammerton, A. James. 1992. *Cruelty and companionship: Conflict in nineteenth-century married life.* London.

Hanlon, Gregory. 1985. Les Rituels de l'agression en Aquitaine au 17e siècle. *Annales ESC* 40 (2): 244–68.

Harris, Leonard. 1992. Honor: Emasculation and empowerment. In *Rethinking masculinity: Philosophical explorations in light of feminism*, ed. Larry May and Robert A. Strikwerda, 191–208. Lanham, Md.: Rowman and Littlefield.

Hausen, Karin. 1976. Die Polarisierung der "Geschlechtscharaktere." In *Sozialgeschichte der Familie in der Neuzeit Europas*, ed. Werner Conze, 363–93. Stuttgart.

Helsley, Alexia Jones. 1988. Harbison College: Metamorphis of a dream. *Proceedings of the South Carolina Historical Association*, 14–26.

Herlihy, David. 1985. *Medieval households.* Cambridge: Harvard University Press.

Higginbotham, Anne. 1989. "Sin of the age": Infanticide and illegitimacy in Victorian London. *Victorian Studies*, 319–37.

Hirsch, Susan. 1987. *Roots of the American working class.* Philadelphia.

Hodes, Martha. 1993. The sexualization of Reconstruction politics: White women and black men in the South after the Civil War. *Journal of the History of Sexuality* 3:402–17.

Holloway, Charles T. 1860. *The chief engineer's register and insurance advertiser.* Baltimore.

Howe, Adrian. 1994. *Punish and critique: Towards a feminist analysis of penality.* London.

Ihering, Rudolf von. 1872. *Der Kampf um's Recht.* 2d ed. Vienna.

Ikegami, Eiko. 1995. *The taming of the samurai: Honorific individualism and the making of modern Japan.* Cambridge: Harvard University Press.

Ingram, Martin. 1987. *Church courts, sex and marriage in England, 1570–1640.* Cambridge: Cambridge University Press.

Jannone, Giovanni. 1912. *Il duello Pepe-Lamartine su documenti inediti.* Terni: A. Visconti.

Johnson, Paul E., and Sean Wilentz. 1994. *The kingdom of Matthias.* New York.

Jouanna, Arlette. 1977. *Ordre social: Mythes et hiérarchies dans la société française des XVIe–XVIIe siècles.* Paris: Hachette.

Kant, Immanuel. 1968. *Anthropologie in pragmatischer Hinsicht. Kants Werke,* vol. 7. Berlin.

Kantrowitz, Stephen. 1995. The reconstruction of white supremacy: Reaction and reform in Ben Tillman's world, 1847–1918. Ph.D. diss., Princeton University.

Karus, H. 1888. *Schläger, Säbel, und Pistole.* Halle.

Kelley, Robin. 1990. *Hammer and hoe: Alabama communists during the Great Depression.* Chapel Hill: University of North Carolina Press.

Keunen, Annemieke, and Herman Roodenburg, eds. 1992. Schimpen en schelden: Eer en belediging in Nederland, ca. 1600–ca. 1850. *Volkskundig Bulletin* 18 (3): 289–441 (special issue).

Kiernan, V. G. 1988. *The duel in European history: Honour and the reign of aristocracy.* Oxford: Oxford University Press.

King, Peter. 1996. Punishing assault: The transformation of attitudes in the English courts. *Journal of Interdisciplinary History* 27 (1): 43–74.

King, Peter, and Joan Noel. 1993. The origins of "the problem of juvenile delinquency": The growth of juvenile prosecutions in London in the late eighteenth and early nineteenth centuries. *Criminal Justice History* 14:17–41.

Kingsdale, Jon. 1973. "The poor-man's club": Social functions of the urban saloon, working class. *American Quarterly* 25:472–89.

Klein, Ernst Ferdinand. 1805. Über Verbrechen gegen den Staat, besonders den Zweykampf. *Archiv des Criminalrechts* 6 (2): 134–48.

Kloek, Els. 1990. *Wie hij zij, man of wijf: Vrouwengeschiedenis en de vroegmoderne tijd. Drie Leidse studies.* Hilversum.

Knelman, Judith. 1993. Class and gender bias in Victorian newspapers. *Victorian Periodicals Review* 30:29–35.

Knigge, Adolph von. 1978. Über den Zweykampf. In *Sämtliche Werke,* vol. 17, ed. Adolph von Knigge, 108–23. Nendeln.

Knuttel, W. P. C., ed. 1908–16. *Acta der particuliere synoden van Zuid-Holland, 1621–1700.* 6 vols. The Hague.

Koelman, Jacobus. 1690. *Spiegel der wet: Aan de conscientien voorgehouden tot ontdekking der zonden tegen de tien geboden. Nu laatst veel vermeerdert en verbetert.* Amsterdam.

Koorn, Florence. 1987. Illegitimiteit en eergevoel: Ongehuwde moeders in Twente in de 18e eeuw. In *Vrouwenlevens, 1500–1850: Jaarboek voor vrouwengeschiedenis 8,* ed. Ulla Jansz et al., 74–98. Nijmegen.

Krünitz, Johann Georg. 1806. Ökonomisch-technologische Encyklopädie, oder allgemeines System der Staats- Stadt- Haus- und Landwirthschaft, pt. 83. Brünn.

Kuehn, Thomas. 1991. *Law, family, and women: Toward a legal anthropology of Renaissance Italy.* Chicago: University of Chicago Press.

Kußmaul, A. 1899. *Jugenderinnerungen eines alten Arztes.* 3d ed. Stuttgart.

Laborie, Bruneau de. 1906. *Les Lois du duel.* Paris: Manzi Joyant.

Lagrange, Hugues. 1993. La Pacification des moeurs a l'épreuve: L'Insécurite et les atteintes prédatrices. *Déviance et Société* 17:279–89.

La Mantia, V. 1884. *Storia della legislazione italiana,* vol. 1: *Roma e Stato Romano.* Turin.

Lane, Roger. 1975. *Policing the city: Boston, 1822–1885.* New York.

———. 1979. *Violent death in the city: Suicide, accident, and murder in nineteenth-century Philadelphia.* Cambridge: Harvard University Press.

Laqueur, Thomas. 1990. *Making sex: Body and gender from the Greeks to Freud.* Cambridge: Harvard University Press.

Laurie, Bruce. 1980. *Working people of Philadelphia, 1800–1850.* Philadelphia: University of Pennsylvania Press.

Lavori preparatori del codice penale e del codice di procedura penale. 1929. Rome: Mantellate.

Leach, Robert. 1985. *The Punch and Judy show: History, tradition, and meaning.* London.

Lees, Clare A., ed. 1994. *Medieval masculinities: Regarding men in the Middle Ages.* Minneapolis: University of Minnesota Press.

Leo. 1787. Über Zweikämpfe und ihre Schädlichkeit. *Deutsches Museum* 2 (7): 15–22.

Levine, Phillipa. 1993. Rough usage: Prostitution, law, and the social historian. In *Rethinking social history: English society, 1570–1920, and its interpretation,* ed. Adrian Wilson, 266–92. Manchester.

Loen, J. M. von. 1751. *Gesammelte Kleine Schriften,* vol. 3. Frankfurt.

Lovati, Carlo. 1939. *Il duello: Conversazioni di un avvocato.* Milan: Corticelli.

Luckenbill, David F. 1977. Criminal homicide as a situated transaction. *Social Problems* 25:176–86.

Luebke, David Martin. 1993. Serfdom and honour in eighteenth-century Germany. *Social History* 18 (2): 143–61.

Lynch, Thomas R. 1880. *The volunteer fire department of St. Louis.* St. Louis.

McAleer, Kevin. 1994. *Dueling: The cult of honor in fin-de-siècle Germany.* Princeton: Princeton University Press.

Macaloon, John J. 1981. *This great symbol: Pierre de Coubertin and the origins of the modern Olympic games.* Chicago: University of Chicago Press.

McCreary, George W. 1901. *The ancient and honorable Mechanical Company of Baltimore.* Baltimore.

McCurry, Stephanie. 1995. *Masters of small worlds: Yeoman households, gender relations, and the political culture of the antebellum South Carolina low country.* New York.

Macdonald, Michael, and Terence R. Murphy. 1990. *Sleepless souls: Suicide in early modern England.* Oxford: Oxford University Press.

McGowen, Randall. 1986. A powerful sympathy: Terror, the prison, and humanitarian reform in early nineteenth-century Britain. *Journal of British Studies* 25: 312–34.

———. 1987. The body and punishment in eighteenth-century England. *Journal of Modern History* 59:651–79.

McHale, V. E., and J. Bergner. 1981. Collective and individual violence: Berlin and Vienna, 1875–1913. *Criminal Justice History* 2:31–61.

MacLean, Nancy. 1994. *Behind the mask of chivalry: The making of the second Ku Klux Klan.* New York.

Maconi, G. 1991. *Storia della medicina e della chirurgia.* Milan.

Mahood, Linda. 1990. *The magdalenes: Prostitution in the nineteenth century.* London.

Mariani, R. 1983. *I veri bulli di Roma: Cento anni di cronaca della malavita romana.* Rome.

Marsilje, J. W., et al. 1990. *Bloedwraak, partijstrijd en pacificatie in laat-middeleeuws Holland.* Hilversum.

May, Margaret. 1978. Violence in the family: An historical perspective. In *Violence and the family,* ed. J. P. Martin, 136–67. New York.

Mayer, Arno. 1981. *The persistence of the old regime.* New York: Vintage.

Mays, Benjamin E. 1987. *Born to rebel: An autobiography.* Athens: University of Georgia Press.

Medem, R. 1890. *Die Duellfrage.* 2d ed. Greifswald.

Meiners, Cristoph. 1788. Von den außergerichtlichen Duellen, die durch ehrenrührige Reden, und Thätlichkeiten veranlaßt wurden. *Göttingisches historisches Magazin* 3 (4): 591–678.

Meyr, G. K., ed. 1784. *Sammlung der Kurpfalz-Baierischen allgemeinen und besonderen Landesverordnungen,* vol. 1. Munich.

Michaelis, J. D. 1973. *Räsonnement über die protestantischen Universitäten in Deutschland,* vol. 4. Frankfurt, 1776; reprint, Aalen.

Miller, Vivien. 1994. Loyal wives and evil temptresses: Women and executive clemency in Florida, 1890–1910. Paper presented at the IAHCCJ-colloquium Violence and Context, Paris, 3–4 June.

Mohrmann, Ruth-Elisabeth. 1977. *Volksleben in Wilster im 16. und 17. Jahrhundert.* Neumünster.

Molinini, Niccolò. 1934. Il suicidio e il duello nella concezione fascista. Bari: La Disfida.

Mommsen, Wolfgang J., and Gerhard Hirschfeld, eds. 1982. *Sozialprotest, Gewalt, Terror: Gewaltanwendung durch politische und gesellschaftliche Randgruppen im 19. und 20. Jahrhundert.* Stuttgart.

Monholland, Cathy. 1989. Infanticide in Victorian England. Master's thesis, Rice University.

Monkkonen, Eric. 1982. From cop history to social history: The significance of the police in American history. *Journal of Social History* 15 (4): 575–91.

———. 1989. Diverging homicide rates: England and the United States, 1850–1870. In *Violence in America,* vol. 1: *The history of crime,* ed. Ted Robert Gurr, 80–101. Newbury Park: Sage.

Morgan, Sharon. 1993. Women and violent crime in London, 1800–1830. Master's thesis, Cambridge University.

Möser, Justus. n.d. Also sollte man den Zweikämpfen nur eine bessere Form geben. In *Sämtliche Werke,* vol. 7, ed. Justus Möser, 115–18. Oldenburg.

Mosse, Werner. 1993. Nobility and middle classes in nineteenth-century Europe. In *Bourgeois Society in Nineteenth-Century Europe,* ed. Jürgen Kocka and Allen Mitchell, 70–102. Oxford: Berg.

Muchembled, Robert. 1985. *Popular culture and elite culture in France, 1400–1750.* Baton Rouge: Louisiana State University Press.

———. 1987. Anthropologie de la violence dans la France moderne. *Revue de synthèse,* 4th ser., no. 1 : 21–55.

———. 1989. *La violence au village: Sociabilité et comportements populaires en Artois du 15e au 17e siècle.* Turnhout.

Müller, Friedrich von. 1982. *Unterhaltungen mit Goethe.* 2d ed. Munich.

Muir, Edward. 1993. *Mad blood stirring: Vendetta and factions in Friuli during the Renaissance.* Baltimore: Johns Hopkins University Press.

Murray, Henry A. 1855. *Lands of the slave and the free.* London.

Nash, Roy. 1916. The Lynching of Anthony Crawford: South Carolina Declares an End to Mob Rule. New York *Independent,* December 11.

Neal, Diane. 1976. Benjamin Ryan Tillman: The South Carolina years, 1847–1894. Ph.D. diss., Kent State University.

Negri, C. de. 1908. La delinquenza in Italia dal 1890 al 1905. *Annali di statistica,* ser. 4, vol. 110, *Atti della Commissione per la statistica giudiziaria e notarile,* sessione del luglio 1907. Rome.

Neilly, Andrew. 1959. The violent volunteers: A history of the Philadelphia volunteer fire department, 1736–1871. Ph.D. diss., University of Pennsylvania.

Nye, Robert A. 1993. *Masculinity and male codes of honor in modern France.* New York: Oxford University Press.

Ownby, Ted. 1990. *Subduing Satan: Religion, recreation, and manhood in the rural South, 1865–1920.* Chapel Hill: University of North Carolina Press.

Padovan, G. 1988. Le sentenze criminali emesse a Padova alla fine della Repubblica di Venezia, 1780–1797: Dati e considerazioni. *Studi veneziani,* n.s., 16:228–35

Painter, Nell Irvin. 1988. Social equality, miscegenation, labor, and power. In *The evolution of southern culture,* ed. Numan V. Bartley, 47–67. Athens: University of Georgia Press.

Penzenkuffer, C. W. F. 1819. *Über den Zweikampf: Eine philosophische Abhandlung.* Nuremberg.

Peristiany, J. G., and Julian Pitt-Rivers. 1992. *Honor and grace in anthropology.* Cambridge: Cambridge University Press.

Perrot, Michelle. 1975. Délinquence et système pénitentiaire en France au 19e siècle. *Annales ESC* 30 (1): 67–91. Translated and republished in *Deviants and the abandoned in French society,* ed. Robert Forster and Orest Ranum. Baltimore: Johns Hopkins University Press, 1978.

Perry, Mary Elisabeth. 1990. *Gender and disorder in early modern Seville.* Princeton: Princeton University Press.

Pessina, E. 1906. Il diritto penale in Italia da Cesare Beccaria sino alla promulgazione del codice penale vigente, 1764–1890. In *Enciclopedia del diritto penale italiano: Raccolta di monografie a cura di Enrico Pessina,* vol. 2, 638–70, 685–708, 733–64. Milan.

Picca, P. 1907. Il coltello a Roma. *Nuova Antologia: Rivista di Lettere, Scienze, ed Arti* 42, no. 862 (November): 259–75.

Pierer, A. H. 1835. *Universal-Lexikon oder vollständiges encyclopädisches Wörterbuch,* vol. 13. Altenburg.

Polk, Kenneth. 1994. *When men kill: Scenarios of masculine violence.* Cambridge: Cambridge University Press.

Pompejano, D., I. Fazio, and G. Raffaele. 1985. *Controllo sociale e criminalità: Un circondario rurale nella Sicilia dell' '800.* Milan.

Porter, Roy. 1991. Bodies of thought: Thoughts about the body in eighteenth-century England. In *Interpretation and cultural history,* ed. Joan H. Pittock and Andrew Wear, 82–108. London.

Pouchelle, Marie-Christine. 1983. *Corps et chirurgie à l'apogée du moyen age: Savoir et imaginaire du corps chez Henri de Mondeville, chirurgien de Philippe le Bel.* Paris.

Preising, R. 1959. Nachrichten über ein Duell in Werl. *Soester Zeitschrift* 72:55–59.

Prince, Carl E. 1985. The great "riot year": Jacksonian democracy and patterns of violence in 1834. *Journal of the Early Republic* 5 (1): 1–19.

Prokowsky, D. 1965. Die Geschichte der Duellbekämpfung. Ph.D. diss., Bonn.

Prost, Antoine. 1992. *In the wake of war: "Les Anciens Combattants" and French society.* Trans. Helen MacPhail. Oxford: Berg.

Pusch, G. 1887. *Über Couleur und Mensur.* Berlin.

Reddy, William M. 1993. Marriage, honor, and the public sphere in postrevolutionary France: *Séparations de Corps,* 1815–1848. *Journal of Modern History* 65 (3): 437–72.

———. 1994. Condottieri of the pen: Journalists and the public sphere in postrevolutionary France, 1815–1850. *American Historical Review* 99 (5): 1546–70.

Reinhold, Karl Leonhard. 1796. Über die Duelle auf Universitäten. In *Auswahl vermischter Schriften,* vol. 1, ed. Karl Leonhard Reinhold, 122–45. Jena.

Reitsma, J., and S. D. van Veen, eds. 1892–99. *Acta der provinciale en particuliere synoden gehouden in de Noordelijke Nederlanden, 1572–1620.* 8 vols. Groningen.

Renan, Ernest. 1871. *La Réforme intellectuelle et morale.* Paris: M. Levy frères.

Riches, David, ed. 1986. *The anthropology of violence.* Oxford: Oxford University Press.

Rock, Howard B. 1979. *Artisans of the New Republic.* New York.

Roodenburg, Herman. 1981. Predestinatie en groepscharisma: Een sociologische verkenning van de conflicten tussen Calvinisten en andere gelovigen in de Republiek, ± 1580–± 1650. *Amsterdams Sociologisch Tijdschrift* 8:254–84.

———. 1990. *Onder censuur: De kerkelijke tucht in de Gereformeerde gemeente van Amsterdam, 1578–1700.* Hilversum.

Rooijakkers, Gerard. 1994. *Rituele repertoires: Volkscultuur in oostelijk Noord-Brabant, 1559–1853.* Nijmegen.

Rosoni, I. 1988. *Criminalità e giustizia penale nello Stato pontificio del secolo XIX: Un caso di banditismo rurale.* Milan.

Rossetti, B. 1978. *I bulli di Roma: Storie e avventure d'amore e di coltello da Jacaccio ar più de l'urione: Quattro secoli di vita sociale e di costume.* Rome.

Roßhirt, Conrad Franz. 1819. Über den Zweikampf. *Neues Archiv des Criminalrechts* 3 (3): 453–77.

Rotundo, E. Anthony. 1993. *American manhood: Transformations in masculinity from the Revolution to the modern era.* New York.

Rousseaux, Xavier. 1993. Civilisation des moeurs et/ou déplacement de l'insécurité? La violence à l'épreuve du temps. *Déviance et Société* 17:291–97.

———. 1994. Ordre moral, justice et violence: L'Homicide dans les sociétés européennes, XIIIe–XVIIIe siècle. In *Ordre morale et délinquance de l'antiquité au XXe siècle,* ed. Benoît Garnot, 65–82. Conference proceedings, 7 and 8 October 1993. Dijon.

Ruggiero, Guido. 1980. *Violence in early Renaissance Venice.* New Brunswick, N.J.: Rutgers University Press.

Ryan, Mary P. 1990. *Women in public: Between banners and ballots, 1825–1880.* Baltimore: Johns Hopkins University Press.

Sabean, David Warren. 1984. *Power in the blood: Popular culture and village discourse in early modern Germany.* Cambridge: Cambridge University Press.

Salvisberg, P. von. 1896. *Das Duell und die academische Jugend.* Munich.

Santini, Aldo, and Nedo Nadi. 1989. *Personaggi retroscena e duelli della grande scherma italiana.* Livorno: Belforte.

Saraceno, P. 1984. Le statistiche giudiziarie italiane: Saggio bibliografico. *Clio* 20 (1): 133–44.

Scacchi, D. 1981. *Roma tra Ottocento e Novecento: Studi e ricerche.* Rome.

Scaglione, Giuseppe. 1869. *Riflessioni e consigli sul duello ed osservazioni sul giurì d'onore.* Bologna: G. Monti.

Schalk, Ellery. 1986. *From valor to pedigree: Ideas of nobility in France in the seventeenth and eighteenth centuries.* Princeton: Princeton University Press.

Scharf, John Thomas. 1874. *The chronicles of Baltimore: Being a complete history of Baltimore town and Baltimore city from the earliest period to the present time.* Baltimore.

———. 1883. *History of St. Louis City and County.* Philadelphia.

Schleiermacher, Friedrich. 1846. Gelegentliche Gedanken über Universitäten in deutschem Sinn. In *Sämtliche Werke,* 1:535–624. Berlin.

Schlosser, Johan Georg. 1776. Über die Gesetzgebung gegen die Duelle. *Deutsches Museum* 2 (11): 1128–30.

Schlözer, A. L. 1786. *Stats-Anzeigen* 9 (33).

Schneider, Robert A. 1984. Swordplay and statemaking: Aspects of the campaign against the duel in early modern France. In *Statemaking and social movements: Essays in history and theory,* ed. Charles Bright and Susan Harding, 265–96. Ann Arbor: University of Michigan Press.

Schreiner, Klaus, and Gerd Schwerhoff, eds. 1995. *Verletzte Ehre: Ehrkonflikte in Gesellschaften des Mittelalters und der frühen Neuzeit.* Cologne.

Schweninger, Loren. 1990. *Black property owners in the South.* Urbana: University of Illinois Press.

Scotti, J. J. 1821. *Sammlung der Gesetze und Verordnungen in den ehemaligen Herzogtümern Jülich, Cleve und Berg,* vol. 1. Düsseldorf.

Seronde-Babonaux, A. M. 1983. *Roma: Dalla città alla metropoli.* Rome.

Shilling, Chris. 1993. *The body and social theory.* London.

Simpson, Antony E. 1986. The "blackmail myth" and the prosecution of rape and its attempt in eighteenth-century London: The creation of a legal tradition. *Journal of Criminal Law and Criminology* 77: 101–50.

———. 1988. Dandelions and the field of honor: Dueling, the middle classes, and the law in nineteenth-century England. *Criminal Justice History* 9: 99–155.

Sleebe, Vincentius Cornelius. 1994. In termen van fatsoen: Sociale controle in het Groningse kleigebied, 1770–1914. Ph.D. diss., Groningen.

Smith, Greg. 1995. Law reform and the culture of violence in eighteenth-century London. Manuscript.

Smith, Roger. 1981. *Trial by medicine: Insanity and responsibility in Victorian trials.* Edinburgh.

Spallanzani, A. 1917. Sull' omicidio in Italia dal 1881 al 1911 (Ricerche di statistica giudiziaria penale). In *Ministero di Grazia e Giustizia e dei Culti: Atti della Commissione di statistica e legislazione, Relazioni e verbali delle discussioni della sessione del dicembre 1915*, 475–676. Rome.

Spierenburg, Pieter. 1984. *The spectacle of suffering: Executions and the evolution of repression: From a preindustrial metropolis to the European experience.* Cambridge: Cambridge University Press.

——. 1987. From Amsterdam to Auburn: An explanation for the rise of the prison in seventeenth-century Holland and nineteenth-century America. *Journal of Social History* 20 (3): 439–61.

——. 1991a. *The broken spell: A cultural and anthropological history of preindustrial Europe.* New Brunswick, N.J.: Rutgers University Press.

——. 1991b. Justice and the mental world: Twelve years of research and interpretation of criminal justice data, from the perspective of the history of mentalities. *IAHCCJ-Newsletter* 14 (October): 38–79.

——. 1994. Faces of violence: Homicide trends and cultural meanings: Amsterdam, 1431–1816. *Journal of Social History* 27 (4): 701–16.

——. 1996. Long-term trends in homicide: Theoretical reflections and Dutch evidence, fifteenth to twentieth centuries. In *The civilization of crime: Violence in town and country since the Middle Ages*, ed. Eric A. Johnson and Eric H. Monkkonen, 63–105. Urbana: University of Illinois Press.

Stansell, Christine. 1987. *City of women: Sex and class in New York, 1789–1860.* Urbana: University of Illinois Press.

Stearns, Peter. 1979. *Be a Man! Males in modern society.* New York.

Stephen, James Fitzjames. 1884. *History of the criminal law of England*, vol. 3. London.

Stewart, Frank Henderson. 1994. *Honor.* Chicago: University of Chicago Press.

Stone, J. M. 1894. The suppression of lawlessness in the South. *North American Review* 158 (April): 500–506.

Stone, Lawrence. 1965. *The crisis of the aristocracy, 1558–1641.* Oxford: Oxford University Press.

——. 1983. Interpersonal violence in English society, 1300–1980. *Past and Present* 101:22–33.

Svarez, Carl Gottlieb. 1960. Über Duelle. In *Vorträge über Recht und Staat von Carl Gottlieb Svarez*, ed. H. Conrad and G. Kleinheyer, 411–18. Cologne.

Tarde, Gabriel. 1892. *Etudes pénales et sociales.* Paris: Masson.

Tavernier, Adolphe. 1885. *L'Art du duel.* New ed. Paris: Marpon Flammarion.

Teellinck, Willem. 1622. *Davids wapen-tuygh ende loose der vromer Crijgs-lieden.* Middelburg.

Thernstorm, Stephan. 1975. *The other Bostonians.* Cambridge: Harvard University Press.

Thimm, Carl A. 1896. *A complete bibliography of fencing and dueling.* London: John Lane.

Thompson, E. P. 1972. "Rough music": Le Charivari anglais. *Annales ESC* 27: 285–312.

———. 1991. *Customs in common.* New York.

Tilly, Charles. 1990. *Coercion, capital, and European states, A.D. 990–1990.* Oxford: Oxford University Press.

Tolnay, Stewart E., and E. M. Beck. 1995. *A festival of violence: An analysis of southern lynchings, 1882–1930.* Urbana: University of Illinois Press.

Treitschke, Heinrich von. 1912. *Briefe,* vol. 1. Leipzig.

Trumbach, Randolph. 1978. *The rise of the egalitarian family.* New York.

Tyson, Timothy. n.d. *Radio Free Dixie.* Chapel Hill, forthcoming.

Udemans, Godefridus. 1658. *Praktijcke: Dat is werckelijcke oeffeninge van de Christelijcke hooft-deugden (. . .). Den vijfden druck (. . .).* Amsterdam.

Velzen, H. U. E. Thoden van. 1982. De Aukaanse (Djoeka) beschaving. *Sociologische Gids* 29:243–78.

Venosta, Giovanni Visconti. 1906. *Ricordi di gioventù: Cose vedute o sapute, 1847–1860.* Milan: L. F. Cogliati.

Villeneuve, Hébrard de. 1894. *Propos d'épée, 1882–1894.* Paris: A. Lahure.

Waardt, Hans de. 1996. Feud and atonement in Holland and Zeeland: From private vengeance to reconciliation under state supervision. In *Private domain, public inquiry: Families and lifestyles in the Netherlands and Europe, 1550 to the present,* ed. Anton Schuurman and Pieter Spierenburg, 15–38. Hilversum.

Waldorf, Dolores. 1944. Baltimore fire laddie—George Hossefross, *California Historical Society Quarterly* 23:69.

Walkowitz, Judith. 1980. *Prostitution and Victorian society: Women, class, and the state.* Cambridge: Cambridge University Press.

Ware, Lowry. n.d. A history of Abbeyville. Unpublished ms.

Weber, K. von. 1857. *Aus vier Jahrhunderten: Mittheilungen aus dem Haupt-Staatsarchive zu Dresden,* vol. 1. Leipzig.

Weel, A. J. van. 1977. De wetgeving tegen het duelleren in de Republiek der Verenigde Nederlanden. *Nederlands Archievenblad* 81:282–96.

Weinstein, Donald. 1994. Fighting or flyting? Verbal duelling in mid-sixteenth-century Italy. In *Crime, society, and the law in Renaissance Italy,* ed. Trevor Dean and K. J. P. Lowe, 204–20. Cambridge: Cambridge University Press.

Welcker, Carl. 1838. Geschlechtsverhältnisse. In *Das Staats-Lexikon,* 6:629–65. Altona.

Wells-Barnett, Ida B. 1991. *On lynchings.* Salem, N.H.

Werner, Randolph Dennis. 1977. Hegemony and conflict: The political economy of a southern region, Augusta, Georgia, 1865–1895. Ph.D. diss., University of Virginia.

White, Deborah Gray. 1985. *Ar'n't I a woman? Female slaves in the plantation South.* New York.

Wiener, Martin. 1990. *Reconstructing the criminal: Culture, law, and policy in England, 1830–1914.* Cambridge: Cambridge University Press.

Wiesner, Merry E. 1991. Wandervogel and women: Journeymen's concepts of masculinity in early modern Germany. *Journal of Social History* 24 (4): 767–82.

———. 1993. *Women and gender in early modern Europe.* Cambridge: Cambridge University Press.

Wilentz, Sean. 1984. *Chants democratic: New York City and the rise of the American working class.* New York.

Wrightson, Keith. 1982. *English society, 1580–1680.* London.

Wunder, Heide. 1992. *"Er ist die Sonn, sie ist der Mond": Frauen in der frühen Neuzeit.* Munich.

Wyatt-Brown, Bertram. 1982. *Southern honor: Ethics and behavior in the Old South.* Oxford: Oxford University Press.

Ylikangas, Heikki. 1976. Major fluctuations in crimes of violence in Finland. *Scandinavian Journal of History* 1:81–103.

Zanazzo, G. 1908. *Tradizioni popolari romane,* vol. 2: *Usi, costumi e pregiudizi del popolo di Roma.* Turin and Rome.

Zedler, J. H. 1750. *Grosses vollständiges Universal-Lexicon aller Wissenschaften und Künste,* vol. 64. Leipzig.

Zedner, Lucia. 1991. *Women, crime, and custody in Victorian England.* Oxford: Oxford University Press.

Zehr, Howard. 1976. *Crime and the development of modern society: Patterns of criminality in nineteenth-century Germany and France.* Totowa, N.J.

CONTRIBUTORS

DANIELE BOSCHI completed his dissertation on homicide in nineteenth- and early twentieth-century Rome at the University of Rome in 1996.

TERENCE FINNEGAN received his Ph.D. from the University of Illinois at Urbana-Champaign in 1992. He is currently teaching at William Paterson College in Wayne, New Jersey.

UTE FREVERT is professor of modern history at the University of Konstanz, Germany. Her publications include *Krankheit als politisches Problem, 1770–1880* (1984); *Frauengeschichte* (1986, English trans. 1988); (editor) *Bürgerinnen und Bürger* (1988); *Ehrenmänner: Das Duell in der bürgerlichen Gesellschaft* (1991, English transl. 1995); *Mann und Weib, und Weib und Mann: Geschlechter-Differenzen in der Moderne* (1995); (editor) *Militär und Gesellschaft im 19. und 20. Jahrhundert* (1997).

AMY SOPHIA GREENBERG is assistant professor of history at the Pennsylvania State University. She is the author of a forthcoming book with Princeton University Press: "Cause for Alarm: The Volunteer Fire Department in the Nineteenth-Century City."

STEVEN HUGHES is professor of history at Loyola College in Baltimore, Maryland. His studies focus on problems of criminal justice and public order in modern Italy, and he is currently working on a book-length monograph on dueling in Italy after the Napoleonic period.

STEPHEN KANTROWITZ is assistant professor of history at the University of Wisconsin-Madison. His essay in this volume is part of a larger project entitled "The Reconstruction of White Supremacy," which uses the life and career of Ben Tillman to explore the transformations of manhood, violence, and politics in the postbellum South.

ROBERT NYE is the Horning Professor of the Humanities and Professor of History at Oregon State University. He teaches intellectual and cultural history, and he is currently working on topics in the history of sexuality and on medical ethics in modern Britain and France.

PIETER SPIERENBURG is affiliated with the History Department of Erasmus University, Rotterdam, the Netherlands. His publications include *The Spectacle of Suffering: Executions and the Evolution of Repression: From a Preindustrial Metropolis to the European Experience* (Cambridge, 1984); *The Broken Spell: A Cultural and Anthropological History of Preindustrial Europe* (New Brunswick, N.J., 1991; Dutch edition 1988); *The Prison Experience: Disciplinary Institutions and Their Inmates in Early Modern Europe* (New Brunswick, N.J., 1991); *Zwarte Schapen: Losbollen, Dronkaards en Levensgenieters in Achttiende-Eeuwse Beterhuizen* (Hilversum, 1995). He is currently working on the long-term history of violence in its sociocultural context.

MARTIN J. WIENER is the Mary Gibbs Jones Professor of History at Rice University. He is the author of *Between Two Worlds: The Political Thought of Graham Wallas* (Oxford, 1971); *English Culture and the Decline of the Industrial Spirit, 1850–1980* (Cambridge, 1980); and *Reconstructing the Criminal: Culture, Law and Policy in England, 1830–1914* (Cambridge, 1990). He is currently writing a book on the treatment of domestic violence in nineteenth-century England, at the Woodrow Wilson International Center for Scholars in Washington, D.C.

INDEX

Abbeville, SC, 240–41, 245–52
Adams, Sam, 246
Amsterdam
    knife fighting in, 103–27
Aschenbrenner, Martin, 45
Ayers, Edward, 21–22, 23, 25

Bahr, Hermann, 49
Baker, Benjamin, 159
Baltimore, MD
    and violence among firemen, 161–72
Beard, William P., 240, 246, 252
Blease, Coleman, 246
Blok, Anton, 104–5
Boschi, Daniele, 14, 99–101
Breittmayer, Georges, 91–93
Britain
    and violence, 197–212
Brown, Richard Maxwell, 24
Bruce, Dickson, 23
Burts, R. M., 245–46, 249

Cohen, Thomas and Elisabeth, 115
Cooper, Robert, 246
Crawford, Anthony
    career of, 245–48
    family of, 250–51
    lynching of, 20, 21, 248–50
criminal law
    in nineteenth-century Britain, 197–212

Dawson, F. W., 226
Denmark, SC, 228–32, 234
Dewey, D. A., 250, 251
domestic violence, 206–8
    See also violence
Douglass, Frederick, 219, 220, 225
drinking
    and violence, 204–6
duels (official)
    in American South, 23
    in Amsterdam, 116–17
    characteristics of, 33–35

and civilization, 8–10, 39–40
decline of, 74–75, 82–83
defense of, 89–91
in France, 82–95
in Germany, 37–63
incidence of, 48, 66–68, 73–74
in Italy, 64–81
and journalism, 68–69
and the law, 44–45, 49–51, 72–73, 204
by military men, 70–73
and nationalism, 69–70
origins of, 38–39, 65
and social stratification, 7–8, 50–52,
    83–86
by students, 42–43, 52–55
suppression of, 22–23
and war, 91–94
duels (popular)
    in Amsterdam, 103–27
    characteristics of, 99–101, 103–5
    definition of, 13–14
    incidence of, 148–49
    origins of, 16–17
    in Rome, 128–58
    See also knife fighting
Dupont-Bouchat, Marie-Sylvie, 199

Elias, Norbert, 10, 16, 23, 24, 25, 39, 121,
    200

Finnegan, Terence, 19–21, 194–95
fighting
    among firemen, 159–89
    See also duels (official); duels (popular);
        knife fighting; violence
fire companies
    attitudes toward, 170–72, 176–80,
        185–86
    in Baltimore, 161–72
    characteristics of, 163–64
    and honor, 14–15, 165–66
    in literature, 159–60
    in New York, 163

fire companies (*continued*)
    in Philadelphia, 163–64
    riots by, 167–70, 172–76, 180–84
    in St. Louis, 172–80
    in San Francisco, 180–85
France
    dueling in, 82–95
France, Anatole, 88
Freeman, Joanne, 76
Frevert, Ute, 8, 9, 10, 15, 17, 22, 33–35, 85
Fries, Jakob Friedrich, 49
Fritschius, A., 42

Gamble, C. C., 247, 249–51
Garve, Christian, 45
Gelli, Iacopo, 8, 64–65, 66–68, 71–74
gender
    historiography of, 1–2
    and honor, 2, 5
    See also masculinity; violence: and
        gender
Germany, 37–63
Goblot, Edmond, 85
Goethe, Johann Wolfgang von, 45
Gonzales, Narciso, 231
Greenberg, Amy S., 12, 15, 99–101
Greene, W. P., 245

Hemphill, James C., 226, 227
homicide
    character of, 107, 120, 138–40
    decline of, 150–53
    legal categories of, 134–38
    in nineteenth-century Britain, 199–210
    quarrels leading to, 140–43
    perpetrators of, 144–46
    rates of, 105–6, 129–30, 131–34
    in Rome, 128–58
honor
    in American South, 21–22
    and the body, 4
    gendering of, 2, 5
    and social stratification, 10–12, 72
    spiritualization of, 5–7
    See also duels (official), duels (popular)
Hughes, Steven, 8, 10, 23, 33–35

Ihering, Rudolf von, 49
Italy
    dueling in, 64–81
    Rome, 128–58

Kant, Immanuel, 44
Kantrowitz, Stephen, 12, 19–21, 23, 194–95
Kiernan, V. G., 82

Klein, Ernst Ferdinand, 44, 46
Klettenberg, Johann Hektor von, 40–41
knife fighting
    in Amsterdam, 103–27
    attitudes toward, 128–29, 146–47
    decline of, 120–21, 123–24
    defense against, 109–10
    reconciliation after, 114–15
    rituals of, 111–14
    in Rome, 128–58
    and social stratification, 107–9, 110–11,
        149–50
Knigge, Adolph von, 47

Lamartine, Alphonse de, 65
Laqueur, Thomas, 4
loan-sharking, 17
lynching
    of Major Clarke, 241–43
    context of, 193–95
    of Anthony Crawford, 248–50
    of Wilder McGowan, 244, 245
    newspapers' views of, 225–27, 231–33,
        240–41, 245, 251–52
    opposition to, 224–25, 227–28
    of John Peterson, 230–31

Manning, Richard, 245–46, 252
masculinity, 2, 6, 55–60, 87–88, 93, 117–18,
    161–63, 197–98, 241
Meiners, Cristoph, 47
Miller, Thomas E., 225
Möser, Justus, 45
Muchembled, Robert, 115, 198

New York City
    and violence among firemen, 163
Nye, Robert, 5, 8, 9, 10, 33–35, 66, 68, 70,
    71, 75

Pepe, Gabriele, 65
Perrin, Jack, 250–51
Philadelphia, PA
    and violence among firemen, 163–64

rape-lynch complex, 20–21, 218–21
Reinhold, Karl, 43
Rodgers, James, 247
Rome, 115, 128–58
Rostand, Edmond de, 88

St. Louis, MO
    and violence among firemen, 172–80
San Francisco, CA
    and violence among firemen, 180–85

Savigny, Friedrich von, 50
Scaglione, Giuseppe, 64
Schleiermacher, Friedrich, 53
Schlosser, Johann Georg, 45
Sheppard, John C., 227
Shubuta, MS, 241–43
Smith, J. Allen, 245, 250
South Carolina
    lynching in, 19–20
    political violence in, 217–18
    See also Tillman, Ben
Spierenburg, Pieter, 99–101, 138, 199
Stark, J. S., 250
Svarez, Carl Gottlieb, 43, 44

Tarde, Gabriel, 66
Tillman, Benjamin Ryan
    attitudes to lynching and the law, 12,
        19–21, 23, 213–14, 221–24, 233–35
    and Denmark lynching, 228–32
    rise to power, 214–18
Tourgée, Albion, 228
Treitschke, Heinrich von, 54

Velzen, B. Thoden van, 3
vendetta, 15–16

violence
    in Britain, 197–212
    church's attitude to, 119–20, 121–22
    and civilization, 200–202
    criminalization of, 202–4
    domestic, 206–8
    and drinking, 204–6
    and gender, 37, 198–99, 204–6
    after insults, 116
    present-day, 25–26
    prosecution of, 209–10
    relationship to honor, 3
    and ritual, 12–13
    and ritual disfiguration, 115–16, 118–19
    and the state, 18–25, 122–24, 193–95
    See also duels (official); duels (popular);
        homicide; lynching

Weizsäcker, Carl Heinrich von, 58
Wells-Barnett, Ida B., 219, 225, 233
Wiener, Martin, 6, 18–19, 193
Wiggins, MS, 244
Wyatt-Brown, Bertram, 21–22, 75

Zion, A.M.E., 225

THE HISTORY OF CRIME AND CRIMINAL JUSTICE SERIES

DAVID R. JOHNSON AND

JEFFREY S. ADLER, SERIES EDITORS

The series explores the history of crime and criminality, violence, criminal justice, and legal systems without restrictions as to chronological scope, geographical focus, or methodological approach.

MURDER IN AMERICA

A History

Roger Lane